"This book is so full of powerful exercises and ideas, I could not put it down. A wonderful guide to energy healing."
— James P. Ericson, D.C.

Chakra Breakthrough

The familiar, seven-chakra system was just the beginning of our understanding of the holistic human. Now, in *New Chakra Healing*, Cyndi Dale greatly expands upon this traditional knowledge, providing a complete picture of thirty-two human energy centers: twelve chakras within and outside of the body, plus twenty other energy points that exist in the spiritual plane.

This book is loaded with original concepts and sound, hands-on methods for removing energy blocks, supported by real-life examples from the author's successful counseling practice. You can use these revolutionary methods and exercises to heal disturbances and disruptions in all of your subtle energy bodies: the aura, rays, even your karma.

Millions search for the "reality behind the reality." You will understand your role as a conduit between the material and the spiritual when you experience first hand the holistic miracle of *New Chakra Healing*.

"We know of no other book that explores in such depth, conciseness, and understandability the chakra system and its effect on our physical, emotional, and spiritual health. *New Chakra Healing* should be required reading for any alternative healing class."
— Drs. Loren and Diane Mickelson

About the Author

Through her business, Life Systems Services, Cyndi Dale has provided intuitive-based consulting and life issues counseling to more than 3,000 people in individual sessions, small classes, and large-scale seminars. She has helped many of these individuals use the thirty-two-center energy system make powerful life changes and heal personal problems.

She originally developed this unique, innovative, approach to healing for herself as a method of psychic self-defense. Finding herself vulnerable to the psychic information and energies of others, she sought training from other psychics, healers, and energy workers around the world. When these methods failed to provide boundaries and self-definition, she developed the thirty-two-center energy system on her own.

Cyndi discovered her natural psychic abilities at an early age, when she was able to manipulate materials, speak with unseen presences, see energy fields in and around other people, and hear others' thoughts. She "turned off" this ability during adolescence, then experienced a range of self-destructive addictions and behaviors. During twelve years of therapeutic assistance, she once again "turned on" her psychic abilities, enhancing, managing, and using her own intuitive energy system.

To Write the Author

If you wish to contact the author or would like more information about this book, please write to the author in care of Llewellyn Worldwide, and we will forward your request. Both the author and publisher appreciate hearing from you, and learning of your enjoyment of this book and how it has helped you. Llewellyn Worldwide cannot guarantee that every letter written to the author can be answered, but all will be forwarded. Please write to:

Cyndi Dale
c/o Llewellyn Worldwide
P.O. Box 64383, Dept. K200-3, St. Paul, MN 55164-0383, U.S.A.

Please enclose a self-addressed, stamped envelope for reply or $1.00 to cover costs.
If outside the U.S.A., enclose international postal reply coupon.

Llewellyn's Whole Life Series

New Chakra Healing

The Revolutionary 32-Center Energy System

Cyndi Dale

2001
Llewellyn Publications
St. Paul, Minnesota 55164-0383, U.S.A.

FIRST EDITION
Sixth printing, 2001

Cover design by Tom Grewe
Interior illustrations by Wendy Frogge't and Anne Marie Garrison
Interior editing, layout, and design by Amy Rost

Library of Congress Cataloging-In-Publication Data
Dale, Cyndi
    New chakra healing : the revolutionary 32-center energy system/
Cyndi Dale.
        p.   cm.   — (Llewellyn's whole life series)
    Include bibliographical references.
    ISBN 1-56718-200-3
    1. Mental healing.   2. Chakras.   I. Title.   II. Series.
RZ401.D28 1996
615.8'9—dc20   96-13288
                                                                      CIP

Llewellyn Worldwide does not participate in, endorse, or have any authority or responsibility concerning private business transactions between our authors and the public.

    All mail addressed to the author is forwarded but the publisher cannot, unless specifically instructed by the author, give out an address or phone number.

Llewellyn Publications
A Division of Llewellyn Worldwide, Ltd.
St. Paul, MN 55164-0383
www.llewellyn.com

Printed in the United States of America

About Llewellyn's Whole Life Series

Each of us is born into a body, but many of us lack anything beyond the most utilitarian connection with our physical beings. Being in touch with the body—being aware of the senses' connection to our thoughts, emotions, dreams, and spirits—is integral to holistic living.

Instead of taking the intellect or the spirit as a starting point, books in Llewellyn's Whole Life Series focus on the how the health and sensations of the physical body are inextricably linked with the health of our minds and souls.

What does the physical have to do with the emotional or the spiritual? Everything. We are as much beings of the earth as we are beings of the stars. The connection to our bodies and our senses is just as integral to physical, mental, emotional and spiritual well-being as the connection to our higher selves. It is impossible to truly feel that we are part of the universe—as much as the ground we walk on and the air we breathe—until we entirely accept our own full natures as physical and spiritual creatures.

This book will help further your journey to wholeness, to the place where body, mind, heart, and spirit are integrated and healed. Its techniques will help you tap into your internal sources of wisdom, love, and healing in order to heighten your mind/body awareness. This book will help you see past the sum of your parts to your complete, your whole self.

To my father, whose death taught me about life,
and to my son, Michael, whose life taught me about love.

Table of Contents

Illustrations

The Human Condition

At first glance, the human condition is easy to understand. After all, don't we all have the same needs? We feel feelings, dream dreams and hope against hope that our days will bring us love, prosperity, fun, and good health. Every day, all over the world, people wake up, get dressed, make plans and carry them out in order to achieve these desires. As part of the human family, we all participate in these endeavors.

With so many people searching for the same experiences, we would predict at least a satisfactory degree of success; we might even expect more. After all, more people searching means more people helping, we might assume. Why then does it seem that life brings more thorns than buds, more pitfalls than pit stops, more tears than rainbows? Why, when we muster pictures of the human condition, do snapshots of starving children, broken bodies, and bombed-out cities dominate?

The truth is, when most of us consider the human condition, it is these painful realities that surface. The upside of acknowledging these realities is that we can try to change them. We might serve as volunteers, select service careers, or give money to alleviate the struggling suffered by so many. The downside is, whatever we do just doesn't seem to be enough. These facets of the human condition tug at our hearts.

What does this have to do with a book about energy systems? Part of the problem with the human condition is that we can't understand it nor help humanity unless we understand what it means to be a human being.

The Search for Full Humanness

Understanding our humanness is an individualized endeavor. Yes, we have much—if not everything—in common with other people. However, unless we look inside ourselves, then to our immediate surroundings, we lack the necessary knowledge, feelings, awareness, and honesty to relate to anything or anyone else. This educational process needs to involve more than a quick page-through of a basic anatomy text, spiritualist directory, or self-help book. It requires learning about all three basic aspects of our being—the body, mind, and soul. It requires learning about our spiritual nature, not just material needs. This self-reflection can help us diagnose and heal the chasms between these various aspects of our own being. When an individual becomes whole within him- or herself, the entire culture benefits, for one reflects the other.

Getting the basic information we need regarding our own bodies, minds, and souls can be an excruciating process. Each discipline, while true unto itself, seems to try to cancel out the respectability of other disciplines. Textbooks approved by the American Medical Association (AMA), while outlining the basics of the human body, offer little or no insight into the effects the mind has on our well-being. There is certainly no mention of a soul in these books. For the most part, the academic world also disregards the impact of the body and the soul on our well-being. This disregard limits our learning abilities, especially when we are young, since the mind learns best when the body is active. Though aware of the mind/body connection, the psychological arena has yet to fully embrace the existence of the soul. If our real problem or issue lies in our spirit, then working with the mental/physical connection alone will not suffice. Many of us turn to religious institutions for assistance with the soul and soul issues, yet doubt the validity or effectiveness of particular religious approaches. We are in desperate need of an approach that integrates body, mind, and soul, and we do not know where to turn.

Fortunately, all is not bleak. For centuries, Eastern doctors have taken a spiritualist approach to human concerns, including healing, and many Eastern traditions incorporate concepts of the mind, body, or soul in their views of and hopes for humanity. These societies are not perfect, however. Many Eastern spiritual systems (and economic structures) are based on a class system, which limits access to this more holistic approach.

In our Western world, where access to health care, education, and religious studies are supposedly non-class oriented, we see an explosive change in attitude toward and awareness of the non-traditional. Consider the various metaphysical, holistic, and spiritual principles which have been incorporated into chiropractic and massage therapy. Several mental health professionals have advanced theories which locate the origin of trauma not only in current-life experiences, but also in those predating birth. They incorporate past lives and even soul healing into their work. Many spiritual and lay groups are borrowing philosophies and healing methods from our wise, collective ancestry, legitimizing views from shaman-based societies and goddess-worshipping cultures among others. Clearly, there is a movement and paradigm shift going on around us. Is it enough? Is it even wise? Are we treading on dangerous ground?

Those of us dedicated to personally surviving and thriving in the midst of contemporary pressures and realities might question the validity of these paradigm changes. We still lack a solid, hands-on, definitive approach to working with our bodies, minds, and souls. Yes, we can study the enormous bulk of knowledge explaining our human anatomy. We can probe the vast recesses of the mind through Freud and friends. We can connect with our souls with the rest of the New Age. We can walk hand-in-hand with our gurus and saints. We can even explore our invisible energy systems by clearing our chakras or energy centers and tracking the snake of kundalini, a well-known, life-giving energy. However, to what central place can we go to learn about all these different parts of ourselves and our humanity? How can we then link this knowledge with a sense of purpose, our need to help humanity, and need to acknowledge a greater Spirit?

A Holistic Approach

The New Chakra Healing: The Revolutionary 32-Center Energy System has been created with this need in mind. As an intuitive consultant and counselor, I have helped thousands of individuals address and heal personal, professional, and physical issues. I have worked with and taught people from all walks of life, including executives, computer technicians, body workers, homemakers, actors, and children.

On the surface, each of these individuals have been just that—a true individual. Mary doesn't look like Sue, and Jack has different goals than Harry. Underneath, however, there are several common threads. First, my clients and students have all wanted to learn more about themselves, how they functioned, what made them tick. Second, they have all sought less pain and more pleasure in their lives. Third, they have all wanted to help other people and have sought a sense of purpose to guide and shape their decisions.

In order to facilitate the healing and awakening process of these individuals and in myself, I have worked with many techniques and approaches. I have integrated principles from business with spirituality. I have formed partnerships with AMA doctors and shamans. I have connected warriorism with feminism. I have blended chakra clearing with exercise. I have made decisions using intuition, rationality, and just plain common sense. At some point, I began to connect these various theories, techniques, and approaches.

After much work and experimentation, a system began to unfold, a system which combines the esoteric, intuitive, and invisible with the medical, practical, and concrete.

The basis of this system is the belief that there is a human condition and there is a human system. This system is not flat or two-dimensional, as our medical world might have it, nor is it completely mystical or far-out, as our metaphysical pioneers might assert. Rather, it is a blend of both. It must be, for the human being is both. Each of us is a material and spiritual universe unto ourselves. We are each significantly imperfect and wholly divine at the same time. We are both in this world and in another simultaneously. We are **revolving doors** between the base and the divine, the visible and the invisible, the known and the unknowable. We are, in short, human.

You as a Revolving Door

As revolving doors, we are continually stretched. When are we supposed to get angry or when are we to be forgiving? When are we supposed to get work done and when are we to be silent?

This book can't make those decisions for anyone. Instead, it is meant to serve as an outline of the energetic properties, quotients, and philosophies which can help individuals make those decisions for themselves. Though complex and loaded with data, lists, diagrams, and theories, its aim is to give you the opportunity to understand and fully love the human that you are—the simple human who has a body, mind, and soul, all at the same time. Ultimately, this book should enable you to comprehend just how important you are to humanity and to a Divine Source. By knowing yourself, you can move forward, get to know other people, and open yourself to the path of purpose which is yours, and yours alone.

Chapter One

The Revolving Door:
The Human Energy System

When you look in the mirror, you see an image. Most of us believe that this image shows what we really look like. Sometimes we like what we see, sometimes we do not. Regardless, we perceive that the "me" staring back from the mirror is a statement of fact. We are so sure of the mirror's correctness that some of us even believe that the picture staring back is a reflection of who we really are.

The truth is, there is much more to us than what we see in the mirror. An anatomist would point out that our perceptions are only skin deep, and that, from the surface, we cannot see the myriad of blood vessels, muscles, bones, or organs that make our bodies function. A professor would outline other invisible truths and note that from a mere image, we cannot see the depth of knowledge, learning, or intelligence which underlies our thought processes and belief systems. Our mothers might tell us of other non-apparent truths which have made us who we are, such as the escapades that defined us, the scoldings that shaped us, or the hugs that supported us. A pastor, priest, rabbi, or spiritualist would challenge us with another obvious limitation, saying that from the physical, we cannot imagine the soul, the light, the spirit, the divinity that makes each of us unique. There is much more to us than what we can see in any mirror, snapshot, portrait, or single situation.

Does this mean the mirror is wrong? No, it is only operationally limited. The mirror lacks the ability to fully explain ourselves to ourselves, because it does not have the capability to reveal our full physical, mental, emotional, or spiritual realities. Does this mean we must smash all our mirrors and stop relying upon them? If I said yes, most people would shut this book right now. How else are we to check out our make-up or outfits, and assuage our vanity? The point is that the item we use most often to evaluate ourselves can at best provide us with only a fraction of the truth.

The Visible Versus the Invisible

We are each unique and whole beings composed of the visible and invisible. However, in our society, we tend to ignore the invisible in favor of the visible. We fantasize about others based on appearances. We reach conclusions about emotional states based on voice inflections. We evaluate intelligence from framed certificates. We judge souls by the church attended.

The visible holds clues to the invisible, but it is not the whole truth. It is just the mirror image, the portrait someone has chosen to present to the world. The visible is a reflection of what lies underneath. This outer reflection may accurately illuminate inner truths or it may disguise them. While one person with a low self-image may dress poorly, stutter, or avoid relationships, another with equally low self-esteem may wear sequined dresses, boast a Yale diploma, or have been married three times. The problem with relying solely upon the visible to determine the personality, needs, or truths about others or ourselves is that we can hide as much as we can flaunt.

We hide, disguise, and plagiarize for many reasons. One reason is society. We have become a society of mirror-images freed from our looking-glasses, but perhaps we are no more real than the reflections still stuck in the silver backdrops. This is not a condemnation, but a confession. We are a society plagued by abuse, low standards, and confusion. Newspaper headlines emphasize our fascination with death, indiscretion, and betrayal. Businesses armor themselves against good-will to protect their self-interests. Politicians blame the bad economy for personal ineffectiveness, while economists blame the bad economy on the ineffective politicians. Underneath these mirror presentations are people who have cut themselves off from invisible truths, people who have largely lost their connection to nature, Spirit, and love. They have substantiated the visible, but not the invisible.

Another reason for the chasm between our inner and outer selves lies in our family patterns. Estimates state that anywhere between seventy and ninety-nine percent of our families are dysfunctional. Many of us have grown up in families affected by abuse of some sort, and most of us have directly or indirectly experienced neglect or physical, sexual, verbal, or emotional abuse.

Patterns of abuse appear in many forms, including alcoholism or substance abuse, and drug or food addictions. Abuse is also present in any situation involving physical endangerment, ranging from being beaten to being threatened. It can include emotional and mental traumas arising from constant criticism and put-downs or a lack of acceptance or support. Any disregard for one's rights, individuality, or privacy is abuse. Any extreme system, whether it involves rigidity or lack of boundaries, is abusive. Spiritual abuse, while less frequently discussed, can be equally damaging, whether it stems from forced denial of a divinity and an essential belief system, or forced adherence to a dogmatic and judgmental system. The telltale yardstick is that anything that makes us feel we are a bad person is abuse. Which of us has not experienced at least some conditions that left us feeling inherently bad, guilty, or flawed?

Most of us coped with our childhood difficulties by stunting, stuffing, ignoring, or hiding our invisible self, the self that:

- Is sensitive.

- Is vulnerable.

- Wants to be loved and nourished.

- Instinctively loves other people and wants to nourish them.

- Understands animals, plants and nature.

- Is connected to the Divine Source (a highest power or divinity as you understand it), spirits, and the Universe.

- Knows the invisible language of the inner soul, of nature, of the Divine Source.

- Is intuitive, can see pictures, hear voices, feel feelings, and know things at the deepest level of truth.

None of us have fully succeeded in secreting away this invisible self. If you ever find yourself feeling hurt, happy, loved, wanting to be loved, walking alone outside, or wondering at the beauty of the stars, you are still connected to your invisible self. While externally, many of us may want to repress this internal self, in order to protect, destroy, or conceal it, none of us can completely do so. Being alive is about having our visible and invisible parts joined together and mutually supporting each other. If we are alive, it is because at least some aspects of our visible and invisible selves are working together. If we are alive, it is because at least part of us really wants to be, no matter how bad life may have been or may now seem. Disease, disorders, depression, denials, problems, predicaments, plagues, stress, traumas, confusion, doubts—all these stem from incomplete connections between our visible and invisible selves.

I call the visible self the **material self**, and I call the invisible self the **spiritual self**. Disease (dis-ease or lack-of-ease) such as low self-esteem, post-childhood trauma, sexual dysfunction, addictions, money problems, relationship ills, and lifestyle confusion, originates with misunderstandings and disconnections between these material and spiritual selves.

Healing and Soul Work

Healing is the process of joining the material and spiritual selves, the visible and invisible. The healing process may involve rejoining parts of ourselves that, although previously bonded, experienced a trauma so great they disconnected or forged bonds where none existed. In the former case, we may need to work with memories, energies, and belief systems; experience long-held and hurt feelings; soothe injured body parts; or sort out old and current relationships. In the latter case, we may need to look at aspects of our soul, mind, or body that have never been examined. In either case, true healing—the process of becoming fully alive and happy—relies on merging our material and spiritual selves.

How are we to do this? The key lies in the paradox of the mirror. Although our mirror image fails to accurately or fully reflect the material or spiritual being, in it we are to search for the three essential aspects of identity—our body, mind, and soul. We are also to look for the points-of-contact, the doorways or portals, the revolving doors, that link the visible and invisible truths of our body, mind, and soul.

In *The Rays and Esoteric Psychology*, Zachary F. Lansdowne says, "Following birth, a human being learns to integrate the etheric body with the dense physical body, and then the mental body with the emotional body. After learning how to coordinate all aspects of the personality, we begin the process of integrating personality with soul" (Lansdowne, Zachary F. York Beach, ME: Samuel Weiser, Inc., 1989, 33).

Essentially, we are trying to figure out how to do soul work and how to be revolving doors. Working with these revolving doors can be hard, calling for painful self-examination, tough corrective actions, and critical maneuvering. However, by re-forging the bonds between the material and spiritual aspects of our being, we free ourselves from the fetters that keep us from complete expression. We free ourselves to become truly real, open, and happy. We free ourselves to heal.

Opening the Doors

To enter our revolving doors is to enter the realm of **purpose**. I believe each of us has been born to achieve a certain purpose. That purpose is our ultimate calling. It originates in our spirit or our essence, the self that was and is one with the Divine Source and the energy behind creation. We each have a different purpose, because we were each unique creations.

Here is my snapshot of the creation process. Upon separating from the Divine Source, we each received a torch representing one of the truths or principles of the Universe. That torch becomes our essential purpose, and our soul's job was to carry our purpose forward until we achieved it. However, as our soul added new dimensions, including a mind and eventually a body, it obviously became hampered by blocks and resistance. That is why our souls have entered one life after another; each life has presented the opportunity to live out different life tasks designed to clear any issues, beliefs, or experiences that prevent achievement of the essential purpose.

Living our purpose is the dynamic process whereby we heal our blocks and misperceptions, while expressing our true selves. Seen practically, living our purpose is fully expressing ourselves, expressing our spiritual self in the material world. Living our purpose is proof that we have achieved completion. It is the goal, and it is the process whereby we achieve completion. Our spiritual self provides the direction. Our material self creates concrete reality. When these parts of ourselves are fully linked, we are being all that we can possibly be. That is the key to happiness.

Because we each have a different purpose, each of our healing processes requires self-reliance. As we go about re-claiming our visible and invisible selves, we learn to accept responsibility for understanding our invisible self and healing any misunderstandings we hold about it. How?

"The first step is to find peace and balance within ourselves, to put aside those energies of doubt, of anger, of separation and fear that keep us from manifesting our whole potential...," says Cherokee medicine woman and leader Dhyani Ywahoo in *Voices of Our Ancestors*. "It is for each of us to sing out the light. It cannot be done for you. You cannot abdicate the responsibility of your holiness" (Ywahoo, Dhyani. Boston: Shambhala Publications, 1987, 257).

We must accept responsibility for bringing this internal, spiritual self into our external, material reality. Becoming self-responsible may mean knowing when and how to protect or reveal our inner truths. It may mean acquiring practical skills that will help guarantee success. It will certainly mean healing the barriers between our material and spiritual selves. Fully understanding not only the nature of our purpose, but also the nature of our energy systems, becomes imperative, because through our body, mind, and soul we acquire knowledge of self and our abilities.

Learning about these energy systems will require understanding more than a science textbook can provide. Understanding terms such as **chakra**, **energy center**, **kundalini**, **mana**, and **intuition** becomes important because they are means we can use to blend our material and spiritual selves. Understanding and accepting our own individual fears, challenges, and opportunities also becomes important, because it requires a willingness to destroy the limitations which narrow our sights.

On my own path, I have faced many hurdles and challenges in order to break free of the rules governing my limited perceptions. Growing up in an upper-middle class family, I knew myself as my family and culture knew me. My body was composed of organs, tissues, and blood, and it needed food and clothing. My mind required textbooks and instruction. My soul needed salvation, which was guaranteed by my weekly Sunday School attendance.

It wasn't until my twenties that I began to question the validity of these concrete rules. I went through two near-death experiences for which doctors could not diagnose the causes. Though I did the "right things," I wasn't happy in my marriage. Although full of intelligence and ideas, books and universities couldn't answer my questions.

The past fourteen years have involved a search that has taken me from the jungles of Peru to the Tor of Glastonbury, England, from anatomy texts to Hindu mysticism. Along the path of my search, I have met many fellow journeyers. One truth has emerged, one which other travelers have repeated: understanding the self depends on accepting that there is much, much more to us than the physical shell we have been told is reality. Ywahoo has a beautiful way of describing this truth. "We are the days and the nights, and we are the stars that illumine the starry chambers. We are holy beings. To recall this truth is to sense the sun and the moon within our body as dancing spirals, great mysteries of mind unfolding" (Ywahoo, 100).

In addition to self-reliance, I believe the journey into the self requires that we learn to work within the human family and the forces of nature and change. Just as our purpose is a doorway for our own self-expression, it is also an opportunity to help others. Because of this opportunity, fulfilling our purpose, living our dreams, and becoming happy are contingent upon transforming the barriers which prevent complete connection between ourselves and others. Disjointed relationships can be based on a lack of understanding about our own or another's true inner nature, or on actual real-life traumas. Being a revolving door means dealing with the people who are gumming up the works, and opening to the people who keep us in the flow. Because of our interdependence, understanding our relationships with the visible beings and invisible beings (such as angels, spirit guides, and the Divine Source) takes on new meaning.

In *Mutant Message Down Under*, Marlo Morgan passes on the wisdom of her Aboriginal teachers, who are called the "Real People."

"All human beings are spirits only visiting this world. All spirits are forever beings. All encounters with other people are experiences, and all experiences are forever connections. Real People close the circle of each experience. We do not leave ends frayed…. If you walk away with bad feelings in your heart for another person, and that circle is not closed, it will be repeated later in your life. You will not suffer once, but over and over until you learn. It is good to observe, to learn and become wiser from what has happened" (Morgan, Marlo. Lees Summit, MO: MM Co., 1991, 87–88). Concepts such as **karma**, **dharma**, **cords**, **rays**, and **principles** explain our relationships in this broader context.

The idea of interconnectedness and interdependence is not a new one. In my practice, I have seen these truths played out time and time again. One obvious example concerns a client who at age thirty-six expressed considerable dissatisfaction with her life. She wanted a loving husband, a purposeful career, and a healthy body, but felt she lacked the means to get any of them. I began by asking her who she believed herself to be. She couldn't answer. During the course of many months, we used a broad array of means to help her peel away the layers of beliefs and experiences that had defined her.

That stage was painful. She recalled childhood abuse; she remembered being told she was a bad person. She said that her parents often shamed her for what she "just knew" such as that there were "angels" or that the "plants could speak." Gradually, she began to dream about the self she was underneath her life-created self. Instead of voicing complaints to me and her therapist, she began to wonder what she was supposed to do with her life. What were her real gifts? Who was she supposed to help?

Her search within gradually melted away her excess weight. She started her own business by doing what she had wanted to do when she was a child. Through her business, she began to create art forms that helped people know themselves and see their inner natures through external means. She began to talk to angels again and understand that she deserved to be happy. The last time I saw her, she was preparing to move—with her new husband.

This spiral between our spiritual self and our material self, this unveiling of our being, is a journey we must all undertake if we are to be our true and happy selves. It begins by understanding that there is more to ourselves than meets the eye. We are holistic beings—beings who are whole and who live in wholeness. Happiness involves achieving this reality.

The Holistic Human

An ethical physician will tell you that drugs only work sometimes, tests only reveal so much, and treatments only help some people. An honest therapist will acknowledge that you can't just think yourself rich, thin, or happy, nor does feeling happy pay the rent or cure a sick relationship. Even a spiritualist will warn you that faith can only take you so far. Miracles can work wonders, but faith doesn't guarantee you will receive a miracle.

To create change powerfully, one must powerfully change. Change occurs when we braid together all four human dimensions: physical, emotional, mental, and spiritual. These are the four dimensions which interact to create the tapestry of self and life.

The idea that each human being is composed of physical, mental, emotional, and spiritual dimensions is not new. This concept has been referred to as **holism.** Supported and researched through disciplines ranging from physics to medicine to spiritualism, holism is the belief that a person is composed of a number of different aspects, and each aspect interrelates with the others. In fact, each aspect is reflected by and projected upon the other aspects. While the divisions between our body and mind are distinct at a superficial level, at another, deeper level these distinctions blur. For example, our body may hold, reflect, or act out that which is being experienced by the mind. When healing one part of someone, such as a broken leg, we are also indirectly making a change on all other levels, say the mind or soul. Fixing this leg might require the participation of feelings, thoughts, and spirit if it is to really work. If our mind says, "Let's stay sick. I like taking time off work," the broken leg will certainly be a long time mending.

This mind/body connection has recently received considerable documentation. One recent study has determined that the key ingredient in healing from broken bones is not as scientifically based as we might assume. Is it the quality of care, the ability of the doctor, or the speed of the bone setting? No, the most crucial recovery factor is whether or not someone likes his or her job. (This fact has been documented through studies available at the Northwestern College of Chiropractic in Bloomington, Minnesota.) Non-Western and ancient cultures have long known about the power of the mind, often adding a soul connection to the mind/body link.

Describing the setting and supposedly miraculous healing of a broken leg in *Mutant Message Down Under*, Morgan says, "In setting the bone earlier that day, the two native physicians worked by sending the thoughts of perfection to the body. There was as much going on in their heads and hearts as in their hands.... What would happen in America if physicians put as much faith in the healing ability of the human body, as they do believing drugs can or cannot cure?" (Morgan, 89.)

Many East Asian, African, and South American practitioners first look for the disease in the spirit before trying to mend the body. Several Japanese and Native American approaches first examine the families, lifestyles, or environments of the stricken person. Early Polynesians believed that "most internal illnesses other than obvious temporary upsets...were supernaturally induced by spirits and demons because of the breaking of some tapu by the individual or some member of his family" (Whistler, W. Arthur. *Polynesian Herbal Medicine*. Kauai, HI: National Tropical Botanical Garden, 1992). Although Western civilization has been a bit slow to come around to these ideas, the proof is there, as many alternative caregivers and receivers will attest.

The body/mind/soul connection is, interestingly enough, being played out and explored in contemporary physics and mathematics. Many leading physicists now assert that the holographic theory, the larger paradigm in which holism is housed, explains much of the universe, as well as our human condition. In *The Holographic Universe*, Michael Talbot, a well-known writer on new physics, says, "Our brains mathematically construct objective reality by interpreting frequencies that are ultimately projections from another dimension, a deeper order of existence that is beyond both space and time: the brain is a hologram enfolded in a holographic universe" (Talbot, Michael. New York: HarperCollins, 1991, 54). Thinking of the universe as a hologram assumes that the universe as a whole is reflected in its parts, and that each part holds a picture of the universe as a whole.

If we work the same way, it stands to reason that a dis-ease in a part of our self—an illness, a stress, a bad relationship—points to an illness in our entire being and vice versa. A spiritual belief of being bad can make us feel bad, think bad thoughts about others, and ultimately, feel bad physically. Obviously, this can only happen if the body, mind, and soul are interconnected. Here again we see the idea that revolving doors exist to connect points between the visible and invisible, the material and the spiritual.

When we think like this, objective and subjective reality begin to blur. Long-held ideas about our physical bodies, ourselves, our immaterial soul, and our emotional reactions begin to slide away, like tectonic plates shifting. Doors open. Mirrors cloud.

When these paradigms slip, we can become confused and need to establish a new model. Let's stop perceiving ourselves as collections of parts. Instead, let's picture circles existing and expressing in a series of waves. Our physical body flows into our emotional reality, which connects to our thought forms, which link to our spiritual or intuitive processes, which flow right back into our physical body.

We can substantiate this wave theory by understanding the existence of quanta. Quanta are sub-atomic particles, considered by some to be the basic "stuff" from which everything in the universe is made. Minute energy units, quanta are able to exist both as waves and particles, and flow from one form to the other. Talbot points out that quanta usually operate in waves—freely streaming and unbroken energy flows. He says, "The only time quanta ever manifest as particles is when we are looking at them" (Talbot, 34). Invisible quanta become visible when their effects are measured.

When applied to ourselves and our lives, the implications of this concept are stupendous. If we, like everything else in the universe, are made of quanta, suddenly, it is not only possible, but likely, that we can be composed of both visible and invisible energies. We can exist in material and spiritual form simultaneously. What we are depends upon how we perceive ourselves. Our mirror image changes as we change our views. We can occupy real space and other, non-apparent space simultaneously. We can exist in one era and another simultaneously. We can be healed and still need healing simultaneously.

The crux of healing and of being happy is working with our quanta, the energy units capable of going back and forth between the visible and invisible, that are able to become or connect with an organic cell, feeling, thought, or piece of our soul. To effectively operate at this level, however, we must be able to bring our body, mind, and soul into unity. We must be able to open the revolving doors between the various parts of ourselves. We must update our ideas about our human energy system—the body, mind, and soul—to accommodate the responsibility of being both spiritual and material. Being able to do this not only speeds our own healing processes, but also affects the lives of others.

We are speaking now of wholeness, a philosophy explained by Ywahoo, in reference to her own Cherokee people. "Indian mind always looks to the whole," she says. "Treatment of disease is never to a particular energy center, but for the whole being sensing that person as a continuum. If we are thinking 'part' then we are giving energy to the problem. It is better to know wholeness" (Ywahoo, 263).

This book accepts as basic the belief that we are material and spiritual beings and exist on both planes simultaneously. Given that these two aspects of being can interrelate, and therefore affect each other positively or negatively, we need an operational set of principles, tools, and rules that would enable us to both connect these two selves for our good.

The thirty-two-chakra system is such a system. We will examine it and corollary concepts in order to maximize the positive contacts between our spiritual and material selves. Just as important is the discussion about the aspects of our self that should be making the decisions about what could and should happen. The emphasis on soul purpose is deliberate and definitive, because the soul is the aspect of our self which carries our purpose from our Divine Source—God, Buddha, Spirit, Creator, Christ, or other Higher Power. Therefore, this is the aspect of the self to put in charge.

This book assumes that there is indeed a higher spiritual power, a Divine Source to which all souls are connected. Strengthening and maintaining this connection through the soul is essential to being fully human. Because of our common spiritual background, I and many of my clients refer to this Divine Source as "God." However, I encourage all my clients—and readers—to derive their soul work from their own spiritual traditions.

The Full Human Energy System

One thing missing in alternative, metaphysical, or AMA-approved health care explanations of healing endeavors has been a clear picture of the human energy system, a picture of not only the spiritual or material sides of our being, but of these revolving doors between the material and spiritual realms. *New Chakra Healing* presents a view of the visible and invisible aspects of our beings, and highlights various methods that can be used to open these portals.

Chakras and Energy Points

Through my work, I have perceived thirty-two energy centers upon which the holistic human is based. Twelve of these centers are chakras, the skeleton of our physical system. The other twenty energy centers exist on the spiritual plane. Understanding the nature of these energy centers is critical to understanding ourselves, our truths, our purposes.

Chakras regulate, maintain, and manage the physical, emotional, mental, and spiritual aspects of our being on the physical plane. Chakras themselves serve as revolving doors or portals between our body, mind, and soul. In *Vibrational Medicine*, Richard Gerber says, "The chakras are specialized energy centers which connect us to the multidimensional universe. The chakras are dimensional portals within the subtle bodies which take in and process energy of higher vibrational nature so that it may be properly assimilated and used to transform the physical body" (Gerber, Richard. Santa Fe: Bear & Company, 1988, 370).

Chakra is actually a Sanskrit term meaning "wheel of light." A chakra is nothing more or less than a wheel of light revolving in and through our energy system. C. W. Leadbeater, in his classic text *The Chakras*, describes chakras this way: "The chakras or force-centers are points of connection at which energy flows from one body of a man to another...all these wheels are perpetually rotating, and into the hub or open mouth of each a force from the higher world is always flowing" (Leadbeater, C. W. The Theosophical Publishing House, Wheaton, IL: 1927, 4–5).

There are major and minor chakras. The major chakras manage our most critical functions and issues; the minor chakras regulate less fundamental needs. All are important, but one could picture their differences like the differences between our arteries and capillaries. Wounding an artery is a catastrophe; we have only a few, and each is critical to our survival. A wounded capillary, on the other hand, results in minor discomfort. There are thousands of capillaries, and though important, the work done by one can be absorbed by others while repair is in progress.

Of the twelve physically oriented chakras, seven are located in the actual physical body. These chakras have been known to most Eastern cultures and several South American cultures (such as the Mayan) for thousands of years, and have recently been employed in the methods of many Western holistic practitioners. However, no practitioner I know has adequately explored the full dimensions of the back sides of these seven in-body chakras, preferring instead to highlight the front sides. This book will illustrate the nature and function of both sides of the in-body chakras, and how the spine and vertebrae serve as revolving-door connections between the front and back sides of these chakras.

The remaining five, out-of-body chakras, associated to our visible existence, have been only vaguely referred to in other material. My awareness of these chakras comes primarily from my work. Together with the seven in-body chakras, they create a system of incredible magnitude with regard to healing and manifesting.

The additional twenty **energy centers**, which exist in the invisible realm, have not been discussed before in any book, except conceptually. This book will explore all the chakras and energy points to locate the revolving-door connections between these out-of-body chakras and our in-body energy centers and systems.

Auras

Another important aspect of our energy system is our **aura**, the bands of light surrounding all living things. Studies at the Neuropsychiatric Institute at the University of California, Los Angeles used high-frequency photography to show blue and white rays emanating from people's fingertips. If a subject became excited during filming, the color changed to a spotty red. In one subject who became drunk, the photographs showed a murky haze around the hands (Stetler, Alfred. *PSI-Healing*. New York: Bantam Books, 1976, 75–76). Several newer studies also support the existence of the aura.

I believe that each auric band is connected to one of the human chakras, and that the chakras themselves are connected to visible organs, and therefore, to our very existence. Barbara Ann Brennan, a former scientist for the National Aeronautics and Space Administration (NASA) and now a respected healer, sees this connection as a seal regulating the energy exchange. "The points or tips of the chakras, where they connect to the main power current, are called the roots or the hearts of the chakras. Within these hearts are seals which control exchange of energy between layers of the aura through that chakra. That is, each of the seven chakras has seven layers, each corresponding to a layer of the auric field" (Brennan, Barbara Ann. *Hands of Light: A Guide to Healing Through the Human Energy Field*. New York: Bantam Books, 1987).

I also believe that as each of our twelve chakras is affected by energies we bring into this life, our experiences within it, and the reflections of the higher twenty energy points, our auras will metaphorically tell us the stories of ourselves. While they hold the projections of all that has happened, is happening, and perhaps will happen, these auric bands serve as input centers for the spiritual energies that can alter or heal our past, present, or future.

Rays

A third major energy affecting us is **rays**, usually defined as waves of energy that are universal in nature. There are many types of rays, for there are many types of universal energies. In my work, I see six major revolving doors or entry points for these rays, plus thirty-two minor entry points. Isolating these entry points in our physical or energetic systems is important, so that we learn how to manage both the incoming and outgoing flow of universal energies. By managing our own ray process, we can effectively work on relationship problems, career questions, physical ailments, and many other issues.

Aligning yourself with certain rays can also be helpful. Your attraction to specific rays will depend upon your overall energy system, personality, healing needs, purpose, and developmental process. Many people find it beneficial to perceive a connection to spiritual beings or entities through these rays. In exploring this possibility, I emphasize alternate methods of taking in and sending out ray energy, because working through another being presents challenges and difficulties that can outweigh the benefits.

Principles

Governing the flow of universal rays and the interaction of spiritual and material energy with our human energetic system is a set of guidelines called **principles**. Principles are not rules, but regulations. The difference is that rules are rigid and regulations are flexible. Understanding the principles that regulate our system can save us a lot of hardship by steering us away from mistakes and toward success. We will explore the principles I work with and various applications of them.

Other Healing Concepts

There are a few additional concepts that are important to understand. Most relate to the need to find your purpose as a means to heal, a process that differs slightly between men and women.

As we work with energies and their applications, we must remember that there are gender differences. There are reasons men and women never seem to understand each other! Knowing how to best work with your own energy system, while following gender-based applications, can clear up much of the current confusion held about energy.

Kundalini

One of the points of gender difference lies in the use of **kundalini**, the life-energy force, often symbolized as a serpent. Kundalini is an explosive energy, often used and well documented in Eastern traditions, many of which see kundalini as the energy of will, passion, and physicality. Other cultures purport similar ideas. For instance, Mayan masters teach that "we are the integration of the seven powers of light, traveling in the form of the serpent, undulating eternally with movement and measure" (Men, Hunbatz. *Secrets of Mayan Science/Religion*, trans. Diane Gubiseh Ayala and James Jennings Dunlapp II. Santa Fe, NM: Bear & Company, 1990, 126).

While the New Age is ushering in a Westernized view of kundalini, misconceptions abound, such as beliefs regarding its inherent dangers and the preparation stages for using it. Confusion regarding this energy, which many believe to be the crucial force behind actualizing oneself, arise from lack of awareness. Most people are not aware that:

1. Kundalini is actually an energy connected to a higher, spiritual energy point.

2. It affects men and women differently.

3. It can be reached and used through material and spiritual access points.

I believe that employing this "snake energy" is critical to achieving growth, maintaining self-awareness, and tapping into our own power. I share Richard Gerber's belief that "the kundalini is the creative force of manifestation which assists in the alignment of the chakras, the release of stored stress from the bodily centers, and the lifting of consciousness into higher spiritual levels" (Gerber, 389). We will explore kundalini as an effective tool or revolving door which actually ties the entire human energy system together, when used in concert with a second, equally effective energy.

Mana

This second energy is **mana** energy. The kahuna healers of Hawaii feel that mana is the life force permeating the universe, and that it is highly concentrated in living things (King, Serge. *Kahuna Healing*. Wheaton, IL: The Theosophical Publishing House, 1983, 62–63). Because of its use in manifesting, performing miracles, and healing, this mana energy is critical to the healing process.

Karma and Dharma

In the exploration of ourselves, we will inevitably travel paths journeyed by other metaphysicians. In doing so, we will explore two other important concepts: karma and dharma. Typically, **karma** is seen as a retributive process whereby we re-experience our mistakes or dilemmas until we get them right. I see karma as a completely different process, one which we can actually choose to engage in or not.

Frederic Wiederman sees karma as "the sum total of the consequences of all our actions...." He says, "Regardless of whether our actions create positive or negative karma, the law of karma assures that we must experience the return of the effects of our actions. While this...may seem binding...it is in reality very freeing." Wiederman views the law of karma as a cosmic feedback system which allows us to become conscious of our deeds, and therefore learn from them (Wiederman, Frederic. *Between Two Worlds: The Riddle of Wholeness*. Wheaton, IL: The Theosophical Publishing House,

1986, 76–77). I cleared up some of my own confusion about karma by perceiving the following:

1. There is a karmic center connected to an actual energy body (a chakra). Working with this energy center is the key to clearing misperceptions about ourselves.

2. Karma can be changed through revolving-door points in any of the energy centers or chakras.

3. Karma is only important because it leads us to dharma; the dharmic conversion process is the only one that can help us transform karmic energy (from pain to wisdom).

If karma is the process which pulls us back toward our past, **dharma** is the process which pulls us forward toward our future. Dharma is actually another word for purpose. Wiederman explains, "Its duty is to serve life and increase God consciousness in whatever manner best suits the person's talents and level of attainment. The soul's calling can be viewed as a blueprint which contains information as to why we are here" (Wiederman, 76). When karmic energy is harnessed appropriately, it can speed up our dharmic process, which in turn speeds up our healing process. Dharma is almost always connected to the soul and the soul-body, which must be effectively integrated with our mind and physical body to be fulfilled. We will explore means of achieving this integration.

Cords

One other theme woven throughout this book is the idea of **cords**. Cords are energetic connections between people, beings, or parts of ourselves that serve as negative relationship contracts. Purpose and relationship are two sides of the same coin. We need people to achieve our purpose, and purpose to clarify our relationships. Cords are formed when we contract with another person to meet our needs. This contract may seem beneficial on the surface, until we realize that these contracts are usually formed out of fear and self-destructive beliefs. These beliefs result in patterns that create self-destructive habits and limit the bonded relationships to a low standard of quality.

Cords are especially dangerous because they can be carried forth across time. They may be formed soul to soul, mind to mind, or body to body during our existence (past lives or this life), or in any other soul/mind/body configuration. They may directly or indirectly affect us, but are almost always detrimental. (The exception is a cord between a mother and newborn.) Cords generally gum up our energy system, filling holes that need to be there, clouding mirrors that need to be clear, and damaging barriers that need to be strong. In short, we cannot work efficiently—or at all—with our energy systems if we do not address our cords and the reasons we are holding them.

All of these terms—chakra, aura, rays, principles, kundalini, mana, karma, dharma, and cords—have been introduced to make you more comfortable with learning about your energy system. They may be new to some, but old hat to others. Regardless of their familiarity, they are presented as an invitation to experience one of the most important events of your life. It is an invitation to come through the doorway of yourself—to meet yourself.

Exercises: Through the Doorways of the Self

We each have the ability to know ourselves, to express ourselves, to be ourselves. Exercises can help us gain access to the innermost areas of ourselves, the areas that are sometimes the most difficult for us to see and feel. The following exercise can help you delve within. It is a six-step series of processes for gaining access to your intuition, your access point to uncovering the invisible you.

1. **Grounding** — The process of bringing yourself fully within your body. When grounded, you will be able to feel all parts of your physical body, from your toes to your head. You will also be able to feel the full extension of your energy system, including parts of you above and below your feet and head.

2. **Centering** — The process of bringing yourself to your center or middle. To be centered is to be fully connected to the part of your body that serves as the meeting ground for all your energies. This meeting ground is usually found within the abdomen, solar plexus, or heart.

3. **Protecting** — The process of clearing, repairing, and erecting energetic boundaries in order to keep yourself safe. The safer you feel regarding visible and invisible elements or beings, the more intuitive you can be.

4. **Opening** — The process of opening your energy centers. You may remain open after an exercise (if you are appropriately protected) or chose to close back down when finished.

5. **Accessing** — Accomplishing what you set out to accomplish, such as performing a healing or obtaining data.

6. **Closing** — The reverse of opening. It includes appropriately closing energy centers, re-protecting, centering, and grounding.

EXERCISE
Meditating on Your Energy System

The best way to learn how to use your energy system is to practice. You may perform this guided meditation by yourself by first reading it through then trying it, by taping it then playing it back, or by having someone read it to you.

A. Prepare yourself by finding a comfortable position in which to rest. With your feet touching the floor, begin to breathe deeply. Concentrate first on the in-breath, picturing a soft, yellow light entering your body with each breath. See or feel this light circle around your chest, opening and clearing.

B. With each additional in-breath, this light moves further within your body, swirling first into your neck, your shoulders, then through your arms and hands. The light passes through your hands, bringing with it any energies you feel ready to release. The light continues spreading upward, moving into your head, gently pushing all the way to the top of your head, then outward. Here too, the light brings out all the energies you no longer need, clearing your sense of self, your inner vision, your own truth and light.

C. The light then begins to move downward, pulsing, clearing, opening as it travels into your solar plexus, your abdomen, moving into your hip area. It parts into two beams at it stretches down into your legs, finally pooling at your feet. It continues downward, finding a path, a channel, into the earth. Here, below, you find a part of yourself awaiting you, an energy center open to this energy. The light passes into, then through this energy center, carrying with it all the substances that you no longer need, passing them into the earth for transformation.

You rest your attention on this part of you underneath the ground, and find that it begins to breathe at the same rate as your lungs are breathing. In, then out. In, then out. You notice that the out-breaths above and below are now removing of all energies, emotions, thoughts, colors, experiences, that have ceased to serve you. Your upper and lower breaths occur in rhythm to each other.

D. You are now grounded. You can feel yourself from your head to your feet. You are safe. You are now able to move your conscious awareness elsewhere, bringing it to your center. Simply allow yourself to find your center, that part of yourself in which you feel most at home. Linger here for a while. Experience the warmth, the colors, the feelings, the knowledge that you hold about yourself there. Bring some light into this aspect of yourself. Allow it to expand; allow yourself to be at one with it.

E. As you grow comfortable inside of yourself, you become aware of the aura, the energy bands, around you. Draw your attention outward and ask to see any discolorations, markings, colors, or shadows that indicate a hole or block. If you see anything, ask for the appropriate color or shade with which to repair your aura. You may also ask your inner self or an outer guide to tell you if there is a part of your aura that needs attention. If there is, ask for help in repairing it. You may also allow yourself to simply expand your energy out into your aura, bringing with you the feeling of light you have spread throughout your body. Let this light fill in any gaps or holes. Let it push out any unwanted energies or people. Let it warm and protect you. When you feel safe, bring your attention back to your center.

F. Centered again, picture a light switch, the center control switch for your energy centers. Flip on the switch. By doing this, you are awakening your intuitive abilities to see, hear, or know what you need to understand. Safely opened, you can now gain access to information.

G. Right now, concern yourself only with your center. Ask your internal self what awareness would help you stay centered more often in everyday life. Give yourself a minute to see, hear, feel, or sense an answer. Take time to follow any provided instructions.

H. It is now time to close. You will remain grounded and centered throughout this process, and after you have regained full consciousness. Examine your aura again. Are there any now-apparent or new holes, blocks, or problems to address? Heal anything preventing you from living a full and active life. Once again, imagine your central light switch, this time picturing it as a dimmer switch. Adjust the dimmer up or down, selecting the intensity that feels safest for you. Bring your awareness back to your breath, feeling your in- and out-breaths as they continue to move through and around your body. Feeling your hands, your feet, your head, your heart, let your breath guide you back to a full and conscious awareness of yourself. When you are ready, open your eyes.

Chapter Two

You as Infinity:
Your Twelve Chakras

Energy centers are doorways revolving between our material and spiritual selves, and between the material and spiritual universes. The first twelve centers are connected to the **material self**. They help us bring the **mana** or energy particles of the invisible world into physical form. Seven of these energy centers are clearly **chakras** or spinning wheels of light particles, because they are body-based and operate according to physical laws. The next five are also chakras. Though their connection points lie outside the physical body, they still operate according to physical principles. (See figure 2a, color pages.)

The other twenty centers are spiritually based; they are located outside this time/space continuum. Of course, you might wonder how I know they exist, if they can't be seen, felt, or heard. As with many hypothesis, the test of this reality is causal. Through my work, I have seen the existence of such points demonstrated. There are also references to these points in esoteric literature and in indigenous practices and various spiritual traditions. These top centers are not officially chakras, for they comprise energy that, if measurable, I believe would rotate faster than light itself. Although they lack physical attributes, these spiritual energy points help us transmute physical energies into immaterial energy and vice versa. They provide us with guidelines to stretch beyond our normal, human limitations.

Describing Our Energy Centers

All of the energy centers contain clues to everything that affects us. In fact, they perfectly mirror all that has ever occurred, is occurring, or might occur. They cannot help but do it, because each energy center functions as a complete unit unto itself, while serving the whole energy system. Holism, at its best, is portrayed through the human energy system. Regardless of their locations (or lack of one), all energy centers have the following in common:

Purpose — All energy centers regulate the human energy system and seek to maintain an equilibrium of health while assisting the mind's, body's, and soul's need to grow, develop, and heal.

Function — All energy centers link the visible and invisible aspects of an individual's body, mind, and soul, and exchange energy between the two dimensions as needed.

Energy Form — All energy centers are composed of quanta (energy that moves slower than the speed of light) or tachyons (energy that moves faster than the speed of light), both of which move in spiral-like motions from material to spiritual form and vice versa.

Frequencies — Each energy center operates at its own optimum frequency. Generally, the more physical and the lower the center, the lower its frequency. All these frequencies are interrelated, however. If one is out of synch, all others will be, too.

Effects — All energy centers affect an entity's physical, mental, emotional, and spiritual well-being by storing, analyzing, dispersing, and transforming data regarding these processes.

Communication Vehicles — Each energy center has a built-in mechanism for communicating to the other energy centers and to the organism as a whole. This feedback process is a psychic process which involves receiving, encoding, sending, and deciphering data between centers and the mind, body, or soul of the organism. In short, all energy centers double as intuitive centers, each using its own peculiar form of psychic process.

While the energy centers have a lot in common, they also differ greatly. While each serves the greater purpose, each also meets a particular function. While each affects our physical, emotional, mental, or spiritual well-being, each also regulates a separate process. While the in-body, out-of-body, and top spiritual energy centers are members of the same family, each group has its own distinctions. Part of the differences between the individual centers and the three major groups of centers lies in how they affect or assist our drive to purpose. By examining these differences close-up, we can gain a better understanding of what is going on inside and outside of us all the time, usually without our immediate knowledge.

In this chapter, we will look at the human chakras—seven in-body chakras and five out-of-body chakras. In Chapter Three, we will explore our twenty spiritual energy points.

How the In-Body Chakras Work

The seven chakras located within the human body are the most well-known chakras, and they ought to be. As people, we live, breathe, eat, love, and die within our physical forms, so it makes sense that we would associate foremost with our physical chakras.

The in-body chakras are shaped like conical funnels. Their point of contact with the physical body lies in the spine (figure 2b). Because they move up the spine, the names of these chakras are relatively easy to remember. Beginning at the hip area, they are:

Chakra	Physical Location
One	Hip/genital area
Two	Abdomen
Three	Solar plexus
Four	Heart
Five	Throat
Six	Forehead
Seven	Crown (the baby's soft spot)

The lower six chakras are actually two-sided, with one side spinning out the front and the other out the back. I perceive that the highest chakra, which emits from the crown, has a back side as well. This back side is less apparent because it opens into a higher dimension than the others.

In this chapter, we are going to examine the front side of the chakra system; Chapter Five is devoted to the back sides. You are probably either intellectually or intuitively familiar with the front side of the in-body chakric system, since it is the part regulating the conscious process. Within the front-side chakras we find:

Records — Of all we have experienced in this lifetime, including experiences we have brought into this lifetime and key experiences from our ancestors and relatives.

Storage — Of our own memories; unexpressed feelings; operating beliefs and patterns; soul beliefs and patterns; desires, hopes, and dreams; other people's energies, experiences, hopes, dreams, beliefs, and opinions.

Regulatory Functions — Of key physical organs and systems; major belief systems; emotional actions and reactions; the soul's integration with and input into the body and mind.

Communication Functions — Through the physical process, the psychic process, and the intuitive process.

Figure 2b.

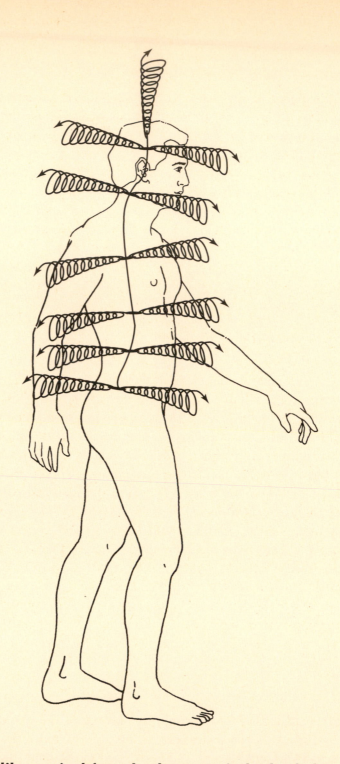

Shaped like conical funnels, the seven in-body chakras connect with the physical body at the spine.

"Chakras are shaped like spirals, the point of the spiral rooted in the central nervous system at the spine, and the vortex or wide part of the spiral passing through the dense body, at the front." — Diane Stein, from *Women's Psychic Lives*

Records

As recording centers, the chakras work much like brain cells do. Let's say that early in life, we experience trauma (such as sexual abuse) in the first chakra, located in the genital and hip area. The first chakra will record or lock in the memory of this trauma. I have seen very dramatic examples of this recording process. One client experienced replays of her father's abuse whenever her husband touched her genitalia in the same way her father once did. Another client, a sixteen-year-old girl, told me that after her first sexual encounter, she was flooded with abuse memories. The first chakra (and all the others) record memories that result from being hurt or touched in its physical locality—the genital/hip area in the case of the first chakra. As you will see, however, the first chakra also regulates a number of other systems, including the skin. Therefore, first chakra issues, such as response to sexual violation, can have a widespread impact. For this reason, I recently helped a client with a skin disease by intuitively guiding her into her first chakra. Through this approach, she began to remember sexual abuse issues, for which I referred her to a therapist. Her skin condition cleared up during therapy.

As recording centers, our chakras also imprint memories that are not ours or that stem from a different lifetime. I worked with one client who for her entire life had been plagued with dreams in which she experienced miscarriage. Having never miscarried, she was puzzled and concerned that these dreams were premonitions. Finally, I asked her to find out if her mother had ever miscarried. She found out that her mother had miscarried twice before my client was conceived, but had never thought that it was important to tell her daughter.

Another client, a therapist, was convinced that her fears about sex stemmed from her most recent past life as a Holocaust victim. She says that since birth, she has been terrified of hangers and other similar articles. She now believes these were instruments of rape in her past life. Under controlled hypnosis (not with me), she has re-lived these horrifying experiences. These memories were imprinted in her chakric system.

Storage

The storage function of the in-body chakras is similar to that of the recording function, but broader. As we have seen, we can record or store our own memories, memories of our physical ancestors, and memories from our past lives (memories from ancestors or ourselves). Storing is different from recording. To record is to imprint; to store is to hold the energy of something intact. We might record something to learn from it. However, storing the energy of that thing preserves it, sometimes so we can learn, but other times to prevent damage or to hold onto it until we can safely deal with it later.

For instance, we can store emotions, beliefs, physical experiences, and spiritual misperceptions that might be too negative or self-destructive to deal with right away. If we were often physically struck as a child, we may sub-consciously decide not to immediately deal with that trauma. Perhaps react-ing would invite further wrath, so we encapsulate the experience and hide it from ourselves. I've met many people who have forgotten entire blocks of time until the memories are suddenly and wholly triggered years later.

Therapists often report this phenomenon. One of my friends, a psycholo-gist, said, "People frequently come to me only after they have become strong or safe enough to deal with their pasts." He says that at this point, intact memories, feelings, and experiences frequently emerge through flashbacks, dreams, or therapeutic discussions.

Where did these memories and experiences go? I believe they have been stored in the chakras themselves or in parts of the body near the primary chakras. I learned this during the early stages of my healing training. Once, while practicing therapeutic touch, my touch on a client's shoulder provoked an outbreak of anger and memories of an event she had forgotten. My sense was that, in order to protect the physical heart itself, she had stored—intact—that experience in her shoulder. She fully remembered it only when her heart had become strong enough to handle it.

The trouble with this process is that these unexpressed memories, feel-ings, and beliefs, whether ours or someone else's, can draw detrimental cir-cumstances to us and cause further unhappiness. If we hold on to mental perceptions such as "I am powerless," "I am a dirty person," "The world isn't safe," or "All women/men are out to get me," these beliefs can generate a whirlpool of problems until we uncover and release them. We may avoid healthy relationships and opportunities in favor of ones that underscore our self-destructive opinions. We may experience secondary physical and psychic effects which, depending on which chakra is affected, could include heart disease (heart chakra), PMS (abdomen chakra), migraines (hip/genital chakra) or more. Our propensity to store information can also affect our soul, because the soul is affected by each and every circumstance endured by our body and mind. If our soul already mistrusts our body's sexuality, our childhood experience may be just another nail on the coffin of our resistance to purpose.

One of the most dangerous side effects to storing energy occurs when what we hold isn't ours. I believe that our chakric ability to hold the energies of oth-ers is a cultural predisposition. Many native tribes, for example, believe mem-ories may be passed down "through the blood." I have unearthed memories that have affected my life, but these memories haven't been mine. I can remember feelings and experiences from my mother to female ancestors sev-eral hundreds of years back. Some of these memories have helped me by teaching me about strength and love, but many have harmed me, because they have reiterated already detrimental conclusions about being bad or powerless.

In cultures that acknowledge stored memory, such as the American Indian, Peruvian, and Central American tribes I've seen, there are systems for working positively with this phenomenon. In Peru, for instance, a shaman I know helps his patients bring forth his or her ancestors, helps heal them, forces the negative spirits onto another plane, and makes the positive ones promise to help his patients. We have no such process in Westernized civilization, except in various charismatic or evangelical movements; therefore, storing another's energy is typically problematic. Because we lack the cultural understandings or methods for recognizing or dealing with this process, we are victims of the blurring of our own patterns, beliefs, feelings, and needs with those of others.

I believe this blurring was the issue facing one of my clients. At age forty, he began to question why everything he did seemed so closely to mirror what his father had done. They shared similar professions and habits, and had married similar women. We intuitively explored each chakra and, using imagery, began to separate his desires, experiences, and feelings from his father's. He removed intact beliefs and experiences from his father's past. After six months of this work, my client barely resembled the self I had first met. He began to dress, stand, and act differently. He was exploring other career options, and he started marriage counseling with his wife. His last words to me were, "I've spent my whole life being my dad. Now I'm just going to be me."

Storing another's reality can create yet another problem. Since we didn't cause or participate in the experiences we have stored, we cannot cure or heal them. However, they can operate within us as if they were our own feelings and experiences. One of the first things I do when working with clients is ask them to separate their issues, energies, and feelings from someone else's.

Regulatory Functions

Besides serving as a storage unit and emotional clearinghouse, each chakra has individual physical or regulatory functions. For instance, the first chakra reigns over the organs and body parts located in the hip and genital area. It directly affects our sexual processes and genitals, the large intestine processes, and sacral vertebrae area. The second chakra, located in the abdomen, maintains the small intestines, kidneys, and appendix, and the uterus and ovaries in women.

Communication Functions

Because chakras dictate or assist with physical, mental, emotional, and spiritual processes, they function like revolving doors between these four dimensions of our humanness. Your emotions can affect your physical health; your self-judgments can alter your relationship with the Divine Source; your physical well-being can have an impact on your effectiveness in the world. Therefore, the chakras also serve a communication function. Basically, each chakra can communicate with our internal and external worlds, which means that each chakra has separate **physical**, **psychic**, and **intuitive** means of expressing its needs and desires, and the needs and desires of our whole being (figure 2c).

Figure 2c.

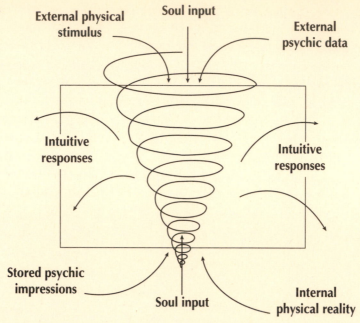

Chakras use physical, psychic, and intuitive communication.

Physical communication is the process of soliciting, processing, or sending sensory (measurable) energies through the physical body to express needs regarding the physical or emotional processes. It is also the process of receiving assistance through the physical/sensory body to meet our needs.

Psychic communication is the process of receiving, processing, encoding, and sending invisible (currently immeasurable) energy to meet our needs, usually in regard to mental understandings and processes.

Intuitive communication is the process of receiving, processing, encoding, and sending psychic data in a managed way in order to meet our needs or receive direction regarding important matters, usually in regard to spiritual or soul-based understandings and processes.

In short, we use:

- Physical communication to meet our physical or emotional needs.
- Psychic communication to meet our mental needs.
- Intuitive communication to meet our spiritual needs.

For instance, say you are hit on the head with a baseball bat. Your head hurts, and you are sad. The fifth chakra, located in the throat, can express both the pain and sadness by being verbal. You will cry, rant, rave, and ask for help. The process may turn into a psychic one to gain an understanding about what happened. If you are aware of your psychic abilities, you may ask an invisible guide why the injury occurred and be told, "You weren't paying attention to the game." A less aware person may simply hear a song in his or her head—guidance coming through the fifth chakra seemingly unbidden—with lyrics such as, "Didn't see it coming, didn't see it coming, pay attention next time." The soul may involve itself by "speaking" later about this event if you sit down and meditate, self-reflect, use a journal, pray, or ask for guidance from the Divine Source. You may then "hear" a voice in the head that says, "That hit in the head was to tell you there is something coming in your life you have to watch out for."

The Seven Individual In-Body Chakras

When looking at each of our seven in-body chakras, we will consider certain key indicators about each:

Location — The site of the physical center of each chakra.

Color — The color psychics typically associate with each chakra. The color indicates the type of frequency or tone affiliated with each chakra. Each color could be turned into a musical note or a mathematical frequency. In general, the lower the chakra is located within the body, the lower its tone or color. The lower the tone, the stronger the effect that chakra has on our material self (versus our spiritual self).

Descriptors — Symbols which have been linked to the various chakras. Each chakra has a predominate yang or male theme, which concerns the energy output and its effect on the world, and a yin or female theme, which concerns energy input and its effect on our self.

Source of — A list of what comes from each chakra; an indication of what each chakra adds to the system as a whole.

Seat of —The ultimate purpose of each chakra.

Key Word — A word about a particular chakra to help differentiate it from the others. If you remember any word about a particular chakra, this would be it.

Energy Type — The type of energy that flows in and out of each chakra.

Physical Communication Style — How we express or receive measurable, tangible data through each chakra. This data is usually recognized as physical sensations.

Psychic Communication Style — How we express or receive intangible data, which when processed through a chakra produces a physical or emotional effect. This data is currently scientifically immeasurable and not always confirmable by others.

Intuitive Communication Style — How each chakra relays spiritual information to us or receives information designed to meet our soul's needs.

Problems — A partial list of the most typical ailments associated with each chakra, particularly those illnesses stemming from imbalance within the chakra itself.

Contains — Suggestions of what information is stored within each chakra and could be reached by communication with it.

First Chakra (The Root Chakra)

The first chakra, the root chakra, is critical to our survival. "Psychologically speaking, the root chakra is linked to the basic survival instincts. It is connected with primal feelings...and is the prime mover behind the so called fight-or-flight response," says Gerber in *Vibrational Medicine* (Gerber, 389).

Located in the genital area, the first chakra receives its basic programming from our family. Through this programming, we make decisions regarding our right and will to survive. Our earliest experiences are also recorded here, resulting in the awareness or repression of our most primal feelings.

In *Wheels of Light*, Rosalyn L. Bruyere says, "In the first chakra, to be aware is to be tactile. Nothing happens until it happens in the first chakra; and nothing has happened until we sense it, until we feel it in a tactile way, until it touches us.... Our interaction with our environment is dependent upon our own body's ability to simultaneously record and make us aware of the occurrence of some event or experience" (Bruyere, Rosalyn L. *Wheels of Light: A Study of the Chakras*. Ed. Jeanne Farrens. Arcadia, CA: Bon Productions, 1989, 152). As we move through life, this chakra regulates our physical existence and needs, including issues surrounding sexuality and passion, and the availability of our most basic needs—money, housing, food, clothing, and loving relationships. The first chakra also regulates the physical realm in which it dwells, including our sexual functions.

Location — Lower hips, genital area (figure 2d).

Color — Red.

Descriptors — Images of a serpent, snake, dragon, or "holy fire," similar to the flame of the Holy Spirit. The yang aspect of the chakra relates to how we put ourselves out into the world and how successful we are at surviving. The yin component concerns how able we are to receive material assistance and keep our "will to live" alive.

Source of — Passion; raw, primal feelings, including rage, terror, joy; survival energy; material energy for achieving life purpose; fundamental programming about what we deserve in and out of life.

Seat of — Existence on the physical plane; the will to live.

Key Word — Awareness.

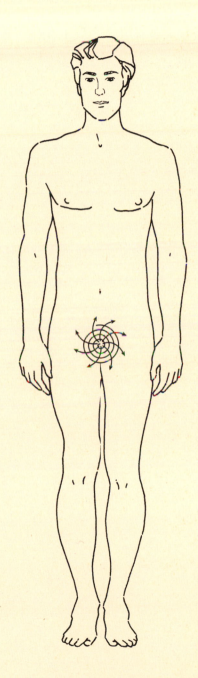

The first chakra.

A fully functioning first chakra gives this awareness: "I am."

Energy Type — Fed by fire energy from inside and outside ourselves. It is the recipient chakra for kundalini, the raw, earth energy feeding our life force and assuring survival.

Physical Communication Style — Communicates physical or emotional needs through real-life sensory impressions: aches and pains, physical awareness, touches, smells, vibrations, movements, feelings. May involve getting sick as a means to becoming aware of a problem.

Psychic Communication Style — Conveys information regarding our mental needs through physical empathy, the registration of physical and feeling-based sensations from sources that are perceived as not there. Can include feeling physical pains, illnesses, and feelings that belong to someone else; getting hit with smells, nausea, touches, vibrations that seem to come from nowhere. I associate abilities such as psychometry, the act of reading physical objects, with this chakra.

Intuitive Communication Style — Receives or sends physical sensations that make us look at a soul or spiritual issue or need, causing us to sometimes experience an imaginary reality, as if we were really there. While these experiences are woven from psychic energies, they usually involve a higher learning and call for a significant change in lifestyle.

Problems — Root area for addictions and compulsions; sexual dysfunctions (physical, behavioral, or emotional); nervous system diseases or disorders; urinary tract disorders; rectal problems; some circulatory, skin, or reproductive issues; headaches. Family dysfunctions and gender role confusion; any childhood abuse issues; money, career, and finance issues; questions about housing, food, and basic needs.

Contains — Our roots, including family values, beliefs, and heritage; original feelings about ourselves, our right to exist, our right to occupy space, our right to be loved, our right to get our needs met; programming affecting our basic needs, including the needs for money, love/being loved, sex, food, air, water, housing; material energy for achieving life purpose.

Second Chakra

Our second chakra, located in the abdomen, is the center of our feelings and creativity. Through this chakra, we begin to understand our reactions to our inner and outer worlds, and decide how we are going to express these reactions. Feelings originating here are generally "softer" than feelings stemming from the first chakra, and the most healthy way to work them out is through creative or emotive expression. This center is particularly important to women, who, I believe, store most of their life energy within it. Regarding physical processes, it is linked to the intestines, abdominal organs, and female reproductive system.

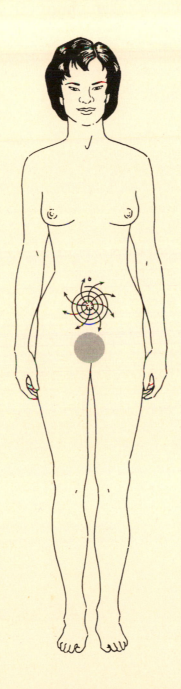

The second chakra.

A functioning second chakra brings us this awareness: "I am feeling."

Location — Abdomen (figure 2e).

Color — Orange.

Descriptors — Water elements and water animals, such as fishes and lizards. Its yang element involves how we express feelings to others and create within the world; the yin aspect involves absorbing or interpreting others' feelings; making self-judgments about our own feelings and creativity; and being able to take in the life energy needed to feel and create.

Source of — Feelings; creative energy; birthing and gestation activity (for babies, businesses, ideas, projects—anything); *women's power*.

Seat of — Feelings and our awareness of them (feelings being the language of the body); creative abilities; *female identity*.

Key Words — Feeling, creativity.

Energy Type — Chi energy, which is seen as life energy in the Chinese system.

Physical Communication Style — Involves feeling and expressing our feelings through the appropriate physical medium, such as crying, screaming, laughing.

Psychic Communication Style — Known as feeling empathy, the ability to experience our own or another person's feelings for the purpose of understanding and clearing self-destructive beliefs. This gift helps us dissect emotions, which are feelings joined with thoughts (as in, "I am angry, therefore, I am bad").

Intuitive Communication Style — Uses feeling empathy to learn a soul lesson or help integrate the soul more fully into the body. It could involve experiencing the feelings of someone we hurt or actually experiencing our soul's feelings as it more fully integrates into the body.

Problems — "Itis" issues, such as diverticulitis and colitis; appendix disorders; kidney problems (childhood issues); fertility issues; women's issues, such as PMS, candida, ovarian disorders, uterine problems; issues from stored, stuck, or unexpressed emotions from self or others; co-dependency (literally taking on or storing another's feelings); creative blocks.

Contains — Feelings of self and others.

Third Chakra (The Solar Plexus Chakra)

The third chakra is highly complex. Known most commonly as the "power center," it functions as the storage house for the judgments, opinions, and beliefs we have gathered about ourselves and the world. These judgments, in turn, affect our self-esteem and self-confidence. Perhaps this is why this center is seen as the source of cognition, the "knowingness" that tells us how to operate within the framework of school, society, and the world. In *Women's Psychic Lives*, Diane Stein describes this center as a "psychic energy pump"

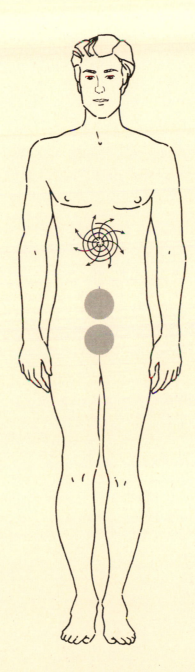

The third chakra.

A functioning third chakra will result in this awareness: "I am feeling and thinking."

for the physical and non-physical bodies. She says, "Emotional and psychic balance are located at this center and thought-forms are produced here" (Stein, Diane. St. Paul, MN: Llewellyn Publications, 1988, 33).

This center is especially important for men, who, I believe, must rely on it as their decision-making point instead of the first chakra. This chakra also correlates to our digestive process and interrelates with the organs located within it.

Location — The solar plexus region (figure 2f).

Color — Yellow.

Descriptors — Air elements and airborne entities, including birds. The yang presence involves expression of self in the world; the yin aspect concerns opinions and judgments about self and other.

Source of — Personal power; self and other judgments; intellectual understanding of physical/worldly existence; *men's power*.

Seat of — Self-esteem; power; directed will; ability to discern; *male identity*.

Key Words — Power, discrimination.

Energy Type — Mental, intellectual.

Physical Communication Style — Perceived as ideas, thoughts, or intellectual understandings that register at gut-level to help us succeed, interface in the world, deal with people, and make effective decisions.

Psychic Communication Style — Known as mental empathy or clairsentience (clear sensing), the means of knowing or sensing something that while it can be justified, isn't rational. This information usually applies to working through issues of personal power and self or other judgments.

Intuitive Communication Style — Use of mental empathy to effectively achieve a position in the world which will help the soul achieve its purpose. Data received or generated usually creates situations, opportunities, and events to benefit the soul and self as a whole.

Problems — Digestive and metabolic disorders; weight issues; feelings of confusion or craziness; power issues. When linked with heart, co-dependency and caretaking (mixing up love and power needs). Different issues for different organs—liver problems indicate anger with men or male self; spleen disorders indicate female anger and defense issues, or faulty use of female power; stomach problems indicate swallowing others' opinions or thoughts; gallbladder troubles indicate resentments, grief about men, our male self or achievement in the world; pancreas disorders indicate the ability to take in or hold the "sweetness" in life or having been smothered, over-mothered, or under-nurtured. The adrenals and kidneys are shared with the second chakra, and so reflect issues of power and feelings—the adrenals hold beliefs regarding our creative reactions to perceived dangers or opportunities; the kidneys hold childhood perceptions regarding emotional needs.

Contains — Opinions, differentiated beliefs.

Fourth Chakra

Since time began, the heart has been seen as the center of the human body, the melting pot for the divine energy of the crown and the life drive of the genital area. In the Cherokee tradition, Dhyani Ywahoo says, "Much of our transformation process, especially at the level of emotion, occurs through the lungs and the energy bridge or doorway behind the heart" (Ywahoo, 116). Indeed, most of our decisions would be prosperous and authentic if they were to be made by the heart, the center of relationships, love, and compassion. Some would say human success depends upon evolving our hearts.

The change in the psychic energies of the evolving heart could indicate this. At birth, the heart is green, indicating an inborn healing ability and energy. During our productive adulthood years, it should be seen as pink, the integration of the white (purpose) color of the crown and the red (passion) color of the first chakra. Finally, we are to achieve gold, the color of universal love. On a more mundane level, this chakra affects the physical processes involving the heart and lungs (circulation and respiratory functions).

Location — Heart (figure 2g).

Color — Green, pink, gold.

Descriptors — Earth-type elements and mammalian animals. The yang function pertains to relationships with others and what we are giving to the world; the yin aspect relates to the relationship with self and what we are willing to receive from the world.

Source of — Healing energy; our innermost desires; our dreams.

Seat of — Compassion, relationships.

Key Words — Love, healing.

Energy Type — Astral (connects to the astral plane and the dream world).

Physical Communication Style — Communicates about physical and emotional needs through actual physical sensations, including heart pains, pangs, and emotional tugs. Source of healing energy used in hands-on healing, hugging, and physical touch. The heart is communicating or receiving whenever we are doing what we love to do.

Psychic Communication Style — Receives messages from aspects of self and guides through dreams, out-of-body experiences (astral projection), receiving and sending healing energy, guided or automatic writing, and journaling.

Figure 2g.

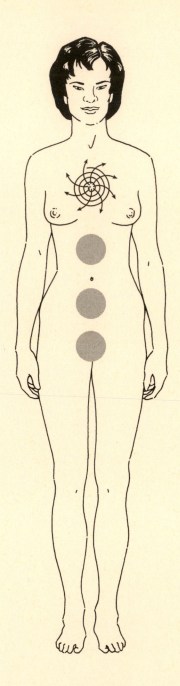

The fourth chakra.

**When fully functioning, the fourth chakra adds this perspective:
"I am feeling and thinking lovingly."**

Intuitive Communication Style — Occurs when working with higher frequencies and energies through the heart, such as channeling guides, rays, principles, out-of-body chakric energy, and, when fully mature, Divine Source or Christ, as individualized to our uniqueness. Soul issues, such as giving and receiving or living our heart's desires, are input, guided, and healed through this center.

Problems — Heart or circulatory diseases or disorders; blood pressure problems; lung-related problems, including asthma, allergies, bronchitis, and pneumonia; relationship problems; sleep disorders. With the third chakra, co-dependancy and caretaking issues.

Contains — The ability to relate.

Fifth Chakra

The fifth chakra is very useful for manifesting and for self-protection. Through it, we express what we think, feel, see, desire, and detest. The front of this chakra is often known as the "seat of responsibility," for through it we say "yes" or "no" to life's options. Also linked with the soul, this chakra is seen as a vehicle for the soul's expression of its desires. Of great psychic importance, this chakra allows us to share the information we are receiving from the invisible self. Its physical presence involves the throat and auditory processes.

Location — Throat (figure 2h).

Color — Blue.

Descriptors — Figures relating to the etheric element or humanity. The yang function relates to expressing and voicing truths; the yin aspect is attuned to receiving guidance.

Source of — Truth.

Seat of — Wisdom; responsibility.

Key Word — Expression.

Energy Type — Etheric, an emotional energy that has been charged with spiritual awareness.

Physical Communication Style — Uses language, sounding, singing, toning, or any other verbal means of communication to express the experiences, needs, or emotional states of our physical awareness. Gathers information regarding these matters by hearing or reading.

Psychic Communication Style — Center of clairaudience (clear hearing), the ability to hear or speak psychically to ourselves, spirit guides, or other people. Abilities such as guided writing, channeling, trans-mediumship, and telepathy are linked with this chakra. It ideally uses these abilities to

Figure 2h.

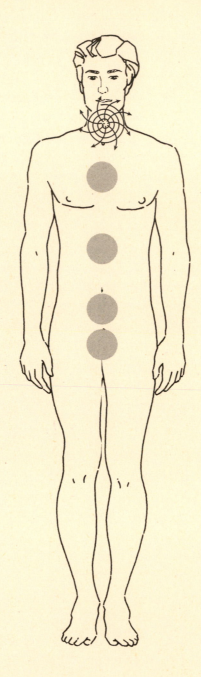

The fifth chakra.

A functioning fifth chakra will enable us to say:
"I am feeling, thinking, and lovingly expressing."

clarify and clear debilitating mental belief patterns, and eliminate cords that feed it "old tapes."

Intuitive Communication Style — Often seen as the "seat of the soul," the entry point for a non-integrated soul on a daily basis. The soul speaks verbally or psychically through this chakra to help us create the circumstances necessary to achieve purpose. The soul will also send or receive guidance from higher beings through psychic channels available to this chakra.

Problems — Any disorders affecting the throat area, including the jaw or mouth, thyroid, larynx, tonsils, and thymus; inability to say "no" or "yes"; victimization from non-assertion; issues of under- or over-responsibility.

Contains — The ability to define ourselves in the world.

Sixth Chakra (The Third Eye)

Revered since ancient times, this chakra, also called the "third eye," is our inner and outer visual center. Through it, we obtain, record, and send pictures, symbols, colors, and images that represent reality. Linked to the pituitary gland, this center regulates many of our hormonal and endocrine functions, basing its physical health on our self-image and goals. As Gerber says, "The endocrine glands are part of a powerful master control system that affects...the body from the level of cellular gene activation on up to the function of the central nervous system. The chakras are thus able to affect our moods and behavior through hormonal influences on brain activity" (Gerber, 370).

Location — Forehead (figure 2i).

Color — Purple.

Descriptors — Figures pertaining to the spiritualized human, such as saints, spirits, and gurus. The yang aspect pertains to ability to see and reach the future, and perform strategic planning measures; the yin function relates to self-image and self-perception.

Source of — Insight.

Seat of —Visions and visioning.

Key Word — Vision.

Energy Type — Cerebral; the front of the third eye draws energy from the brain and the seventh chakra.

Physical Communication Style — Uses ability to see, draw, or otherwise project images to communicate or determine physical or emotional needs or desires.

Psychic Communication Style —Called clairvoyance (clear seeing), this chakra can help us internally visualize images, including colors, symbols, forms,

Figure 2i.

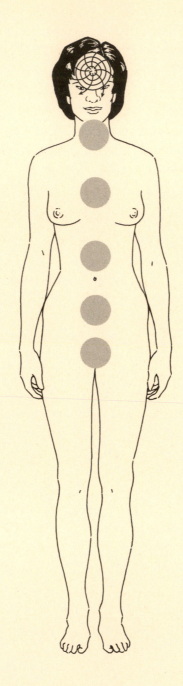

The sixth chakra.

When the sixth chakra is fully functioning, we can say:
"I am feeling, thinking, and lovingly expressing my vision."

metaphors and literal or figurative pictures of beings, events, or ideas from the past, present, or future. This ability also pertains to being able to send this type of visual data. Some people are able to perform clairvoyant functions with their physical eyes. Work done with this ability usually applies to clearly seeing and working with the imagination.

Intuitive Communication Style — The means employed by the soul to communicate desires for the future, and to present views that need to be changed to reach it. Advanced intuits can actually create their projections with the use of imagination or "i-magic-ation." Insight, inspiration, and other visually based abilities are based here.

Problems — Glandular or endocrine issues (this chakra is linked to the pituitary gland); hormonal imbalances; growth or development issues; difficulty in planning for the future; eyesight issues; headaches in the brow indicate a problem with the third eye, either from over-use or under-use; adolescent issues.

Contains — Self-image and the means of correcting/shaping one's view of self and the world.

Seventh Chakra (The Crown Chakra)

Connected to the pineal gland, cerebral cortex, and our higher chakras, this chakra regulates many in- and out-of-body functions. Gerber says, "Currents of energy are taken into the body through a stream entering the crown chakra" (Gerber, 371).

The "psychic center" for higher knowing, it receives the spiritual energies and guidance necessary to activate our purpose. Because it is connected to higher planes, the seventh chakra is seen as the center of our divinity, the place through which we know our unity with the Divine Source and all other spiritual beings.

Location — The crown (the baby's soft spot; figure 2j).

Color — White or clear.

Descriptors — Spiritual entities and essences, such as spirit or god forms, angels, or powers. Contains the yang ability to live our divine identity by expressing purpose, and the yin ability to take in energies essential to feeding our spiritual nature.

Source of — Divine awareness.

Seat of — Our oneness with all.

Key Word — Divinity.

Energy Type — Ketheric, a materialized form of spiritual energy originating beyond the earth's space/time continuum.

Figure 2j.

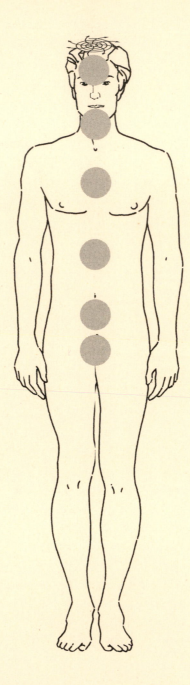

The seventh chakra.

A fully functioning seventh chakra results in this awareness:
"I am feeling, thinking, and lovingly expressing my vision of divine purpose."

Physical Communication Style — Describes our physical needs and emotional desires through our thoughts and any actions that feed our purpose.

Psychic Communication Style — A higher level of kinesthetic awareness felt as divine inspiration, metatonic or peak experiences, spiritual awakenings and the like.

Problems — Immune system disorders; cancers; bone disorders; nervous system disorders. All problems relating to the pineal gland, which operates as the psychic attunement and purpose center, and as an immune system regulator. Learning disorders or difficulties; schizophrenia, multiple personality disorder, neurosis or psychosis; major depression. Headaches; dizziness or light-headedness. Dissociation or being ungrounded; imbalance of any type; lack of self-understanding; lack of direction.

Contains — The receptive means for understanding path and purpose.

The Five Out-of-Body Chakras

In order to fully understand the human, physically based energy system, we must learn about the top five human chakras. These five chakras connect to the physical body, but are not located or based within it. Rather, they serve as intermediaries between the higher, invisible chakras and the in-body chakras. Their presence firmly validates C. W. Leadbeater's belief that "chakras naturally divide into three groups...respectively the physiological, the personal, and the spiritual" (Leadbeater, 9).

Basically, the lower seven chakras meld our physical, mental, emotional, and spiritual energies with the glue of the physical. Changes made within these seven chakras tend to produce substantial, tangible results. We get a job, get sick, get well, gain or lose a relationship. However, as Gerber observed, the chakras provide a regulatory function for our bodies; there are other bodies or energies affecting us. He says, "Changes in the physical body are merely the observable end result of physiologic events occurring simultaneously on a variety of energy levels" (Gerber, 371). One such level involves the top five chakras, which link the material with the spiritual energy centers. They combine the visible and invisible, working most frequently with elemental and celestial energies.

Elemental energies pertain to the type of quanta creating the earth plane: fire, water, air, and earth. Celestial energies run on a faster, higher frequency, probably through tachyons—particles which move faster than the speed of light. These are the energies relating to concepts, ideas, principles, values, spirituality. I believe that the top five chakras work an alchemy of their own. They are the chakras through which magic is wrought, imagination becomes real, humanity receives salvation. They are the chakras which exchange elemental and celestial energies. Let's examine each of these chakras in depth.

Eighth Chakra

The eighth chakra is incredibly interesting. I find this chakra from the bottom-up; it is located about an inch and a half above the head. Stein says, "Feel it by holding your left palm high above your crown center and notice the energy" (Stein, 36). I perceive it as flat, so it is hard to find from the top-down.

Working with this chakra, I have come to believe that it is our portal into and out of this time/space continuum. Inside it, my clients and students report experiencing the sense of being in space, and they often visualize different stellar or planetary images. The winds, circles, lines, and paths to our own and others' pasts, presents, and futures can be found here.

Here one also finds the Akashic records, the "books" upon which is recorded all we have ever seen, done, or said, in this life or any other. Cherokee teacher Ywahoo calls these records "The Temple of Understanding" which contains "...all the programs of our expression in this life and the other lives that are co-existing" (Ywahoo, 106). Because of this, we can gain access to anything about our past through the eighth chakra. If appropriate, we can read the pasts of others. We can journey to any place that exists in the present or in other dimensions, and probe into potential or destined futures. It is also possible to read alternative pasts, presents, and futures here. When working with clients who have a difficult time separating their issues from those of others, I often guide them into their eighth chakra.

For instance, a CEO spent two sessions trying to determine the cause of his fear of flying, an obvious hazard in his position. I had him feel his eighth chakra, picture his Book of Self (Akashic records), then look up images describing the origin of his fear. He recalled times in his early childhood when his father read aloud newspaper stories concerning airplane crashes. Regaining this information helped my client re-think the decision that planes were dangerous.

This chakra is rich in information about our karma, the slate of issues we have come to work out and learnings we seek to acquire. Because we record in this chakra information about others and their roles in our lives, it is here that we can find many of the cords which currently affect us. We can also trace our patterns (the habitual processes in which we get stuck) through the eighth chakra, making it a valuable access point for healing chronic physical or emotional problems, and difficult relationships. Because it relates to time, many of our time issues can be resolved through this chakra.

Location — About one and one-half inches above the head (figure 2k).

Color — Silver or ultraviolet.

Descriptors — A feminine-based chakra with a male core, most often associated with visual images such as the moon, stars, universal night, planets, other dimensions, and time itself. Its yang elements relate to ways we are

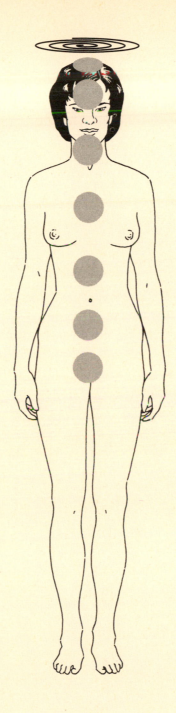

The eighth chakra.

A fully functioning eighth chakra will enable us to say:
"I am feeling, thinking, and lovingly expressing my vision of
divine purpose in a timely manner."

living out karma; its yin aspects are its ability to hold memory and serve as our personal scribe.

Source of — All past knowledge; karmic memory; access to other dimensions and times.

Seat of — Time and timelessness; karma; soul relationships; portals in and through this time/space continuum.

Key Word — Time.

Energy Type — Spatial.

Physical Communication Style — Affects our sense of balance, time, and planning. Keys into the emotions and physical experiences that have occurred in the past.

Psychic Communication Style — Access point for past-life information, present-life data, alternate-reality portals, other dimensions and levels, selected and possible futures.

Intuitive Communication Style — Place that regulates our **destiny points**, the decisions our soul made before we were born regarding life events. Also the place in which we can change these decisions.

Problems — Time issues (being too late, too early); metabolism; difficult relationships; chronic problems, diseases. Any problem that has been carried over from a previous life, whether physical, emotional, mental, physical, relational, or career-related.

Contains — The Akashic Records, the book that records all we have ever done, been, thought, or said in any incarnation.

Ninth Chakra (The Soul Chakra)

Our ninth chakra is the least understood, yet I sometimes believe it is one of our most important chakras. I believe Jungian counselors unknowingly, yet frequently work at this level, for the ninth chakra, functioning as the "seat of our soul," communicates through images, archetypes, patterns, numbers, and other symbols.

Basically, this chakra works just like one of our physical cells. It contains our soul genes, the programs underlying the choices we have made regarding our physical body, emotional states, and mental beliefs. In *Vibrational Medicine*, Gerber refers to these genes as a template, saying, "The etheric body is the energy growth template for the physical. Energetic changes occur at the etheric level before becoming manifest as physical cellular events" (Gerber, 371). Within this chakra lay the fundamental seeds of our soul purpose and information regarding our life purpose and life tasks.

Figure 21.

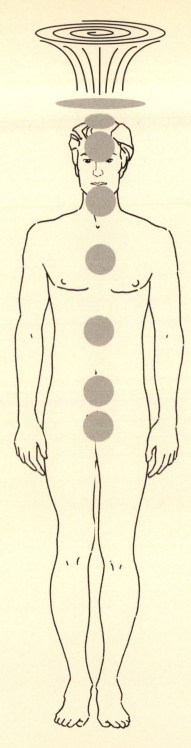

The ninth chakra.

A fully functioning ninth chakra will lead you to know:
"I am feeling, thinking, and lovingly expressing my vision of divine
purpose in a timely manner, while creating all that I am."

All healing must be locked into the ninth chakra to be completely integrated. Only by healing the soul body, which carries all data from one incarnation to another, can we be assured that we are not just going to repeat our lessons over and over.

Location — Approximately one arm's length above the head (figure 21).

Color — Gold or infrared.

Descriptors — Mushroom-shaped; masculine in appearance with a feminine overlay. (Its appearance, of course, depends on the nature of the represented soul.) It contains all symbols, patterns, and archetypes pertinent to a particular person; each symbol functions like a chromosome. Contains the yang ability to imprint and design the physical body and to mold a life for meeting the soul's ends, and the yin ability to channel energy from the Divine Source to create and change the soul itself.

Source of — Creation and change energy; master plans; life seed.

Seat of — Soul genes and templates; personal archetypes and symbols.

Key Word — Soul.

Energy Type — Radioactive.

Physical Communication Style — Helps select the appropriate sperm and egg for this incarnation and oversees the physical and emotional programming functions.

Psychic Communication Style — Speaks to us and external forces through symbols, archetypes, designs, universal and individualized feelings and realities. All symbols refer to our basic beliefs about self.

Intuitive Communication Style — Here, we can tap into representations of the self and soul for healing, insight, and knowledge. From this chakra, we can gain knowledge of soul, life purposes and life tasks, destiny points, significant relationships, and power symbols. It also helps us uncover soul damage for the purpose of healing it.

Contains — Programming of the soul and self.

Tenth Chakra (The Grounding Chakra)

I believe that one of the biggest crimes in the metaphysical movement is the lack of or incomplete teachings about the tenth chakra. We simply cannot be effective in daily life, perform psychic functions, or attempt to fulfill life purpose if we are not grounded.

To be grounded means that we are fully attached to the earth; we are "in" our bodies. Grounded people can draw on their full faculties, abilities, and experiences, and thus, are able to handle any situation. In this way, they are

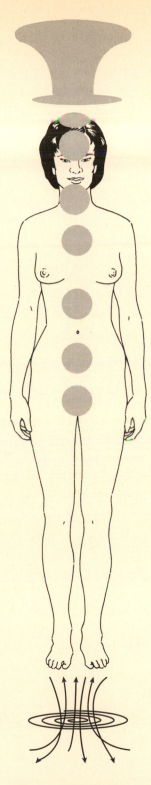

The tenth chakra.

A completely functioning tenth chakra enables us to say:
"I am feeling, thinking, and lovingly expressing my vision of divine purpose in
a timely manner, while creating all that I am, in a grounded, practical way."

comparable to the Shambhallic warrior, the spiritual warrior who lives fully fearless and ready for action.

Ungrounded people are quite easy to spot. They tend to be unfocused, spacey, or out of touch with their own needs and feelings. When I am ungrounded, I usually feel like I am out of my body. This is typically a fear reaction. Many of us dissociate both from an experience and from our self to cope with problems.

In my work, I have found that the tenth chakra works like an earth lung, breathing in elements needed by the physical and emotional body, as well as the chakric and auric systems. It also releases all wastes from these systems into the ground for transformation. When we or others are not grounded, we are probably dissociating from a perceived trauma. When we are not grounded in our tenth chakra, we may experience a light to severe inability to deal with stress or the inability to cope with everyday realities, maintain boundaries, and think with a clear head. We may experience difficulty separating our feelings or reality from those of others. Disconnection from our tenth chakra makes us vulnerable to physical or psychic attacks of any nature. It is also impossible to fulfill our life mission without full assistance from this chakra, because creation requires the full blend of spiritual and material energy; it is through this chakra that we breathe in material energy.

Almost every time I think about this chakra, I remember one of the first times I witnessed its power first-hand. A few years ago, a man came to me asking for help in finding his spaceship. For years, he had been unable to hold down a job or a relationship because of this quest. I psychically saw that his soul was only in his body from the torso up. He had no self in the lower extremities and even complained of frequent leg and foot numbness. Rather than address his request, I asked him if he would be willing to have me help him ground. He agreed. Through breathing and visualization, I had him find and look in his tenth chakra.

His entire demeanor changed. His eyes became focused. He stopped jittering. He began to talk about how painful his life had been, both growing up and into his twenties. After awhile, he admitted that by searching for a spaceship, he didn't have to deal with this pain. We spent a few sessions helping him face the issues and learn how to be grounded. He then consented to long-term therapy with a mental health professional.

This story leads to another interesting function of the tenth chakra. I believe this chakra holds many of our family-of-origin heritage and past-life issues. In fact, I see it as playing a very important role in these matters.

Before and during conception, the tenth chakra, along with the ninth chakra, selects the physical chromosomes regulating our genetic make-up. While the ninth bases these decisions on soul requirements, the tenth substantiates its claims based on our ancestral background, choosing genes from our gene pool that will enable us to meet the physical and psychological challenges we will face.

Location — Approximately one and a half to four feet under the feet (figure 2m).

Color — Earth tones, including citrine, brown, mauve, russet, limestone yellow, olive greens, obsidian.

Descriptors — Contains all four earth elements: fire, earth, water, and air. The yang function pertains to eliminating waste and channeling energy for real life achievement; the yin components pertains to receiving earth energy for the entire system.

Source of — Daily life energy; daily cleansing energy; energy needed to spiritualize the body. Nurturing and sustenance; information on immediate past, present, or everyday life matters. Chooses physical characteristics from our gene pool to help us meet lifetime challenges; through our feet, transports information from our past lives; through our legs, transports information from our lineage.

Seat of — Everyday life energy and information.

Key Word — Grounding.

Energy Type —Elemental.

Physical Communication Style — Dumps waste products from the physical and emotional bodies and from the aura. Also receives elemental energy from the ground and feeds it into the physical energy system. In women, this energy is stored in the abdominal chakra, in men, in the solar plexus chakra. Provides and maintains the influx of energy necessary for "flight or fight" to deal with life's daily occurrences and dangers.

Psychic Communication Style — The key to effective energy receptivity, this chakra is the grounding chakra, keeping all chakras aligned by locking all energies in the ground. Without grounding, the energy body is too frightened to receive or send appropriate information or hold its boundaries.

Intuitive Communication Style — Serves as a locking in or buttoning down place for the soul, which must be fully integrated at all levels of the physical and energy body to accomplish its purpose.

Problems — Foot, ankle, and leg problems. Adrenal problems (not being grounded impinges upon fight-or-flight reactions; shares this function with the second and third chakras). Weight issues (not being grounded causes the body to hold weight to feel safe). Avoidance issues; a sense of being airy or "out-to-lunch"; paranoia, schizophrenia, and other neurosis or psychosis affiliated with dissociation of some sort. Difficulty in staying centered or being in one's body; vulnerability to outside influences, including harmful spirits and dangerous people. Because it holds all denied family issues, it is a critical component in recovering from childhood or inter-generational abuse or abuse patterns.

Contains — Earth memories, needs, and transformational abilities.

Eleventh Chakra

"Other less talked about chakras are those in the palms of the hands and...the soles of the feet," says Stein (Stein, 36). Knowing about the eleventh chakra can be very beneficial energetically. Seen as a pink film around the hands and feet, this chakra can transmute charged external physical or emotional energy into the raw energy our body needs to think, react, and respond. For instance, when tired, we can drink in elemental energy through our feet, soak in the power from a thunderstorm through our hands, or absorb an angry person's negative energy and convert it into strength for our own response. We can also release our own energies through this chakra in order to let go of blocks, resistance, pains, and issues no longer assisting personal growth, or in order to direct psychic or physical energy to affect change.

I have heard many students and clients report success in using this chakra at work. One woman was constantly denigrated by her boss. She started to visualize the energy he sent her as black in color. When he directed this blackness at her, she began to deliberately allow it to enter the pink chakra around her hands. She would then leave the blackness outside of her system, absorb the energy, and reflect his energy back to him as a pink light. She would do this without saying a word. She reported, "It was like the cat would get his tongue! Almost every time I do this, he turns red, swallows his words, shakes his head as if his thoughts were lost, and just plain walks away!"

Healers of any sort, including hands-on professionals, nurses, doctors, or counselors, would do well to learn how to use both the feet and hand outlets of this chakra. They are very useful for converting negative or diseased energies and perceptions, and reflecting them back in a positive way.

Location — Around the hands and feet (figure 2n).

Color — Pink.

Descriptors — Any image related to giving and receiving, such as an open or shut hand. Its yang function relates to energy put out into the world, opportunities grasped or turned away; its yin function pertains to assistance taken in or help received.

Source of — Energy transference; entry point for receiving or sending energy designed to meet our needs or deal with situations.

Seat of — Transmutation for physical energy.

Key Word — Transmutation.

Energy Type — Etheric.

Physical Communication Style — Takes in elemental or emotional energy available in the outside world and converts it into energy needed by the physical or emotional body to respond to any given situation. For instance,

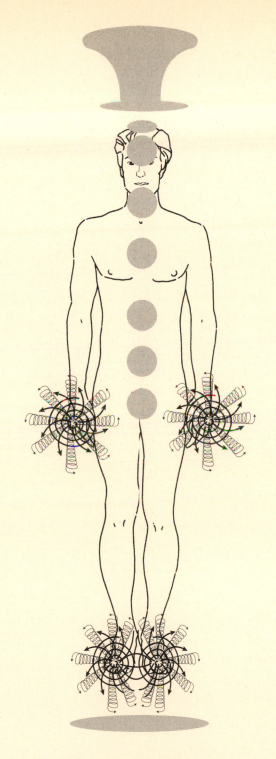

The eleventh chakra.

A fully functioning eleventh chakra enables us to say:
"I am feeling, thinking, and lovingly expressing my vision of divine purpose in
a timely manner, while creating all that I am, in a grounded, practical way that
requires an ability to cope with any situation."

we can soak in energy from a rainstorm or an angry person, and use it to react appropriately to the climactic emergency or dangerous person.

Psychic Communication Style — Reads the energetic properties of outside forces, takes in the actual energy behind the situation, and provides raw energy for psychically responding. This chakra can also send energy out through our hands and feet to deal with this situation.

Intuitive Communication Style — Gives the soul the hands and feet it needs to reach for its desires, protect itself, convert physical energy to spiritualized energy, and receive assistance or data.

Problems — Problems with hands or feet. Problems in reaching for what we want; problems in accepting or receiving help, resources, input; difficulty dealing with difficult or dangerous situations; inability to deal effectively when in fear. Loss of energy when doing psychic work.

Contains — The ability to transmute physical energy into psychic or spiritual energy and vice versa.

Twelfth Chakra (The Secondary Chakra System)

The twelfth chakra is actually a collection of thirty-two points on the body and in the aura. I see these in-body points as the Secondary Chakra System. While most of these secondary chakras are located within our physical body, some of these reach beyond the physical body. The thirty-second secondary chakra, for instance, is in the center of the earth, because our physical survival is contingent on our ability to tap into certain earth elements.

The secondary, in-body points are (figures 2o and 2p):

1. Legs
2. Buttocks
3. Coccyx
4. Sacral vertebrae
5. Lumbar vertebrae
6. Thoracic (dorsal) vertebrae
7. Cervical vertebrae
8. Cranium
9. Silver cord to the soul
10. Bubbling springs in the feet
11. Ankles
12. Knees
13. Thighs
14. Hip bones
15. Navel and sexual organs
16. Appendix
17. Kidneys and adrenals
18. Large and small intestines
19. Pancreas
20. Liver
21. Gall bladder
22. Spleen
23. Stomach
24. Diaphragm and lungs
25. Arms
26. Bubbling springs in palms
27. Wrists
28. Elbows
29. Clavicle
30. Throat (including larynx, thyroid, and tongue)
31. Upper brain (spiritually oriented functions involving cerebrum, pineal, pituitary, hypothalamus, and thalamus glands)
32. Center of the earth

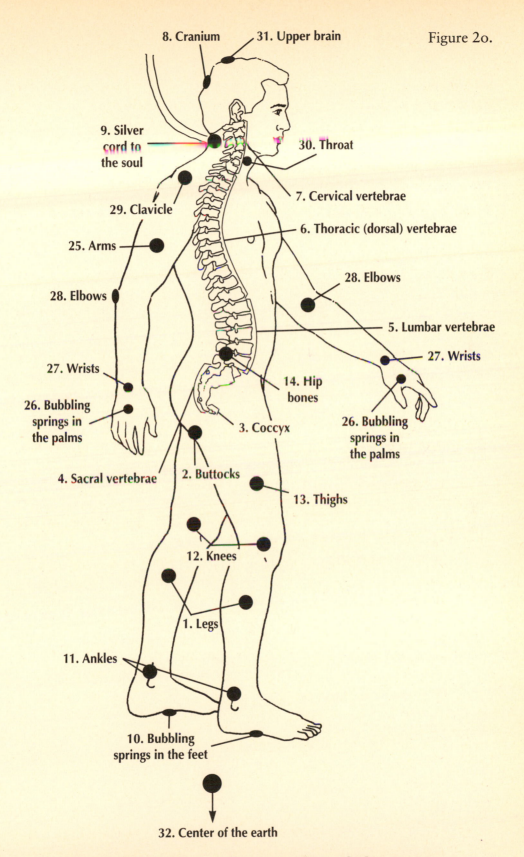

Figure 2o.

The twelfth chakra or the Secondary Chakra System, with its in-body chakra points (1–14; 25–32).

Figure 2p.

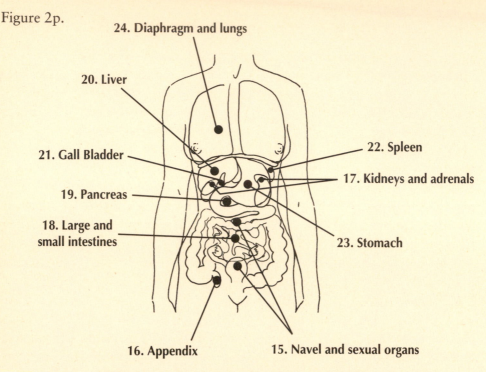

24. Diaphragm and lungs

20. Liver

21. Gall Bladder

19. Pancreas

**18. Large and
small intestines**

22. Spleen

17. Kidneys and adrenals

23. Stomach

16. Appendix

15. Navel and sexual organs

The twelfth chakra or the Secondary Chakra System, with its in-body chakra points (15–24).

Each of these secondary chakras relates to the primary chakra numerically connected to it as well as a particular vertebra on the spinal column. Chapter Ten will explore these access points in more depth. Each secondary chakra is also connected to a specific human archetype.

In general, our twelfth chakra ensures the connection between natural forces and our own body. It determines us as human, because its boundaries are the human visible and invisible energy body. "Man is a soul and owns a body—several bodies in fact; for besides the visible vehicle by means of which he transacts his business with his lower world, he has others which are not visible to ordinary sight," says Leadbeater (Leadbeater, 2).

Linking in with our aura, this chakra effectively encapsulates us while it opens us to non-apparent energies. In this way, it appears similar to the egg-shaped body perceived by anthropologist Carlos Castenada during his training with don Juan, a Yaqui Indian sorcerer. The difference between Castenada's portrait and mine is that I see lines connecting this outer shell to our internal self, thus allowing us to operate as both a closed and open system.

Gaining Access to Our Human Chakras

Ways of experiencing the human chakras are multi-fold. Many of us rely on our intuition to find these centers. We might be able to psychically see, hear, or feel (hands-on or through the "knowing sense") these energy centers. A few people can actually see the chakras with their physical eyes. Studies at UCLA have produced audiotaped sounds of these energy centers.

When working with students, I have them find the chakras using pendulums, devices made of stones or rings hung on a thread or chain. The tester hangs the pendulum over one of the subject's chakras. The subject, willing his or her chakra to open, is usually as surprised as the tester to find the pendulum acquires a life of its own, moving with the frequency and directional flow of the chakra.

Another way to pinpoint these chakras is through a reductionistic or process-of-elimination approach. For example, if you have cirrhosis of the liver, you can deduce you have issues in your third chakra. Knowing that the solar plexus contains the liver, you can examine the functions of the third chakra and begin to reason the non-apparent issues behind your physical disease. The third chakra is the seat of self-esteem and personal power; perhaps you are angry with men for being judged as a child and need to examine your self-esteem in regard to these judgments.

Chakra Combinations

Some chakras pair-up with other chakras to create a strong relationships between the two. It is easy to remember these correlations because the chakric colors are complementary on a color chart. For instance, there is a complementary tie between the following chakras:

- First and fourth (red and green).
- Second and fifth (orange and blue).
- Third and sixth (yellow and purple).
- Seventh and first through the heart (white and red, resulting in pink).

Their functional relationship is logical as well. For instance, the first chakra is our seat of passion. As our life energy vibrates up the spine, it passes through our feeling and thought processes. These perspectives alter our immediate life and death reactions to given situations, and culminate in a heart-felt response, that of com-passion (or being "with passion"), rather than just passion.

Looking at the second and fifth chakras, we could examine the following scenario. Let's say we feel sad because someone insulted us. That sadness originates in the second chakra. Our fifth chakra is the one available for expression of this sadness. We can say, "Don't say that to me," or decide to just swallow our response. Likewise, our third and sixth chakra interrelate. We may store a judgment such as "I am ugly" in our mental chakra, the third. This affects our perception of self, a concept regulated by our sixth chakra. How we see ourselves will have a direct impact what we think we deserve or don't deserve in our future. Hence, our strategic planning skills (third-eye abilities) are determined by our third chakric programs.

There is another pattern we find in chakric interrelationships. Sometimes the chakra holding the block affects the chakras above and below it so much that these chakras, rather than the problematic chakra, are considered to be the chief troublemakers. For example, I worked with a man who was having a difficult time deciding between job options. He admitted that when he was young he was taught that it was bad to make the wrong decision. My sense was that, because job issues, decision-making, and self-esteem fixate in the third chakra, he was experiencing a third chakra block or issue. However, he also reported frequent bouts of abdominal pain and gas and a constricted feeling in his heart, which would worsen when he discussed his career.

I believed that to protect his third chakra, his second and fourth chakras had become blocked, creating his physical discomfort. Rather than address these secondary issues, I took a chance and had him experience the feelings, beliefs, and pictures associated with his third chakra. After three sessions, during which he let himself remember childhood experiences which could be affecting his current attitudes, his second and fourth chakra problems disappeared. He also said he could now feel his stomach and breathe for the "first time, ever!"

Obviously, the interplay between our chakras can be as complicated or as simple as we make it. The most reliable method for working with it is and will continue to be listening to our intuition, that deep, quiet voice within us that knows, sees, and is all.

Other Resources

Most of the information pertaining to these seven in-body chakras corresponds to the systems most widely accepted. If you would like to read more about the chakras, I would suggest the following sources:

The Chakras, by C. W. Leadbeater. Wheaton, IL: The Theosophical Publishing House, 1927.

Hands of Light: A Guide to Healing Through the Human Energy Field, by Barbara Ann Brennan. New York: Bantam Books, 1987.

Wheels of Light: A Study of the Chakras, by Rosalyn L. Bruyere. Edited by Jeanne Farrens. Arcadia, CA: Bon Productions: 1989.

Chapter Three

Your Twenty Spiritual Energy Centers

Although our twelfth chakra rounds out our human existence, it does not limit the extension of our being. There are twenty higher spiritual centers. In fact, there is one more in addition to these that we can reach through the sheer grace of the Divine Source, as we shall see. These spiritual chakras do not have locations, colors, or regulatory functions as we understand them, because they exist outside of the physical framework we call reality. However, they can channel energies so powerful, so intense, that their impact on our physical or emotional bodies can be greater than that achieved through our in-body chakras. Because we can absorb their energies through our physical bodies, we can sometimes experience these energies pictorially, associated with colors, shapes, or forms; physically, having certain predictable, physical sensations; or mentally, making us respond in a logical, repeatable, thought sequence.

In many ways, these higher chakras pertain more to our real self than do our physically based chakras. They have existed in many forms, many ways, and many times, because they do not fluctuate and change when we change bodies. They are the parts of ourselves still held within the Great Divine Source—the Invisible Consciousness, Jung's Conscious Unconscious, Chaos, God, the Buddha, the Atman, the Universe, the Force—whatever we choose to call the unchanging All. Though the Divine Source energy is perfect, our higher spiritual bodies are not necessarily in this same form. Remember, our higher spiritual bodies are intrinsically linked to our lower chakric bodies through our soul, so they record, affect, and are affected by all we experience through our body, mind, or soul. While the Faith energy point, for instance, channels the energy of pure faith through it into all aspects of our being, any issues, fears, misperceptions, experiences, and blocks we hold about faith may warp our perceptions of this energy. We may not receive all the energy available to us, or our imprints may severely affect our impressions of this energy. These energy points, or our perceptions of them, need to be healed, just as our human chakras do.

While examining these energy points, it may be helpful to remember that there is a lot of information not yet known about them. I began developing this system only a few years ago, with little comprehension about what I was doing. My uncovering of these points began because a friend was experiencing tremendous personal distress. Neither medical nor alternative professionals were able to help her, so in desperation she approached me for help. I asked for a dream to provide clarity into the situation.

That night, it seemed to me that a being appeared and showed me a ladder reaching from beneath the ground to the stars above. He told me the human energy system was much broader than anyone guessed and that, yes, many of the rungs were tangible. However, the other guiding forces were far and near, as visible yet invisible as the stars themselves. The next day, I began to use applied kinesiology, intuition, and lucky guesses to help my friend. On myself and on her, I experimented with the different inspirations and systems that came to me.

My appreciation for this work caught fire as I saw various clients respond. A friend was healed of carpal tunnel syndrome during one session. Another cleared up her money issues and began making money the next day. Another received career inspiration. Yet another felt his spine adjust on the table without any physical help. I believe that my work with the thirty-second energy point, Grace, actually saved my life.

I continued to work with and refine the system, knowing that neither this system nor any other will bring forth the key to healing. Rather, the key is our willingness to bring truths through us, so we may live and be them.

To explore these energy points, we will extrapolate information according to the following categories:

- Purpose.
- Function.
- Energy form.
- Communication processes.
- Problems.
- What the energy point contains.

The Higher Energy Centers

13. Yin (female) Energy
14. Yang (male) Energy
15. Balance of Polarities
16. Balance of Similarities
17. Harmony
18. Free Will and Freedom
19. Kundalini
20. Mastery
21. Abundance
22. Clarity
23. Knowledge of Good
    and Bad (the Tree of Life)
24. Creation
25. Manifestation
26. Alignment (with Highest
    Purpose)
27. Peace
28. Wisdom
29. Enjoyment
30. Forgiveness
31. Faith
32. Grace and Divine Source
    Consciousness
    (See figure 3a, color pages.)

Point 13: Yin (Female) Energy

Purpose — To provide the universal female perspective and energies necessary for receiving, processing, protecting, and creating.

Function — To keep us aligned with the forces regulating absorption, gestation, and birthing. Its helps us understand and heal issues regarding pain, negativity, suffering, and trauma, and to transmute these experiences into sources of power and strength. Its yin aspect is the spiritual receptivity to growth and change; its yang aspect concerns decisions about what to do with pain and grief. Related to its functions, this point contains our programs regarding our feminine nature, beliefs about our ability and deservedness about receiving, the effects of our past and current emotions, our spiritual ability to internally and externally create, and our higher intuitive abilities.

Energy Form — Dark power; energies on the low end of the color spectrum. This energy relates to yin in the Chinese system, including cold, contraction, and black. Some people see the major color as magenta.

Communication Process — Linked specifically into the yin function within each chakra. For women, its energies' major entry point is the second chakra; for men, the major entry point is the first chakra.

Problems — Confusion regarding feminine process, female identity, or women's needs and issues; issues surrounding feelings, creativity, and the birthing or gestation of babies, ideas, concepts, projects, or the self; chemical or organic absorption or transmutation concerns; emotions of pain, grief, sorrow, loss; misconceptions around strength, power, feelings, creativity, and deservedness around receiving. Also problems related to gathering and holding the energies needed to dream and manifest, and the primary call for protecting ourselves and our loved ones.

Contains — Our perceptions regarding the female universal energies.

Point 14: Yang (Male) Energy

Purpose — To provide the universal male perspective and energies necessary for expressing, forcing, building, and defending.

Function — To keep us aligned with the forces regulating the expression of dreams, the forcing of change, the building within reality, and the defense of ourselves in the world. This point assists us in comprehending and living out our worldly roles. It is affected by judgments and opinions of self and others, and learned behaviors. Its yin aspect covers that which is held within to determine success; its yang functions relate to the courage and determination required to make dreams real. Related to its purpose, this energy point channels the energy necessary to materialize spiritual energy to meet our needs. Through this point, we connect to our beliefs about power; to our emotions regarding loyalty, courage, and preparedness; to our physical skills and abilities, exhibited in warriorism; and to our call for direct action. Action can include thinking, manifesting, expressing, building, and defending.

Energy Form — Light power; energies on the high end of the color spectrum. The energy relates to the yang in the Chinese system, including heat, expansion, and white.

Communication Process — Linked specifically into the yang function within each chakra. For men, the energies' major entry point is the third chakra; for women, it is the fifth chakra.

Problems — Confusion regarding masculine process, male identity, or men's needs and issues; issues surrounding self-perception, judgments, and skills required for achievement in world. Emotions involving lack, limitation, violence, and cruelty exist within. Beliefs regarding personal and positional power greatly affect the energy channeled through this point and greatly affect physical well-being, including health, status, and career. This point relates to problems in shaping and directing energies needed to achieve success and defend ourselves, our loved ones, and our ideas.

Contains — Our perceptions regarding the male universal energies.

Point 15: Balance of Polarities

Purpose — To align everything within and without us that is polar, tying these complementary energies together to strengthen each.

Function — To create a positive exchange of energies between the seeming dualities, including life and death; female and male; good and bad; absorption and elimination; love and indifference. This point regulates the physical, mental, emotional, and spiritual yin and yang functions within each center by emphasizing the complementary nature of these opposites.

Energy Form — Can be seen as a beam connecting two parallel columns or as the line between the yin-yang symbol.

Communication Process — Links the yang and yin functions within each chakra or energy point. The energy of this point enters every human chakra, specifically through the spinal column.

Problems — Balance problems of any sort and the inability to make peace with any oppositional qualities or natures inside or outside oneself. Symptoms vary greatly. Physically, problems can underlie epilepsy, dizziness, and scoliosis. Emotionally, they could be experienced as conflicting feelings about a relationship. Mentally, they can result in apathy caused by opposite beliefs regarding our needs, safety, self-perception. Spiritually, they can result in the inability to achieve purpose due to internal struggles regarding our desire to be versus do.

Contains — Our perceptions regarding the relationship between seemingly oppositional qualities.

Point 16: Balance of Similarities

Purpose — To align all within and without us that is similar.

Function — To emphasize the similar, and to bond similarities together in a number of ways. This energy point can connect all that is already similar, reveal similarities in that which appears different, or emphasize the individuality in what appears the same. This point's function can be pictured by visualizing the spine. Notice the tissues that are similar in each vertebra, then pretend to adjust the spine by lining up these similar tissues. This center works that same way. Now picture the tissue that is different. Make these differences so vast the tissue actually becomes the same. Yes, this center can also make in-born differences so extreme that they actually curve around and return to the point at which they become the same. This point's function is also comparable to the yin-yang symbol. These separate entities cohabit because they are different and independent (a function of Point 15), but also because the yin also has the yang within and vice versa (Point 16). This point channels the energy necessary to see these similarities and link them, thus uniting the two forms. It also pushes the yin and the yang to reveal the similarities hidden by the differences.

Energy Form — Can be seen as the yin within the yang or the yang within the yin.

Communication Processes — Links the yang and yin functions within each chakra or energy point. Its energy enters every human chakra, specifically the spinal column.

Problems — Any type of balance problem and the inability to make peace with qualities or natures of a similar sort inside or outside of ourselves. Being unable to recognize the similarities between ourselves or someone else, such as similarities in feelings, views, needs, experiences, and souls. When we fail to see or express these similarities, we may experience dis-ease within our physical, emotional, mental, or spiritual systems, such as denial, prejudices, war, spiritual judgmentalism, or any physical symptom that results from our rigidity.

Contains — Our perceptions regarding the interrelation between similar qualities.

Point 17: Harmony

Purpose — To completely align all that appears similar and different in order to achieve the oneness and unity necessary for health.

Function — To transform differences into similarities and similarities into differences in order to merge these two forces on all levels. This energy point is capable of working on all levels. Physically, it alleviates conditions caused by balance disorders, including those involving the breath, lungs, ears, headaches, migraines, eye problems, cranial issues, upper torso, spine, and bones in general. Emotionally, it soothes our internal relationship with ourselves and relationships with others by showing how we are one and the same; it shows that we all have had the same feelings, albeit for different reasons. Capable of rearranging the structure of our thoughts, the energy channeled through this chakra can unite even warring people. What others have done to us, we are capable of doing to them—knowing this is a great leveler. Spiritually, this center brings all back to the Divine Source, to the time when we knew we were all the Divine Source, yet still separate beings.

Energy Form — Opaque, it can call forth any energies necessary to achieve its ends.

Communication Processes — Enters all oppositional and similar functions simultaneously to perform its work. While this energy point speaks most often through revelation, it can also shape experiences to illustrate its points. Energy of harmony may also be channeled in its raw form, especially through the seventh chakra, where it enters through the pineal gland, and results in the production of mana and an advanced psychic awarenesses.

Problems — Any and all problems resulting from lack of harmony or attunement within or between ourselves and the environment.

Contains — The perceptions required to internally unify and authentically express ourselves in regard to the understanding of differences and similarities.

Point 18: Free Will and Freedom

Purpose — To align us with our abilities and our right to choose that which conforms to our higher purpose and essential needs.

Function — To set up situations to help us learn that our deepest needs involve making decisions which align with the deepest yearnings of our essence and the Divine Source within. Most frequently works by showing us our in-born right to live and be exactly as we desire. It defines free will as the state of experience connected with responsibility to self and the Divine Source—just the opposite of being owned by others or the Divine Source. It implies that that freedom of choice is about making decisions that retain free will, but which are authentic at the same time. When existing in true accountability and self-power, we do not need cords; free-will energy can therefore correct relationships with self, others, and the world. It is helpful for healing emotional issues of any sort, especially those regarding blame, self-hatred, victimization, and betrayal. It works frequently for mental processes, including those regarding over- or under-responsibility and abandonment. Spiritually, it forces us to understand our real needs and desires. Physically, it is often linked to the "freedom" organs, such as the lungs and heart.

Energy Form — Clear.

Communication Process — While physical, it most often results in intellectual or intuitive struggles. A sure sign we are working at this level is any physical discomfort in our heart or lung area.

Problems — Lungs or heart area most often physically affected. Mental problems are often experienced as indecision or the questioning of purpose, path, relationship. These feelings are often associated with loss or abandonment; spiritual issues evolve into struggles between responsibility and our own desires.

Contains — Answers to our most burning questions.

Point 19: Kundalini

Purpose — To provide us with the raw energy necessary to materialize the spiritual.

Function — To channel the raw, organic energy we need to perform any physical, mental, emotional, or spiritual function. It helps link our first chakra with our seventh, connecting our material center with our spiritual one. Thus aligned, we bring the material energy to the spiritual realm, allowing the spiritual to become real, solid, tangible. Kundalini energy fuels the entire physical system by traveling up and around the spinal column. It cleanses, opens, and energizes the chakric system. It also activates our emotional and mental processes, ensuring that the energy continues to flow within our systems without getting stuck.

Energy Form — Raw, organic life energy. Often seen as red, it can also have an impact as cobalt blue.

Communication Processes — In men, the energy primarily enters through the coccyx, then weaves its way to the pineal gland. Many men initially experience a torrent of sexual desire or strong feelings culminating in a "white light" or revolutionary experience. Women may undergo the same process; however, I have found it just as likely that the woman's kundalini will enter through the heart, then loop downward into the second or tenth chakras, and upward to the seventh and the ninth. During this process, women may experience intense grieving or connections to their ancestors, plus an awareness of purpose and a full awakening of their psychic/higher intuitive processes. When women's kundalini does strike the first chakra initially, it typically rules her life until brought into the second chakra, from which it can loop into the heart.

Problems — Lack of kundalini affects every area of life. The significant word is probably "energy." Misperceptions can cause us to channel either not enough or too much kundalini energy. Lack in the first chakra can result in sexual inhibitions, low-iron blood, or a lack of money. Emphasizing the first chakra's need for kundalini over the needs of other chakras can create violence, work addictions, and growths. Any and all chakras and systems are affected by kundalini. You could say it is like a family; you can't feed only the father of a family and expect everyone else to be nourished, too. However, starving the father, even when providing for the others, might affect everyone, because father will not then be able to be responsible in other areas.

Contains — The organic energy needed to create and maintain life and its processes.

Point 20: Mastery

Purpose — To achieve self-regulation, self-ownership, and the ability to rule one's own fate.

Function — To enable us to be our own sovereigns. Because each person is an individual, each may choose mastery of different areas. One person may choose to master physical reality, another to become professional at emotions, making magic, or riding horses. Completely mastering one arena is training ground for mastery of the self. To be our own master is to "know thyself," as the Greek god Apollo would say.

Energy Form — Linear and horizontal at the same time. Mastery teaches us to operate logically and inside a larger framework. Mastery helps us spiritualize the material. In process form, we derive the principles, skills, and judgments needed to understand our abilities and rights from our actual experiences and real-world knowledge.

Communication Processes — Can be experienced as a feeling, yet primarily shapes our mind and mental processes. You are what you believe you are.

Problems — Lack of mastery typifies itself as a lack of belief in self or our own worth and any conditions resulting from it. Mentally, it may be experienced as low self-esteem. Emotionally, it may be experienced as depression or general malaise. Spiritually, it may be experienced as the soul's refusal to take a risk or be in the body. Physically, lack of mastery may show itself as lack of success, disuse of muscles, and more.

Contains — The belief the universe holds about us, available for our internal assimilation.

Point 21: Abundance

Purpose — To align with the natural ebb and flow of energies available for us in order to meet our highest purpose and essential needs.

Function — To channel the energies we need to attract situations, people, and resources that will help us achieve our purpose. Conversely, it also opens us to events and circumstances which will help us release that which we no longer need (resources that need to be re-circulated).

Energy Form — Abundance is like a circle between the material and spiritual. While Kundalini helps us materialize our spiritual desires, and Mastery helps us derive spiritual ideals from our material experiences, Abundance ties these two together through the principle of giving and receiving. We allow the material resources we need to meet our purpose to come in, then we release our spiritual dreams into the world to attract their physical counterparts.

Communication Processes — We attract the material through awareness of our higher needs, and we meet our higher needs by releasing spiritual energy into the physical. In other words, Abundance energy helps us think of our desires through the top, in-body chakras; then, through the heart, it activates the abilities of the lower in-body chakras to manifest these desires. This point encourages the lower chakras to cleanse the energy, material goods, emotions, and forms no longer needed. It then fills this empty space with dreams, so that they might become real.

Problems — Any issues of lack or stockpiling. Physical impairments can include not having enough of anything or having so much of one thing that you are impeded. Mental aspects involve beliefs that inhibit free expression of self and energy, especially "I don't deserve…" issues. Emotional components can be felt as envy, greed, sorrow, jealousy, loss. Spiritual problems usually result from beliefs about being inherently evil or bad, or not being loved by the Divine Source. Past-life experiences greatly affect this center. For instance, if someone in a prior existence was hanged for living his purpose, he might be so afraid of similar treatment in his current life that he blocks awareness of his life purpose, refuses to accept help, clings to a job he hates, or lives in terror regarding risk.

Contains — The knowledge of cycles necessary to have all needs met.

Point 22: Clarity

Purpose — To enable us to see things as they really are (not how we might want them).

Function — To shed light on our inner and outer realities. It serves as a vehicle for discernment through which we acquire the skills necessary to know the right questions, plus the ability to differentiate between what is imperative to know, do, feel, or be, and what isn't. Clarity then becomes the basis for making decisions on all levels. Physically, we can now decide whether to go to this doctor or that doctor. Mentally, we can see if we agree with someone else's conclusions about us or not. Emotionally, we can evaluate the basis of our feelings and how we want to express them. Spiritually, we can select opportunities for growth and decide how to operate within them.

Energy Form — Clarity is typically seen as a yellow-gold light because this point most frequently channels into our bodies through the third chakra (yellow), the heart operating at the highest level (gold), or the pineal gland (white).

Communication Processes — Experienced most often as clear thinking and emotional awareness. It can also cause events to align with our soul's purpose, providing us with signs and knowledge about what actions to take in everyday life.

Problems — Any area of life that is confusing, dissatisfying, non-resolved, unclear, murky, or cloudy. Such problems can involve anything from relationship questions and boundaries to an undiagnosed physical complaint.

Contains — The energy necessary to fully see all components of an issue or situation.

Point 23: Knowledge of Good and Bad (the Tree of Life)

Purpose — To reveal the duality inherent in all processes in order to bring them into balance.

Function — To show us the depth of the universal knowledge. This point is connected to our inherent right to choose (Free Will), to channel energy at will (Kundalini), to decide what to do with this energy (Mastery), to use it to get what we want and get rid of what we don't want (Abundance), to see our choices and their consequences clearly (Clarity), and to use these choices to delve into the reasons behind them (Knowledge). Through this center, we find out that our truest motivations may not be that godly, and that our basest, most shame-based motivations may be strivings for something not as bad as we thought.

Energy Form — Extreme light and dark energies. The light energy enters our darker, shadow parts of the self, illuminating the love inside the aspects of which we are most ashamed. The dark energy penetrates our lighter, godly aspects, causing us to question the motivations behind them.

Communication Processes — Religion has made much use of this point's energy. The stories of Adam and Eve, the Kabbalistic Tree of Life, the idea of an all-good God and all-bad Satan, are our cultural attempts to pare down dualities such as good and bad to their essential elements.

Problems — Spiritual questions, moral dilemmas, judgments about our own or the other gender. Problem feelings include shame, guilt, grief, blame. Problem beliefs are any regarding evil versus good. Physical problems result from self-flagellation of any sort or exposure to another's shame-based behaviors. Addictions, violence, rapes, and other harmful situations are directly linked to this energy point.

Contains — The seed of love hidden beneath our beliefs in good and bad.

Point 24: Creation

Purpose — To open us to the energies necessary to create that which we truly desire.

Function — To help us process the desires or knowledge underlying our good and bad selves and other dualities, thus adding to the awareness achieved in the previous point. To create from scratch requires a full connection between the self and our dream/emotional lives. This awareness is our return to innocence, our regression back to the self who wants only love. Spiritually, this center relates to the self as it first emerged from the Divine Source, still pure and hopeful. Mentally, it pertains to our beliefs about our right to exist and create within existence. Emotionally, we re-experience and heal our fears and fantasies within this point. Physically, this center relates most directly to our second and fifth chakras and all the processes connected to them.

Energy Form — Similar to the energy available in and through the second chakra, which is emotive and sensual in nature. The energy of this point would be seen visually as light, felt in the physical body, or felt through feelings.

Communication Processes — We experience this energy center sensually or emotionally. It is linked with the nature of our inborn, inner child, the child of the Divine Source, the child which we are underneath.

Problems — Difficulties in understanding or owning our dreams, desires, fantasies, feelings, or needs. Issues regarding the acceptance of our purity and innocence—impotence, frigidity, emotional imbalances, and lack of love for self or in relationships—and the physical processes connected with these issues) are associated with this chakra. These problems can lead to concerns in our second and fifth chakras.

Contains — The gem of our innocence.

Point 25: Manifestation

Purpose — To add the dark, substantial energies necessary to protect or create that which we desire.

Function — To associate our innocence with our deeper, more substantial dark power. We need this darker, more protective energy to remain safe enough to expose our vulnerable dreams to the world. This center channels our warrior energy—the ability to immediately tap into the power necessary to deal with any situation that arises. This dark power can be shaped and molded as we see fit. We can use it to protect ourselves—to make a sword to stop enemies, to shout "Stop," to shield ourselves emotionally, to make the money necessary to employ a security guard. It is also the energy behind materializing physical resources and objects. We manifest or make real our desires for money, houses, relationships, and other desires by channeling this energy of substance.

Energy Form — Dark power, the deep energy needed to protect, defend, buttress, and actualize physical objects.

Communication Processes — Associated primarily with the first, fifth, sixth, and eleventh chakras. Through the first chakra, we pull in the energy to preserve our life and material goods. Through the fifth, we make statements of desires and assign responsibilities. Through the sixth, we receive and project our dreams and desires. Through the eleventh, we transmute energies for meeting daily goals.

Problems — All issues relating to safety and protection, and to our ability to make good on desires. Symptoms of an incorrectly operating Manifestation point can be similar to those affecting Abundance. To determine which chakra or energy point is affected, we can isolate the inner child available through the Creation point and ask questions. If there are issues that have to do with feeling unsafe, we are dealing with the Manifestation point. If these issues have to do with not believing in meeting needs, we might work with the Abundance point.

Contains — The force necessary to defend our right to actualize our desires.

Point 26: Alignment

Purpose — To bring our dark and light, child and adult, material and spiritual selves into full alignment, allowing us to be an open channel for achievement of purpose and the energies required to fulfill it.

Function — To link our seeming incompatible, yet highly interdependent aspects of the self. Getting all parts of ourselves to work together is the key to receiving the assistance, energies, and situations necessary to know and live our purposes.

Energy Form — Both light, dark, and grey at the same time. An appropriate image is the spine. When all processes and chakras are in their right places, the spine becomes a lightning rod for the physical, mental, emotional, and spiritual energies that make us complete.

Communication Processes — In the physical body, alignment energy works to line up the crown chakra with the first chakra, and the tenth chakra with the ninth. In our everyday lives, we know we are in alignment when everything flows smoothly, and when, upon hitting obstacles, we can nurture the child aspect of the self while calling upon the warrior self to direct us around or through the problem.

Problems — Ultimately, any dissatisfaction or lack of harmony is an alignment issue. Absence of harmony should not be confused with the occurrence of problem issues. Because others have free will, they can attempt to gum up the works. Being in alignment doesn't mean we never get problems or have crises. It means we can call on the powers and abilities we need to deal with them.

Contains — Respect for the process of alignment and the energies necessary to flow with it.

Point 27: Peace

Purpose — To help us accept ourselves—our pasts, present, and desired future—with respect and honor.

Function — To allow us to unearth the unlovable aspects of our being and honor them. To do this, the center channels the energy of the Divine Source's acceptance of us and all we have been/done. The major vehicle for this process is letting go, which culminates in a serene acceptance of all aspects of our own and others' beings. Letting go involves releasing the belief that we are in control, that somehow, we could have made it all different, or can make it all work out. By wrestling with the resultant feelings of hopelessness and powerlessness, we can open ourselves to enthusiasm and power.

Energy Form — A feeling of awareness rather than a physical substance, the energy channeled through this point is both static and dynamic at the same time, comparable to the stillness of a pond surface underneath which life teems. Color-wise, pink would be a typical color, because it blends the different energies of white and red.

Communication Processes — The energy behind this point can enter at any level at any time, but is only completely utilized when all chakras and energy points integrate it.

Problems — Any judgments or thought processes that keep us stuck prevent access to peace energy. Fundamentally, all physical diseases are symptoms of lack of peace or serenity because they disturb the flow. Clearing our resistance to peace energy doesn't mean we won't have feelings of sorrow, anger, or fear. Instead, we accept those feelings. Not needing to resist them prevents them from getting blocked or stored. In peace, we may still experience self-doubt or criticism, but we are capable of working through our false belief systems, using clarity to sort through and make new conclusions. Spiritually, the acceptance of the peace energy allows us to begin assuming our full place within the universe.

Contains — Acceptance of self mirrored by the Divine Source's full acceptance of us.

Point 28: Wisdom

Purpose — To enable us to claim the learnings from our experiences (which is the definition of wisdom) while fully releasing the traumas and feelings associated with them.

Function — To enable us to define the growth, strengths, and knowledge gained on our path, and free us to make decisions about other ways to learn in the future. This point works by helping us boil our experiences down to core beliefs, and by breaking the patterns resulting from these experiences.

Energy Form — Linked to understanding, this center chiefly relates to the energies associated with our mental processes. However, it mainly channels through the heart, because our heart is the true revolving door connecting our seemingly opposite selves.

Communication Processes — Wisdom must be stored in the brain; therefore, our higher brain functions are involved with this energy point.

Problems — The inability to learn from our past and our mistakes in particular. This disability can result in any number of disorders, such as getting into the same predicaments over and over again, experiencing relationship difficulties, exhibiting victim/victor patterns, and countless other situations.

Contains — The collected learnings of the ages, available for our own growth.

Point 29: Enjoyment

Purpose — To teach us that the boldest lesson to be learned is that life is not about lessons, but about enjoyment. Having released our past through peace and having claimed our learnings via wisdom, we can move into the opportunities that will bring us real enjoyment. Following our purpose is always about following our bliss.

Function — To channel the energy fueling our enjoyment. This point is a direct link to the Divine Source and its wishes for us.

Energy Form — Feeling-based, this energy point is extremely potent. Behind the face of enthusiasm lurk powerful manifesting energies.

Communication Process — This energy enters when we believe we deserve it, and manifests through feelings such as enthusiasm, the soul's desires for love, and pleasurable physical experiences.

Problems — Anything—a situation, belief, reality, feeling, relationship, job, or endeavor—that fails to produce joy signifies a block in this center. Failing to own this joy results in these blocks; paradoxically, owning our joy can relieve them.

Contains — The knowledge that we deserve joy.

Point 30: Forgiveness

Purpose — To forgive or to give up our hold on process or outcome. We get hurt or hurt others because we try to be in control. When we give up this control to something greater, we are able to clear the blocks that keep all energy centers below this one from being fully active.

Function — To confront us with this single question: are we willing to fully surrender to higher spiritual energies or not? Most people think that forgiveness is a process. Getting to forgiveness is a process, but it is not forgiveness. Forgiveness is our decision to surrender.

Energy Form — Questioning in nature, decisive in effect.

Communication Processes — The decision to be made comes from within. This energy point, more than any before it, channels directly into the Divine Source self, our essential self.

Problems — Non-specific, lack of surrender can lead to any and all difficulties.

Contains — The right for us to decide to become what we want to be or not.

Point 31: Faith

Purpose — To enable us to live completely in the faith that all we are already exists. By choosing to believe that we are something, we will truly become it.

Function — To erase our revolving doors once we have forgiven. We eliminate the perceptions that there are differences and similarities, that there is separation between our material and spiritual selves, that material and spiritual energies are different. This energy point is the key to allowing all that we want (in Divine Source will) to simply manifest without effort.

Energy Form — This point channels all energies preceding it. After completely balancing them, it erases them. Faith energy seems invisible, made of substance, no more material than air.

Communication Processes — This energy must be incorporated into every cell, visible and invisible. If we believe it is incorporated into all parts of ourselves, then it will be.

Problems — Contributes to the problems of all other chakras.

Contains — The self's ability to be itself.

Point 32: Grace and Divine Source Consciousness

Purpose — To channel miracle energy. Though this miracle energy flows from the Divine Source, the existence of this center connotes our own Divine Source-like ability to give ourselves what we need without needing to believe that we deserve it.

Function — To call what we desire into our lives without effort or immediate knowledge of deserving it. Though it awakens all our powers, the energy coming through this point requires none of them to create our well-being.

Energy Form — None and all. Pure love energy.

Communication Process — Known by results, whether it be a feeling, thought, physical sign, or spiritual awareness (either the appearance of a positive one or disappearance of an undesired one).

Problems — All problems can be solved with this energy.

Contains — The meaning of life.

EXERCISE
Meeting Your Spiritual Energy Centers

It is time for you to meet your own spiritual energy points face-to-face. You will need twenty sheets of paper, plus crayons or other drawing utensils.

A. Lead yourself through the intuitive process introduced in Chapter One. Stop at the access point.

B. Now turn to your papers. Label each one with the title of one of the twenty higher points. Allow yourself to freely draw whatever comes to your mind or flows from your hand. You are describing the current relationship between you and this energy.

C. When you finish this survey, take up the last piece of paper. Let yourself draw a picture of what you will look/feel/be like once you have fully healed your connection to these twenty points.

D. When you have finished this exercise, lead yourself through the closing process.

Alternate Exercises

A more concrete exercise is to actually spend time realizing the impact each of these spiritual bodies can have on you.

I. Each day, decide that you want to experience how a connection with each particular spiritual point can have a positive effect your life. Focus on one point each day. Record your observations at night.

   I recommend starting with the bottom of the list and working toward the top of the list, energy point 32. This approach gives you a foundation as each point becomes aligned on top of the next one.

II. Decide which concept, as reflected by these twenty energy points, could best help you solve a problem. Write or speak aloud the solution that comes to you from that point-of-view.

   For instance, if you are experiencing a problem with a male friend, think of the concept of the fourteenth energy point, Yang. From a yang or male viewpoint, what is the real concern? What are the real questions to ask? What are your choices?

   Then come at the issue from yet a higher perception. Move to the fifteenth energy point, Balance of Polarities. If you could represent both female and male perceptions on this issue, how would you do it? What would be the opposing idea(s)? What do these seeming contrasts have in common? You can move up the ladder of energy points until you finalize your response.

Chapter Four

The Developing Self

The previous chapters provided a glimpse into the inner machinations of our basic energy system. Each core unit or energy center operates as a single entity, while ever revolving within the greater whole. Still missing is an explanation of the developmental process of these energy centers. To work with the energy body, to heal our human selves, we must have this information. Lacking it would be like trying to be a therapist with no knowledge of psychology.

Chakra Development

Though we are born with each in- and out-of-body chakra or energy point intact, they are activated or fully awakened in an orderly manner. This is most obvious in the seven in-body chakras. Our first chakra acts as the primary energy center from womb to six months. Our heart, the fourth chakra, awakens for the first time between four and six years of age. Our seventh chakra kicks in during puberty, and our ninth during our later twenties. Eventually, the process cycles around again, leading us back to our first chakra during our later fifties. In short, there is a link between the child and adult development processes and our chakra system.

This process is comparable to the natural development of the physical body. A newborn has a fully formed human body, equipped at birth with everything necessary for an active and productive life. The organs, limbs, nerves, glands, and muscles needed to talk, run, think, make love, or work are all in place. Many of these functions lie dormant, however, until the appropriate moment (which usually involves entering a stage of development). Within the ovaries of an infant girl already lie all the ova she will ever produce; they will begin to be released at puberty, then monthly thereafter. The glandular ability to produce testosterone is already activated within an infant boy. In a healthy child, the level required to produce a full beard and accentuated muscles will increase only during adolescence.

I believe that though our energy centers become active in a logical sequence, we are linked to and can gain access to any of them at any time. In fact, this is how some of us survived traumas in childhood. A survivor of very early abuse, I remember receiving calm, comfort, and a reason to live from the "angels" with whom I could see and talk. The one called Christ talked to me often about faith, the truth I now associate with the thirty-first energy point. The fact that I could see these spiritual beings at all meant that I had awakened my sixth chakra (the clairvoyant ability) earlier than might have been expected. Our energy centers will do what needs to be done to provide for our greater well-being.

In general, our centers are aligned and active just before conception, but go to sleep after conception. Take the top twenty spiritual centers, which I believe play an active role during pre-conception. The beliefs carried by these higher points are programmed into the developing body and even have a say in what type of chromosomes and genes are selected to create the body this time around. Connected to our soul body, many of them go to sleep during the conception process so as to not interfere with the development of the physical body.

Chakras Eight through Twelve, the higher human chakras, may also be neutralized during our very early months and years. Again, much of our childhood energy during this time must be directed into the growth and development of our physical body, awareness of emotions, formation of relationships, and adaptation to environment. These higher human chakras are quite active during preconception, however, working to select physical traits, determine relationship interactions, and set up life events. The Cherokee tradition explains the process as lighting a fire with a purpose (Ywahoo, 205).

From conception onward, our early moments and years are most concerned with the gradual awakening, programming, and use of our seven in-body chakras. In general, they are activated in order from One to Seven, from the most basic, survival-oriented chakra to the higher-order ones.

Chakra	Age
One	Womb to 6 months
Two	6 months to $2\frac{1}{2}$ years
Three	$2\frac{1}{2}$ to $4\frac{1}{2}$ years
Four	$4\frac{1}{2}$ to $6\frac{1}{2}$ years
Five	$6\frac{1}{2}$ to $8\frac{1}{2}$ years
Six	$8\frac{1}{2}$ to 14 years
Seven	14 to 21 years

During the seven-year span of Chakra Seven, the last in-body chakra, we process Chakras One through Seven again.

Chakra	Age
One	14 to 15 years
Two	15 to 16 years
Three	16 to 17 years
Four	17 to 18 years
Five	18 to 19 years
Six	19 to 20 years
Seven	20 to 21 years

Chakras One through Seven will continue to recycle the remainder of our life, generally in seven-year spans that begin at age twenty-one.

Chakra	Age
Eight	21 to 28 years
Nine	28 to 35 years

Contemporary philosophy tells us that our twenties are a time for preparation, a time to lay the groundwork for later success and happiness. This is an energetic truth, as well. Ages twenty-one to twenty-eight find us moving into our eighth chakra, the keeper of the past (and time). These years might as well be called the "years of karma," for during them, we are clearing blocks, changing misperceptions, altering relationship patterns, and confronting spiritual falsehoods that could inhibit future success. All this in seven short years? We hope so, because after age twenty-eight we will be challenged to own, then materialize our soul purpose. That is a large order; by twenty-one most of us have accrued a serious number of issues that could prevent future growth.

Chakra Eight enables this clearing, making way for our destiny. The bottom line is to tap into our gifts through life events, experiences, or relationships. Yet when we weave a tapestry, the loose threads must be tucked under if we are to become who we really are. In order to "trim us up," Chakra Eight activates our unresolved issues—past and current life—and encourages choices that make us face them. No wonder so many early careers, youthful marriages, and mid-twenties lifestyle choices become obsolete during our thirties. The choices seem so necessary, even compulsively mandatory, when we make them, and they are. Maybe you need to marry Mr. X to confront your father's alcoholism. Maybe you need to become an accountant to learn you were too creative for that profession. Maybe you need to live in New York to own your love of the country. Remember, the twenties are about clearing unresolved issues, not just making mistakes.

Chakra Nine is omnipresent from ages twenty-eight to thirty-five. The "seat of our soul," Chakra Nine encourages the awareness of soul and life purpose. Most often, individuals experience this time as one of questioning and questing. We wonder, "Why am I here?" "Is there any meaning to my life?" "Is there something I am uniquely supposed to accomplish?" This search for purpose can be puzzling and confusing, yet if sufficiently embraced, ultimately rewarding. We want to exit this time period with a sense of self and purpose.

Moving into our mid-thirties, we experience the call to action; the impulse to ground our purpose in reality. We have now entered the era of Chakra Ten, the grounding chakra. Chakra Ten, which was also active during pre-conception and conception, is once again rooting our spiritual self in the material world. From ages thirty-five to forty-two, it enables us to manifest our views, values, and purpose into real life. Now, we can actually get the job, start the company, marry the companion, choose the lifestyle, make that geographic jump, that will best align us with our purpose.

As to be expected, this time is often one of many challenges. Our constant measure of success must be internal—are we upholding our soul's integrity of purpose? Because Chakra Ten also holds patterns and programs from our lineage and past lives, we often find ourselves confronting the old, indoctrinated beliefs that inhibit our growth. This time period is therefore often the springboard for the stereotypical mid-life crisis.

Chakra Eleven, ever-present but more overt during ages forty-two to forty-eight, can help us transmute these old negativities and difficulties. The transmutation chakra, this energy converts negative into positive and challenges into opportunities. Those character deficits, financial liabilities, and bad relationships can now be converted to "positive currency," into learnings, lessons, and teachings that enhance our professional and personal lives. For instance, years of suffering as a sexual abuse victim might now be transmuted into a best-selling book on recovering from this abuse. The struggle with depression may formulate as the basis for compassion and the reason our clients work with us rather than another person.

Finally (in terms of the human chakras), we open to Chakra Twelve. Activated from ages forty-nine to fifty-six, this chakra coaxes us into maturity. Many cultures, including the Cherokee, believe that it is impossible to become an adult before this age (Ywahoo, 169). Unfortunately, many of us are children masquerading in adult bodies.

If we better understood the twelfth chakra, the challenges of maturity would be more profitable. Encompassing the entire human body and energy system, Chakra Twelve energetically connects the material and spiritual worlds. As we realize that we truly are revolving doors between spirit and matter, we must ask ourselves what we are to do with this knowledge and the power inherent in having it. Are we going to reach to the sky, toward individual achievement (thus perpetuating the "me generation" mentality) or follow the path suggested by Buddha, which is to give back to humanity. The hope is that we have successfully faced the challenges of our earlier chakric stages and are ethically responsible enough to use our power for service.

After age fifty, we are invited to fully realize the higher energy centers. Energy centers 13 through 32 may have awakened at many points in our life, as we will see later in this chapter.

Reasons Within Reasons

Knowing our chakric development process and awakening points of the individual chakras can help in many ways. By working with this system, we can:

1. Use physical symptoms to define the emotional, mental, and spiritual components of our illness.

2. Trace our emotional issues back to the development of a certain part of our body or to the age of origination. Emotions are the language of the body. If we can re-experience the feeling component and the physical reactions attached to a debilitating situation, we can reprogram self-destructive beliefs and chart a whole new course.

3. Isolate the mental or spiritual beliefs affecting us, thereby healing our emotional or physical issues.

4. Awaken repressed memories, including in-utero and past-life memories, for the purpose of understanding, clearing, and healing.

5. Understand the origin of just about any physical, mental, emotional, or spiritual issue. If you can get to the root cause or formative age, you can unlock the circumstances causing the blocks and prepare to heal them.

6. Become knowledgeable parents to our own children, supporting them in and through each development stage.

7. Better re-parent our own inner child, that natural self within each of us waiting for his or her chance at life.

8. Make appropriate and wise decisions by pinpointing our current development stage.

9. Better understand where, how, and why other people are stuck.

We are searching for two points of awareness when working with this developmental process. First, we want to discover the wonderful aspects of our being, some of which have already awakened and some of which have not. Even if we know that we have positive traits, they might need recognition or revitalization. Many times, we have buried our best qualities beneath a dirge of conflict and misperceptions. That leads us to our second goal, which is to uncover, understand, and change self-destructive beliefs, patterns, and programs. After all, the gems at our core deserve to be dusted off and polished.

Uncovering the Gems

Healing—an uncovering or recovering process—is frequently unconscious, but this unconscious process can trigger conscious healing. Healing occurs when we suddenly discover a secret about ourself and open to the gifts it provides.

Let's say you are a new parent doubting your ability to care for a crying infant. Instead of copping out and leaving the baby to cry herself to sleep, you pull up the wisdom and courage to provide comfort. The baby stops crying and becomes happy or—the ultimate act of faith—falls asleep in your arms. You are amazed!

Real growth can now follow. What if, following this "Eureka!" discovery, you allow yourself to explore further. Perhaps you reflect upon your own basic needs, whether they are currently getting met, or whether they were met when you were an infant. During this reflection, you may uncover issues to heal and strengths previously unknown. Caring for your three-month-old child has awakened your own first-chakra connection to your past and to your own current, primal self.

If we are lucky, life unfolds gently, allowing the abilities and healing needs of our chakras and centers to unfold smoothly and unconsciously. However, life isn't always so gentle. We must revert to a more direct approach if our challenges are severe. The more difficult our life experiences, especially our early ones, the more apt we are to secret our abilities and traits under a blanket of protection.

Two of my clients illustrate this point. Each carried the impact of events that occurred between the ages of three and four, but one client, more severely wounded than the other, had to address his issues on a much more conscious level. As you read their stories, remember that age three relates to the third chakra and our explorations of the world around us. During this time, the messages and reactions we receive from others become fodder for our own beliefs about ourselves, others, and the world at large. Positive messages will substantiate our belief in the world being a safe and loving place, thus encouraging high self-esteem. Negative messages will reflect on the self or in other judgments, inhibiting our personal power.

Now for my two clients, Max and Jimmy. During the period of their third chakric development, both boys exhibited an obvious interest in art. Their interests encompassed everything from coloring in coloring books to creating masterpieces on their bedroom walls. Max's natural curiosity and expression were viewed with excitement by his parents. Though his parents curtailed the painting expeditions involving Max's walls, they continued to support his desires. Max learned that he could safely experiment in his environment and that authority would both support his dreams and provide constructive boundaries regarding their application.

On the other hand, Jimmy's parents deplored what they saw as his messiness. Criticizing his sloppy artwork and ridiculing him for drawing on the walls, they effectively killed Jimmy's interest in art and his belief in his right to express his insides on the outside (the definition of purpose). Jimmy came to me when he was thirty, complaining that he had wasted most of his life and still couldn't decide what to do with it. We talked for quite some time before he admitted that he really wanted to be an artist, but considered that choice as too impractical. In fact, he went to great lengths during his first and subsequent sessions to convince me that art was a stupid profession.

About this same time, Max came to see me. His problem? He couldn't decide whether to stay in the United States and remain a (famous) painter or to relocate to a more remote country so he could paint in peace.

I explored with each of them the ages/origins of their beliefs about art, and their abilities and needs regarding it. Jimmy took months to free his three- or four-year-old self from the environment which had imprisoned him. Gradually, he began to take art classes. He saw a career counselor and began schooling for graphic design.

Max had more fun in our time together. He imagined himself at the young age of four and began to re-experience how he drew, asking under what conditions was he happiest. Was he alone or with playmates? Did he like input or not? He realized that though he liked to create in solitude, he also liked the influx of other people's comments. He began to set aside hours for creativity and to travel more, but decided to remain in society for balance.

Jimmy's earlier experiences, less supportive and more judgmental than Max's, created great havoc in his life. To unravel it, he had to focus solely on digging to his core, feel a lot of pain, and become willing to make significant life changes. His healing required a very conscious commitment and process. Max, on the other hand, was triggered by the natural process of his development. His questions about self rose to the surface because of opportunity rather than difficulty. With relative ease, he applied the chakric development system for self-clarification.

Time and time again, I have seen that what we are exposed to during the development stage of a particular chakra will linger for the rest of our lives until we deal with it. The more severely we are affected, the deeper the wound is and the more conscious our healing process needs to be. Because each energy center is holistic, the effects pervade the rest of our system and the whole of our lives. Being told we are stupid, bad, or untalented at age three will certainly create a false mental belief. It may also masquerade physically as stomach pains, emotionally as fears about our abilities, and spiritually as questions about the love of the Divine Source. Though housed in the third chakra, these issues subsequently affect all the other chakras, and therefore, every other area of our life (due to the holographic storage capability of the entire system).

This inter-connectedness was pointedly illustrated by one of my clients, a therapist, who came to me to examine the origin of twenty years of back problems. Using guided visualization, we went up her in-body chakric system. At each chakra and age, she re-experienced an event or experience that had debilitated her. For instance, as an infant, she remembered feeling like she was the wrong sex. She sat before me on the couch in a near-fetal position. I asked her to tell me how this perception had affected her. She replied, "I decided to close myself away from life. It's too scary."

At each stage, she made a new decision, reporting to me how odd-feeling the energy was following these reconsiderations. When I saw her a year later, she informed me with a smile that her back had caused her almost no problems since that day in my office.

My client displayed the mirrored complexity of the human energy system, the complicated state of our issues, and the possible difficulties involved with becoming and being our true selves. Within this web of complexities, however, lies a very simple truth: underneath it all, our simple, true self is there. We are trying to uncover that true self, to heal it, to make it whole again or or whole for the first time.

Working With the Chakric Development System

We may do a great deal of this salvage and repair work on our own by working with the chakra system. I usually take one or both of the following approaches:

    1. Looking for blocks.

    2. Looking for truths.

Looking for Blocks

Blocks are points of resistance to our own well-being. A block is any physical condition, belief, feeling, or spiritual misunderstanding that prevents us from living our purpose. While a block can be caused by a physical problem, false mental belief, unresolved feeling, or spiritual misperception, it can create havoc in any one or all of our human areas.

Physical Blocks — We all know what physical blocks are. They are usually experienced as physical problems, ailments, disease, or pains. Obviously, physical blocks can prevent full utilization of our physical bodies. A professional athlete can be blocked by a broken leg. Until the cast comes off, he or she is prevented from fully performing as an athlete. A singer can be blocked by a cold. If the illness is severe, it can hold up a concert tour. Being tired can also block our mental capacities, distorting our perspective and inhibiting our effectiveness.

Physical blocks can also affect our feeling state, causing us to be cranky, fatigued, and impatient. In turn, these feelings and other feeling states can greatly affect the health and nature of our relationships and work life. Physical blocks can also impede our spiritual life, causing us to devote more time and attention to material endeavors than conceptual concerns.

Clearing physical blocks may involve doing something physical, such as resting if we are ill or taking an aspirin for a headache. However, it could just as easily require changing a belief system, releasing a blocked feeling, or talking with our highest form of guidance. The general rule of thumb is that if an impairing physical condition doesn't respond to a physical cure, then we must seek solutions in the other areas. We must be willing to look under the covers, to peer under the symptoms.

I had a rather interesting experience regarding the holistic nature of physical concerns with one of my clients, a fifty-year-old woman. She came to me complaining that for two years she had experienced one physical problem after another, including the flu, aches, pains, heart constrictions, and leg numbness. The doctors finally decided she must be a hypochondriac because they had been unable to decipher any organic cause.

Upon further probing, she relayed that these problems had started at the beginning of her marriage, which had taken place two years earlier. Rather reluctantly, she admitted that before their marriage, her husband's health had been poor while hers had been fine. Psychically, I perceived immense cords or energy connections between each of her affected chakras and those of her husband. I also saw a graver matter, an incomplete separation between her mother's second chakra and her own.

This client worked with me three times. When we dissociated her from her husband, she reported feeling better, though he felt worse. We then began to address her relationship with her mother. When I asked her to also work with a therapist, she grew frightened at the thought of possibly hurting her mother and refused. At this point, I felt I had done what was ethically responsible, and could do no more. I don't know what became of her after our last session, but I do know that she felt physically better when she returned energy that wasn't hers to its rightful owner.

Mental Blocks — Mental blocks are beliefs that prevent us from actualizing our inner self. They can cripple us moderately to severely. A mental belief first has an impact on our thought processes, and, through our thoughts, affects our attitudes, emotions, and actions. The kahuna healers of Hawaii define belief as any idea that you accept as true (King, 97). Believing that you are a bad person can leave you feeling first unlikable, then unhappy, and finally afraid to take advantage of opportunities.

Ted Andrews, in his book *Imagick*, speaks of the power of our thoughts. "The mental body has one of the most subtle and powerful effects upon man in the physical…. It is our mental body and its action in the form of our thoughts and words upon the mental plane that most strongly sets the pattern for what we experience in the physical. It forms the matrix or blueprint of what is to manifest within our lives" (Andrews, Ted. *Imagick: The Magick of Images, Paths & Dance*. Llewellyn Publications, St. Paul, MN, 1989, 77). The implications of negative or untrue beliefs programmed into our thought patterns is long-term damage to our psyches and outward, physical lives.

For example, we might, as do many of my clients, believe that we are the wrong sex, that our parents wanted a child of the opposite gender. This belief can inhibit our sexual expression and our enjoyment of day-to-day physical processes. A belief that we don't deserve to have money can keep us from being financially prosperous. A belief we don't deserve to be alive can make us physically sick by shutting down our physical system or preventing us from getting necessary health care. The list can go on and on. To heal, we must become willing to follow the path of the kahuna healer, which is "to help people change their beliefs from unhealthy ones to healthy ones" (King, 47).

When working on my own issues or when helping others with theirs, I often ask myself how I can tell if the origin of the problem is caused by a belief or something else. Although we might experience stuck mental beliefs and their ensuing patterns as obsessive thoughts, attitude problems, or problematic thinking, they may also be clothed as chronic dissociation or physical patterns, even as physical symptoms such as a nervous stomach or a racing heart. We might just as likely find our mental beliefs coded within recurring feelings, reactions, or behaviors.

Anytime we experience a chronic or repetitive condition, the causal issues are least partially based on destructive beliefs. Tracing a particular belief or pattern to its originating chakra can be extremely helpful, given the complexity of possibilities and the sheer number of secondary beliefs that may shoot off a major one.

Feeling Blocks — Feeling blocks involve the destructive presence or absence of feelings. Destructive present feelings are those that have been stored or absorbed, and which need to be expressed or given back to their owners. As we have already examined, we may store our own feelings rather than express them, because we don't believe it is safe to express them. We may also absorb and store the feelings of others as a way to alleviate scary situations and create a sense of safety. These unresolved and unexpressed feelings literally stop up the works, causing physical and psychological damage.

One of my clients, a CEO of a major corporation, was clearly affected by stored, yet unexpressed feelings. He had suffered two heart attacks prior to seeing me and wanted to learn some meditation techniques. I thought it important to do more, and he consented to seeing if there might be some reason behind the attacks. As he moved into a light trance, I guided his conscious awareness into his heart. He began to cry and talk about how his father had not seemed to love him. He had decided to prove his worthiness by working hard—actually working himself to death. The self he related was a five-year-old boy who had, quite literally, decided to hide these feelings away.

I have seen hundreds of other clients uncover stored or unexpressed feelings, typically because their home environment had not provided the security necessary to express them. The most drastic case involved a woman with cancer of the throat and uterus. She vehemently told me that she would be willing to do anything to live. I asked her if she would be willing to feel any unfelt feelings, no matter how horrible and painful. She said "yes."

Knowing how little time she had to live, I pushed her more than I do most clients. We dove right into memories of abuse. With me and on her own, she yelled obscenities at her father, screaming out all the stored anger. Her throat nodules disappeared within two days. She then threw all the shame in her uterus back to her brother and father, shame which was stored where her brother used to punch her and where her current tumor lay. Although the mass didn't disappear, it was found to be benign upon removal. I am convinced that she would have been dead within weeks if she hadn't expressed these feelings.

We may also be affected by absent feelings. At times in our lives, we might disregard or give away certain feelings, if we or others judge particular feelings to be wrong, bad, or dangerous. We must reclaim our right to feel these feelings if we are to achieve our purpose, because the ensuing emptiness leaves us unable to completely be our true selves.

A thirty-year-old male client of mine asked for intuitive guidance about why he couldn't seem to fall in love. My assessment was that loving feelings may have been too scary for him. After our session, I encouraged him to see a hypnotherapist and uncover what may have happened to cause his fear. He called later, and with tears of joy, said he had discovered that his sister had been given all the relationship feelings in the family. As the eldest, she had been the one expected to nurture the younger siblings. He had reclaimed his right to feel these feelings as well, and had never felt better.

Diagnosing our feeling blocks can be confusing, because our feelings are intertwined with other life components. We might realize the presence of a feeling block by observing obvious emotions, such as outbursts of rage or overwhelming bouts of grief. Our feelings may just as frequently be interspersed throughout other, more predominate issues, including problems with lifestyle, addictions, recurring habits, relationships, illnesses, or thought patterns. How do we get to the bottom of our feeling issues, specifically our feeling blocks?

Working with the chakric development system provides the clues necessary to get to the bottom of feeling-based issues. By tracing physical, lifestyle, relationship, thought, or feeling symptoms back to their originating chakras and causal experiences, we can unpeel the layers of feelings to find the one that is really blocked or absent.

One of my clients, Jackie, provides an example of this process. Jackie's father modeled repression of anger, and by the time she was five, she was locked in to a similar pattern. By age forty, she had been in a number of volatile relationships, had a problem with asserting herself, and registered a physical heart disorder. She had been to a relationship counselor and a heart specialist, but had failed to associate her issues with anger. She came to me for an intuitive assessment. Given these clues, I immediately tuned in to her heart chakra. Relationship issues—a heart problem—indicated concerns with this chakra. Taking care not to diagnose, I helped provide her with information which ultimately helped her get to the bottom of her relationship and physical disorders. Jackie chose to combine hands-on healing with regression work. She learned how to bring her awareness to her heart and to ask her heart what it wanted from her. Through her healing work with me and sessions with a therapist, she began to change her patterns of repressing anger. When last I heard from her, she was dating a very kind man.

In Peru, I studied with a shaman who often said that the core of many illnesses lay in childhood or ancestral concerns. In Costa Rica, I met a healer who professed to cure drug addictions by ridding the body of old patterns. The Tsalagi (Cherokee) tradition also believes that many adult problems stem from early childhood patterns or beliefs. Ywahoo writes, "It is a wise practitioner who carefully changes the thought form of habit...pulling threads of early patterns and re-weaving them into a beauteous garment" (Ywahoo, 85). The wisdom of these practitioners comes from hundreds of years of traditions.

Spiritual Blocks — Spiritual blocks are misperceptions about the universe and our place within it. To me, spiritual blocks are perhaps the most powerful and the most important because they underlie every other issue. They can be caused by anything that happens to us, for us, or around us.

I feel the word "spiritual" means just that—spirit-filled. The bravest and most worthy desire we can have as a human being is to be filled with the spirit, the true essence, of ourselves. As this self is really an aspect of the Divine Source, I believe that life is about learning how to accept that we are of the Divine Source (the All, the Great Spirit), and that we deserve to fully express this truth. Living on purpose is about expressing this spirit self.

This spirit self or essence constantly attempts to bring our body, mind, and soul to this understanding. Certain people, such as Fool's Crow, a now-deceased Lakota medicine man, understood this quest. Known for being able to heal anyone of anything, he asserted that this ability came from being able to become like a "hollow bone" or empty vessel through which Wakan-Tanka, the Great Spirit, could pour. One of my own healing teachers, Echo

Bodine, who has written many healing books, always insisted that she healed no one of anything; she just got out of the way. These people illustrate the power of spirit—our own and that of a greater force—and suggest that any physical, mental, or emotional problems may be caused by something which prevents our own or a greater spirit from entering or being fully present.

Often, these spiritual blocks or confusions about our own true goodness lie within the soul. Remember, our soul carries everything we experience from life to life, from chakra to chakra, from cell to cell. The soul registers experiences such as being shamed or praised, judged or supported, rejected or nurtured, being loved, hated, or killed. It records what we learned in Sunday School, and it is affected by the false and true beliefs involving our higher, spiritual energy points. The soul itself imprints these beliefs about life, death, others, ourselves, everything within our temporal being. The downside of this reality is that even if we didn't begin this life with many spiritual issues, by the time we are adults, we probably acquired a lot of them anyway. The upside is that whatever we heal on the soul level becomes healed on all levels.

We can address our spiritual issues through any chakra or energy point. Holism, at its most consequential, is apparent here. Again, one way to effectively find the spiritual issue underneath a problem is to apply the chakric development system, starting by isolating the chakra affected by a negative or traumatic experience. With clients, I typically help them uncover and understand first the physical, mental, and emotional effects of an experience, then turn to spiritual reflection. I always steer them into addressing the deeper, spiritual issue. Unless we address the soul issue, the soul may carry the negative perception through to another level, perhaps affecting a relationship, career, or lifestyle, or, of course, the body part.

Probing for the spiritual issue often frightens people, because it often requires dealing with questions involving goodness and evil, a divinity and the devil, life and death. Many people think this work lies in the realm of the religious institutions. However, I believe that working with spiritual issues need not be a strictly religious undertaking, though the task can be adversely or positively affected by our religious beliefs.

Spirituality differs from religion in that spirituality has to do with our essence—our essential self and our essential needs. Religion provides a structural approach to living, one which hopefully lies in accordance with our essential needs. We might have been raised in a religious atmosphere that supports our essence and its expression; we might just as easily have been exposed to a dogmatic structure that has crushed, molded, or repressed our essence. Whatever the case, anything that prevents the soul from living in and through us is a spiritual issue. Ultimately, we need to acknowledge our soul, which is our invisible self, and the universe for wanting this self to be happy and satisfied. Spiritual blocks are resistance points to accepting this grace.

I have learned to be rather bold when working with clients on spiritual issues. I often use shamanistic tools and techniques I learned in Peru, Japan, Costa Rica, Wales, Morocco, and from several other cultures which account for the presence of a soul. Whether the technique involves helping a client journey into his or her subconscious, talk to an invisible spiritual guide or angel, or picture to his or her own soul and talk to it, I have yet to find a client who disbelieves what he or she sees, hears, or feels. I believe that people inherently believe in the invisible, spiritual part of themselves.

Working with a spiritual issue usually involves uncovering the soul's major misperception and understanding the consequences that result from the misperception. For instance, one of my clients, who had a serious illness, reported that her soul believed it didn't deserve to be alive. When she pictured her first chakra, she cried out that it was almost closed, and that her soul had been keeping it shut since birth. Without first chakra energy, it is difficult for our bodies to be active and vital, for us to make money, or for us to engage in fruitful relationships. In a way, this client's soul had never even been born into her physical body because it was sure that its presence was going to ruin her mother's life. (Her mother had conceived her out-of-marriage at age sixteen.) Disengaged from the living process, this soul had greatly constricted her health and happiness. After convincing her soul that it hadn't ruined her mother's life, it agreed to open up the first chakra. My client reported immediate improvements in her health and well-being.

The impact of spiritual work can be powerful, because the soul enables us to receive help the easy way. The soul is the aspect of our self most capable of attracting spiritual assistance and grace. If the soul rejects life or feels rejected by the body or mind, it may fragment or splinter. Part of it may enter, or journey in and out of our physical system. Part of it may remain caught in a past life or in an observation rather than participant mode. As the saying goes, a house divided cannot stand. With the soul separated, we cannot go one way or another, we cannot set and achieve goals. Life becomes a schizophrenic experience.

Common spiritual blocks are encapsulated by beliefs, each of which can serve as a springboard for almost-as-potent secondary beliefs. For example, some primary spiritual beliefs could be:

"I am bad/evil."

"Women are from the devil."

"God doesn't love me."

"God abandoned me."

"I don't deserve abundance."

"I don't deserve to be alive."

"I have no soul."

"Someone else is better than me."

While the difference between mental and spiritual beliefs can sometimes seem minute, the litmus test is the origin of the belief. Mental beliefs initially stem from lifetime (this life or past life) experiences, and relate to our attitudes or thinking processes. Spiritual beliefs often originate in the soul and sometimes in experiences that pre-date our physical existence. They can stem back to the time we were one with the Divine Source, separating from the Divine Source, or initially experiencing the existence of other soul bodies (the spiritual selves of other people). When soul beliefs do form from lifetime experiences, they are based on reflections the soul makes first and the mind makes second. It is helpful to remember this when working with chakric mental beliefs. If we can trace a mental belief back to a soul belief, we might suddenly find ourselves out of the ordinary and into a one-on-one conversation with the Divine Source, re-experiencing a soul experience, or speaking with a part of the soul that is hovering around the body—a truly unusual experience for most of us raised under Western ways.

Looking for Truths

In addition to a block-oriented approach to diagnosing issues using the chakric development system, we may also heal by uncovering the truths hidden beneath our issues. Truths are either the opposite of or a reflection of the misperceptions causing us difficulty. "Whether one is aware of it or not," says Ywahoo in *Voices of Our Ancestors,* "the ways in which we think and speak about ourselves attract results and become self-fulfilling prophecies" (Ywahoo, 85).

An oppositional truth is apparent in the following situation. Sandy was a client who had gone from one bad relationship to another. Working with her revealed an array of blocks. In her second chakra lay the belief that she didn't deserve to be loved by a man. In her sixth chakra, she held the idea that she was ugly. Rather than fixate on these blocks, Sandy chose to short-circuit the blocks by deciding to adopt the opposite beliefs. Instead of dwelling on the negative belief "I am ugly," she started to tell herself that she was beautiful.

Working with a truth's reflection requires that we address the secondary effects of the causal problem. Rather than do positive affirmations, Sandy could have made herself aware of all the ways she was acting out (or reflecting) the belief that she was ugly. I immediately noticed that she wore unappealing clothes and slumped her shoulders. I might have asked her to alter these reflections by dressing more attractively or standing up straight. This way, she could have tried on a new truth until she was ready to wear it.

More often than not, the block and truth approaches work hand-in-hand. In order to get to the truth, we might need to feel the feelings not originally expressed, claim the false beliefs, remember the original body memories, and unearth the spiritual issues. Understanding all facets of an issue often make it easier to face the truth, which though always positive, usually challenges us to make further changes in our lives. A woman with relationship problems may, for instance, have to alter her entire approach to meeting people. She may have to change how she dresses, or she may have to do without a relationship for a while. She may need to give herself new messages and might also have to work on her soul or childhood issues. She might need to work on all of these changes at the same time. When we do what needs to be done and trust our own sense of it, healing can happen.

The Full Chakric Development System

Using the child development/chakra system helps clarify the holistic aspects of our issues and difficulties. The following is a more complete outline of the in-body chakras and what they affect.

Cycle One

Chakra One

Age — Womb to 6 months.

Mental Belief — Affects those relating to inherited beliefs, gender legacies, safety, and survival.

Feeling Component — Origin of feelings about self and the world, the right to exist, and primal feelings such as guilt, terror, rage, joy, and shame.

Physical Processes — Body and structure developed; affects all processes governing survival.

Spiritual Perceptions — Relates to commitment to life, acceptance of spiritual help and our basic intuitive abilities. Relates to trust in others and awareness of basic needs. Core of worth issues.

Everything that happens to us or our parents while we are in-utero and newly born is locked into our first chakra. During this time, we experience the world through our parents' perceptions and our own physical body. If we perceive a threat to ourselves or to our parents, we might question our right or ability to survive. Threats can include anything from not being fed when hungry to our parents going through bankruptcy. Endangerment can activate rage, pain, grief, terror, and other primal feelings. Unless acknowledged, allowed, and expressed in some manner, these feelings will continue to haunt us for the rest of our lives. Beliefs that could spring out of these experiences include, "The world is dangerous" or "I don't deserve to live." However, if these feelings and awarenesses are processed by our parents or ourselves, we will create beliefs that support our existence and the right to have our needs met. We then become stronger for being able to tap into our primal feelings.

The first chakra also serves as the fundamental point for opening to spiritual guidance. If for some reason we close ourselves off to spiritual guidance at this young age, we become much more vulnerable to experiences of trauma and abuse.

In a nutshell, core issues regarding emotional insecurity and physical security originate in this chakra, as do spiritual perceptions that relate to our right to exist and have our needs met. These core issues become issues regarding career, money, primal feelings, addictions, family of origin, and sexuality at later dates.

Chakra Two

Age — 6 months to $2\frac{1}{2}$ years.

Mental Belief — Awareness of feelings and the right to express them; world/family views about gender roles and sensuality issures. Beliefs about expression and creativity.

Feeling Component — Development of subtle feelings, choices about which feeling bodies to activate and which to become numb.

Physical Processes — Growth, motor skills, owning of our own body and its subtle needs; ability to motivate our own body; development of sensuality.

Spiritual Perceptions — Development of trust in self and our own feelings, plus empathy and beliefs about the right to express and feel. Root of the right to be creative and expressive.

From age six months to two-and-a-half years, we separate ourselves from our mother. Her ability to separate with love and our father's ability to support this behavior will reflect in our second chakra. This separation and our emerging sense of self and relationship can bring up feelings such as sadness, calm, fear, hope, or enthusiasm. Messages we receive regarding our right to have and express these feelings actually affect the development of our feeling bodies.

Feeling bodies are energetic constructs located within the second chakra. Seen this way, we can approach each feeling as an individual entity. Sadness, fear, anger, joy—each feeling is an individual identity, arranged next to each other like colors in a rainbow. Like colors, feeling bodies blur into each other. Sadness, for instance, may flow into grief; contentment slide into happiness. Like colors, individual feelings are gradated. The feeling body of anger can intensify into rage or dissipate into frustration.

When healthy, each feeling body appears full and ready for activation and expression. If a loved one dies, our sadness feeling body will vibrate. We will feel sad until that feeling has been appropriately dissipated. The feeling body will then return to a calmer state.

If we were raised in a healthy emotional environment, the system works. Something internal or external stimulates a feeling-based reaction. One or more feeling bodies vibrate, and we respond. Our internal or external environment shifts. Quickly or gradually, the feeling bodies deactivate. We return to equilibrium.

The key word is "if." *If* we were raised in a healthy emotional environment. How many families are really functional? Expert opinions insist that anywhere between seventy and ninety-five percent of our families are dysfunctional. Most of us received incorrect messages regarding feelings, resulting in the repression, over-stimulation, or actual injury of one or more feeling bodies.

Short-term infliction is the most reparable. For instance, say one of your high school teachers shamed you for failing a test. Embarrassed, you repressed your instinctive response, which was disappointment in yourself. A discussion with a loving parent would alleviate the shame and help you express the disappointment, thus enabling a release—even though it's a bit late. Your disappointment feeling body would probably not suffer long-term injury.

Chronic or severely acute damage, however, often results in a more permanent state of disease. Sexual, physical, emotional, or verbal abuse can cripple one or many of our feeling bodies. Here is a picture of how this works.

A healthy sadness feeling body could figuratively be described as a perfect circle. Let's say that your dad doesn't think sadness is okay to feel; instead of getting sad, he gets angry. Remember, sadness is an actual energy—a frequency in motion. In his desperation to not feel sad, Dad cuts out a section of his sadness feeling body. Where does it go? You pick it up; it has become displaced in you. Now your circular sadness feeling body is mishappen. You have spent most of your life trying to shake off an extreme state of sadness or depression, but to no avail. Depressed, you try therapy, Prozac, vitamins. You attract lovers who hurt you in an attempt to stimulate the sadness away. Nothing works, and you feel even more sad—and helpless.

In Chapter Eleven, we will further explore how damaged feeling bodies and the misperceptions or experiences which caused them affect our material and spiritual well-being. Ultimately, they handicap our entire second chakra.

Chakra Three

Age — 2$\frac{1}{2}$ to 4$\frac{1}{2}$ years.

Mental Belief — Affects beliefs relating to cognitive development, self and the world, and formative beliefs about the world and our place in it. Holds beliefs about power, abilities, and how we affect the environment.

Feeling Component — Origin of fears and self-esteem.

Physical Processes — Gaining control of physical functions and developing the mind/body connection.

Spiritual Perceptions — Relate to the soul's ability to make an impact on the world and achieve success. Origin of issues regarding interplay between life energy and the world.

At age two-and-a-half, we begin to actively explore the world. Natural curiosity has us seeking to understand the way things work, how people react to us, and how powerful we are. Responses from our immediate relationships and from the world at large greatly affect our opinions about self and others, especially with regard to personal power. If these responses are supportive, we will adopt beliefs about the world such as, "I am effective" or "My personality is all right." If the responses judge or shunt our behavior, we might conclude "I am wrong" or "I don't know anything." The third chakra stores and implements biases, judgments, and prejudices about ourselves and others.

As the "mind of the body," the third chakra affects thinking processes, attitudes, and the intuitive process of mental empathy. Significantly linked to the physical body, the third chakra completes the formation of our mind/body connection. This chakra can now pass judgments down to the second chakra, resulting in emotions (the combination of feeling and thought). Given that the third chakra regulates our digestive and regulatory functions, our self-esteem will continue to affect not only these physical processes, but our ability to use life energy to achieve our desires.

Spiritually, our deserving issues tend to get locked in place at this age. If we think we can make an impact on the world and that we deserve to do so, we will be ready to meet and master any challenges. If we don't believe in ourselves—mainly because the important people in our life don't believe in us—our lives may play out differently.

Chakra Four

Age — 4½ to 6½ years.

Mental Belief — Contains beliefs about relationships, love, heart's desires, and universal principles such as giving and receiving.

Feeling Component — Origin of feelings such as compassion and love.

Physical Processes — Time for refining all physical functions and systems. The initial time for distinguishing girl/boyhood differentiations.

Spiritual Perceptions — Issues regarding self-love, love for others, and the overall role of love in life. Here, the soul "heartily" deals with issues about having a body and using it to achieve desires.

The heart chakra is the integration point for the seven in-body chakras. While we've been busy developing our way up the chakric ladder, our spiritual center, the seventh chakra, has been sending energy down, initially through the baby's soft spot. If we and our parents have given this spiritual energy an important role in our life, we will naturally understand relationships and love ourselves. We will know when to give, to receive, to be compassionate, to be firm, and/or to be self-protective. Experiences and beliefs disturbing this natural give-and-take cycle will inhibit the openness of our relationships. Our desires, dreams, and needs may then become stunted, as might our ability to accept love. Part of being loved involves learning how to accept our purpose and our spiritual needs. If we allow our heart's desires to be met, we often find that the dreams of our body, mind, soul, essence, and the Divine Source are all the same. This truth accentuates the heart's role in supporting our fantasies.

Chakra Five

Age — 6½ to 8½ years.

Mental Belief — Issues of self-worth, responsibility, the expression of desires, and our right to manifest and communicate our needs and beliefs. The entry point for positive and negative guidance.

Feeling Component — Stored frustrations, pride, disillusionment, and grandeur, and the mature expression of needs and feelings.

Physical Processes — Development of self-control, completion of the childhood body, and preparation for adulthood.

Spiritual Perceptions — Contact point for communication between the soul, mind, and body. The place where the soul articulates its desires.

Chakra Five is awakened during our mid-childhood years. At this time, all the beliefs, experiences, and training of our early and most critical developmental years come to fruition. We begin to clearly articulate what we really want or do not want. If we are aware of our needs, know we deserve to have them met, and have a desire to interact with the world, our words will become vehicles for expressing and creating from our inner being. Previous blocks or inhibitions and forces currently repressing our self-expression will now manifest themselves as communication problems or disorders. Being told, for instance, that "Good girls/boys are to be seen, not heard" can create a severe block in this chakra. If our culture is modeling behavior that perpetuates co-dependancy or perfectionism, or that supports under- or over-responsibility, our fifth chakra's ability to state who we are and what we want, and to defend these statements, will be affected.

Spiritually, this chakra is the center of manifesting what we want in life. Any misperceptions about our rights or abilities regarding this manifesting, especially those originating in our soul body, will prevent us from being strong enough to create the life we desire.

Chakra Six

Age — 8½ to 14 years.

Mental Belief — Development of beliefs about body-image, self-image, gender potentials, and plans for the future.

Feeling Component — Contains feelings about the self and self-image, plus feelings about our gender and its capabilities.

Physical Processes — Era of sexual development and of our masculine or feminine nature.

Spiritual Perceptions — Origin of the abilities to register and establish the soul's vision of our life.

The sixth chakra pertains to the development of our self-image, as well it might, for it opens during puberty. While our bodies are beginning to mature sexually, this chakra is busy recording the familial and societal standards set for men and women. We are emotionally vulnerable during this developmental period and tend to personalize these messages. If we feel good about ourselves and our gender, later in life we will be able to select visions and goals that serve our highest potential. If the views around us deflate our gender, and therefore our self and body image, our sights will be set too low in areas such as relationships, schoolwork, and goals.

It is interesting that during this time period we also develop our clairvoyance, the ability to see clearly. If we can learn to see ourselves clearly, to see how loving and beautiful we are, we will be able to set goals and solve problems from our truths rather than our blocks. If the opposite occurs, we will have problems the rest of our life with really imagining ourselves as worthy of the good things in life.

Chakra Seven

Age — 14 to 21 years.

Mental Belief — Beliefs registering our place in the world and in the systems around us, our roles, our capabilities, and our career expectations.

Feeling Component — Can be the origin of confusion between self and parts of ourselves setting goals. Linked to all feelings that refer to the sense of belonging and the choices about what groups or systems to join.

Physical Processes — Maturation of the adult body and the outward completion of inner traits.

Spiritual Perceptions — Awareness of purpose and our own guiding principles.

Chakra Seven is actually one of the few in-body chakras fully activated at birth. The spiritual energy emanating from our higher, out-of-body chakras enters our body and the chakra system through the baby's soft spot, the initial crown entry point. Here lies our ability to claim our divinity right from the start. The physical closing of this center symbolizes the need for us to develop as planned, to live the life set forth for us by our human self and our parents.

During our middle puberty ages, our body completes itself. This is the time to completely open to being one with our past, with others, and with our spiritual plan. However, blocks forged on our life journey, plus the family and societal beliefs that fail to support our purpose, can cause these years to be a time for struggle and confusion rather than the unfoldment of grace and purpose. Many of the decisions young people make during this time are unfortunately made out of programmed beliefs about how to fit in, rather than an emerging sense of individuality.

During the seven years that Chakra Seven spans, we reprocess Chakras One through Seven again.

Chakra	Age
One	14 to 15 years
Two	15 to 16 years
Three	16 to 17 years
Four	17 to 18 years
Five	18 to 19 years
Six	19 to 20 years
Seven	20 to 21 years

We then begin processing the next five chakras in seven-year cycles.

Chakra	Age	Key Concept
Eight	21 to 28 years	Karma.
Nine	28 to 35 years	Soul purpose.
Ten	35 to 42 years	Purposeful survival.
Eleven	42 to 49 years	Creative success.
Twelve	49 to 56 years	Powerful mastery.

Chakra Eight

Age — 21 to 28 years.

Mental Belief — All karmic beliefs are now activated, as are issues regarding time and timing of our past life.

Feeling Component — Past-life feelings come to surface, most significantly about karmic relationships and events needing to be cleared.

Physical Processes — Fully mature body may take on past-life characteristics.

Spiritual Perceptions — Karmic struggles. Evolution of soul to greater awareness.

Almost all of the choices we make between twenty-one to twenty-eight are karmic. A bold statement, but often true. At this age, individuals, believing that they are acting independently, draw to themselves a second tier of karmic relationships (the first tier having been chosen by the tenth chakra during pre-conception). Choices made about life-partners, career, lifestyle, schooling, and other choices made during this time period often relate to undiagnosed and incomplete karmic patterns. Our soul's challenge is to reach beyond the levels achieved in previous lifetimes and make new or more effective decisions.

Chakra Nine

Age — 28 to 35 years.

Mental Belief — Major soul beliefs awaken regarding life purpose and life tasks. Family programs may rerun again for a second look.

Feeling Component — Feelings arise from our inner desires, needs, and purpose, as do conflicts between feelings that support and don't support our life purpose.

Physical Processes — Spiritual body may now completely enter physical form.

Spiritual Perceptions — Completion of spirit into form and acceptance of purpose on this plane.

During this time period, we are challenged to open completely to our spiritual purpose. Our soul may be called completely into our body, and we may begin our life work. This time period often begins with or is accompanied by major life changes, such as divorce, changes in career, and giving birth to children. These changes happen because the opening of this chakra brings with it the potential knowledge of our true self. This knowledge is available to any and all who are willing to experience the feelings that inhibit true expression of purpose, address the beliefs that do not support the true self, and make the life changes necessary to move forward.

Chakra Ten

Age — Pre-conception and conception; 35 to 42 years.

Mental Belief — Past-life and generational beliefs are carried by and stored in this chakra.

Feeling Component — Stores unexpressed feelings of self, parents, legacy, and past lives.

Physical Processes — During pre-conception years, changes spiritual self into a material form. At a later age, allows us to fully ground our spiritual self into a purposeful lifestyle.

Spiritual Perceptions — Helps move our spirit into form (we are really just a materialized spirit). Relates to the grounding of our soul and the ability to provide the elemental energy needed to manifest our bodies, dreams, and desires.

Our soul activates our tenth chakra before conception. Even as our parents begin to consider having a child, our tenth chakra is grounding into the earth and channeling energy for our physical existence. During this pre-conception stage, our tenth chakra gathers energies from our past lives, our parents' existence, and our heritage to shape the nature of our physical body. The physical characteristics, emotional equipment, mental processes, and awarenesses we will need to accomplish our life goals are considered by the soul as it energetically selects the necessary chromosomes using our tenth chakra. Are we going to need to be strong during this lifetime? Will we need to learn how to stop being a victim? Our tenth chakra may gather together memories of our own past-life victimizations (situations of abuse suffered by our forebears) to ensure that our soul selects the right body and events to work out our victim issues. In a nutshell, the tenth chakra provides the incoming soul with an initial umbilical cord to the physical plane.

One of my students, having studied with me for five years, tackled, alone and with a therapist, her "I'm not deserving" issues which had been recently triggered by negotiations during her divorce. All her life, she had felt she wasn't good enough and that she really didn't deserve to succeed. From childhood, she also had long-suppressed issues about wanting to be a boy. Another over-riding feeling was an aching sense of loss and of emptiness, even when a partner was present. Knowing all these issues were probably related, she did some meditative exercises which asked her to look back at the time she was a fetus. She did and was overwhelmed by a sense of loss. Continuing to dig, she felt another presence there with her in the womb— a twin. Unable to go any further on her own, she went to a therapist who was able to help her regress to that womb period and the time before it.

The answers she received validate my belief that the tenth chakra selects the genes necessary to carry out the individual's life purpose. My student went to a place where all things were possible. She was told that she indeed had been conceived as a fraternal twin, because at that point it wasn't clear whether a male or female body would be able to best accomplish the task at hand this lifetime. So two souls, with very consistent purposes, agreed to come into the same space/time continuum as twins, until it was decided which sex could best accomplish the life's purpose. Early in the pregnancy, the choice was finalized; the feminine would be able to do the work, so the male twin left. Although the choice had been made by both souls involved, my student was left with a feeling of loss, a sense of being the wrong sex, and a strong feeling she didn't deserve to succeed or to even be alive, for that matter.

Only after integrating the emotions that resulted from finding out she was a twin was she able to accept the role her twin brother had left her with, the one most able to carry out their shared life purpose. She dove into her life's mission with dedication and enthusiasm, knowing she had to honor the choice her brother made and prove that the feminine energy was indeed the correct choice. Within a month of this discovery, she began to seriously pursue her life-long dream of being a writer, and started her own freelance business as an editor.

Sometimes the events, feelings, and energies we are connected to through our tenth chakra are so painful that we cut off this lifeline. This can leave us ungrounded, open to victimization, and lacking the physical and emotional strength we need to deal with scary situations in general. As we proceed through life, we might misuse our tenth chakra on our own. Instead of drawing upon its hidden power and wisdom, we stuff our negative feelings and experiences down into this chakra, thus closing the channels even further. This can result in repressed memories, dissociation, lack of personal power, low energy, or abusive relationships. Learning to be our true selves is about completely reopening this channel. This process is sometimes called uncovering our shadow self, the part of our being we have judged and repressed. Often hidden in our tenth chakra are the feelings and personality traits we have judged to be bad. In truth, our shadow elements provide us with hidden power and wisdom.

During middle adulthood, ages thirty-five to forty-two, Chakra Ten is reactivated. We are challenged to fully ground or realize our true identity through our life work, relationships, and lifestyle. Integrity is the operative concept—ethical integration of all true components of our self. I believe that the reason so many people have middle-age crisis during this time period relates to this calling for truth in our life.

Chakras Eleven and Twelve

I have not outlined Chakras Eleven and Twelve. The function of the eleventh chakra is simple. A pink energy wrapped around our feet and hands, it transmutes energy external to our body into usable energy. It also releases energy no longer needed by our body into the atmosphere.

As simple as this seems, critical malfunctions may occur if the eleventh chakra is not active or is injured. If it is unable to filter others' negativity, our own body may become a toxic waste site. Inability to release unnecessary energetic wastes through our feet can fill up the lower part of our body, causing us to disassociate into our higher chakras. The resulting spaciness—missing safety signals, such as traffic signs—can be more than annoying; it can be dangerous!

On the other hand, Chakra Twelve is too complex to graph. As the energy center surrounding the human body, it connects into each of the thirty-two secondary chakra points. Chakra Twelve therefore affects and is affected by just about everything in our spiritual and material selves.

Processing With the Higher Points

Our chakras continue to open in seven-year spans for the remainder of Cycle One. Within these seven-year blocks of time, each lower chakra is again re-processed. The beauty of this eternal re-processing is that during these seven years, we can more effectively gain access to our higher energy points. We can apply these higher truths to immediately make ethical changes and clear old issues under spiritual principles.

Consider a typical Chakra Ten mid-life crisis. The challenge to live according to our true needs could become an excuse for reneging on previous decisions and to escape current responsibilities. In effect, we would be saying, "Oops! I really don't like this job, want this husband/wife, want to take care of these children. I made those decisions out of family programs, not my true essence, so I guess I'll just skip out."

If we instead approach these realizations from a spiritual perspective, we may still make many changes, but we will make them responsibly. Instead of trying to escape our responsibilities, we might tap into the Abundance point when experiencing constriction. We may then attract new friends or learn about new ways of being. These positive experiences may keep us from chucking our job, marriage, or life goals quite so suddenly. We could also work with our Yin and Yang points to gain insight into our own feminine and masculine selves.

True wisdom can be gained by struggling to incorporate these higher truths, rather than just living blindly. The reflections granted by these higher points call us to not just react against our present reality, but to be responsible for it.

Cycling Within the Cycle

Over time, I found that the chakric development process helped clients diagnose issues, pinpoint the origins of issues, and, thus focused, clear issues. The process just plain made sense. Therapists began to integrate these ideas into their practices; natural healers began to apply these concepts to locate the origins of disease patterns. It seemed to be a system that needed no tampering, as long as I remembered to assist people with the system rather than fit them into the system.

At this point, a new pattern emerged. I noticed that in individuals older than twenty, there were shadow issues—issues that seemed localized in originating chakras, but tied into another chakra as well. At first, I thought that this was another example of holography, the theoretical assertion that the whole is mirrored in its parts and vice versa. The fact was, these shadow issues fit a pattern. Each primary chakra stage seemed tied to a secondary chakra. These secondary chakras evolved in the same sequence as did the primary chakras, every seven years.

For instance, almost everyone making decisions during their Chakra Eight developmental stage, or working through decisions made during that time frame, were also struggling with what could only be called first chakra issues. Chakra Eight is the time of karma, and during this time period, individuals are working through age-old patterns toward the goal of clarifying their soul purpose. Chakra One is about life and survival needs—career, money, primary relationship, lifestyle. When living within Chakra Eight, individuals were clearly living out (and sometimes actually working through) old patterns, using first chakra issues as the base.

I saw a similar pattern in clients in their early thirties. While almost all of them were questioning their purpose and the value of their life and gifts, they were primarily feeling this push emotionally. The purpose quest is a clear indicator of Chakra Nine, the age placement associated with Cycle One. However, the emphasis on feelings throughout this time period is reflected in Chakra Two, the feeling and creativity chakra.

I found that the best way to assist clients through their Cycle One development was to communicate through the language of one of the in-body chakras. This meant, that when assisting clients in Chakra Eight, I emphasized Chakra One needs. When helping clients located in Chakra Nine, I spoke to their feelings (Chakra Two). Clients based in Chakra Ten required Chakra Three support, involving assistance with personal power and success issues. Clients associated with Chakra Eleven were often heavily involved in personal relationship issues, often originating in Chakra Four.

As an example, I worked with a forty-year-old man who was starting his own business. A successful accountant, he felt that his gifts would be better used supporting small business owners rather than corporate giants. He wanted assistance with figuring out how to communicate his changing desires to his loved ones and to his potential clients.

From a chakric development point-of-view, the accountant was easy to slot. His seven-year cycle was notched at Chakra Ten, the time period for grounding purpose. His needs fit the bill. He was attempting to package his skills and gifts in a way meaningful to him and to others. Within this seven-year span of Chakra Ten, he was also cycling between the fifth and sixth chakra. (Remember, we annually replay the seven in-body chakras within the larger framework.) His desire to communicate his self-image showed concerns addressed by both of these chakras. However, his major concentration was about success and work-related concerns, which were third chakra issues.

After detecting the pattern just illustrated, I did some informal research. Most of the intuitive and healing experts I talked with said that they had always been taught that the chakras recycled from one to seven throughout someone's life. Cycle One seemed to exist, but so did what I now called Cycle Two, the recycling of Chakras One through Seven every seven years.

As I worked with both cycles, I found that my work and my client's success at dealing with problems were enhanced. Though complex, working with this additional layer expanded our understanding of their issues and concerns. The additional data caused additional reflection and subsequently, greater breakthroughs.

Cycle Two

As explained, Cycle One involves a developmental progression through the twelve human chakras. Basically, we work our way from the first to the twelfth chakras in linear fashion. Beginning at the seventh chakra, which activates at age fourteen, we leap from chakra to chakra every seven years. Within each seven-year block of time, we annually reactivate our first seven, in-body chakras.

Age	Cycle One	Cycle Two
14 to 21	Chakra Seven	Chakra Seven
21 to 28	Chakra Eight	Chakra One
28 to 35	Chakra Nine	Chakra Two
35 to 42	Chakra Ten	Chakra Three
42 to 49	Chakra Eleven	Chakra Four
49 to 56	Chakra Twelve	Chakra Five

At age fifty-six, Cycle One returns to baseline; Cycle Two continues upward.

Age	Cycle One	Cycle Two
56 to 63	Chakra One	Chakra Six
63 to 70	Chakra Two	Chakra Seven
70 to 77	Chakra Three	Chakra One
77 to 85	Chakra Four	Chakra Two

As we progress in age, we obviously have more issues to process and more chakras through which to process them. I believe, however, that the complexity is not meant to confuse us, rather, it is to further link our material with our spiritual selves. The beauty of the system is that we are constantly provided opportunity to heal wounds from the past, and to transmute them into gifts for our future.

We can illustrate this if we examine how the two cycles might fit together, if we show how the two chakras, when merged or meshed, can lift our awareness to a new level. For instance:

Age	Cycle One Chakra/Concept	Cycle Two Chakra/Concept	Combined Concept
21 to 28	Eight/Karma	One/Awareness	Karmic awareness.
28 to 35	Nine/Purpose	Two/Creativity	Creative purpose.
35 to 42	Ten/Grounding	Three/Success	Grounding success.
42 to 49	Eleven/Transmutation	Four/Relationship (Love)	Transmutation to love.
49 to 56	Twelve/Humaness	Five/Communication and Wholeness	Communicating wholeness of humaness.
56 to 63	One/Awareness	Six/Image, Vision	Aware vision.
63 to 70	Two/Creativity	Seven/Purpose, Spirit	Life definition.
70 to 77	Three/Success	One/Awareness	Life review.
77 to 85	Four/Relationship (Love)	Two/Creativity	Spiritual connectedness.

Our ability and need to connect with the higher chakras becomes greater during our second chakric development cycle. Optimally, our chakric openings will expand as we move closer to age 100. In Cycle One, we will re-open Chakra Five between ages eighty-five and ninety-two; Chakra Six between ages ninety-two and ninety-nine, and Chakra Seven between ages ninety-nine and 106. Because most of us won't live this long, we group our chakras together to fit them into our life span whenever possible.

EXERCISES
Exploring Your Chakra Development

I. Guide yourself into a meditative state. As you focus on one of your chakras, allow yourself to complete these statements:

A. The experience that most affected me at this age was....

B. The major belief locked in this chakra that is keeping me from being my full self is....

C. The feelings I've repressed and must now claim are....

D. The part of my body connected to this chakra needs to tell me....

E. The soul belief at this level that needs to be changed is....

F. The most appropriate new soul belief would be....

G. When fully healed, this chakra will enable me to....

II. What area in your body causes you the most pain or difficulty? See if you can apply the chakric development system to uncover the reasons for this discomfort.

A. First, look up what age tends to relate to that part of your body. Now, see if you can recall any outstanding events, feelings, or experiences from that time period. What was happening? How were you affected? If you can't remember anything, ask your parents, siblings or relatives to help.

B. Put the pieces together by listing the physical, mental, emotional, and spiritual decisions you made during this time. What picture now emerges?

III. Using the picture on the following page, in each circle on the left, indicate which blocks relate to the corresponding chakra. The blocks can include physical (an illness), mental (a belief or attitude), emotional (a feeling about something that happened at that age), or spiritual (the idea you have about your relationship to the Divine Source). In the right circles, write a contrasting truth.

Take these truths and re-write them on index cards. Challenge yourself to read these twice a day.

Blocks   **Chakra Number**   **Truth**

Chapter Five

From Front to Back: Working With Your In-Body Centers

Most references to the human energy system concentrate on the front side of the chakras, which would be sufficient if we were only two-dimensional beings. However, just our bodies have a front side and a back side, so does our chakric system.

Bodies on the Back of Our Bodies

Most of our in-body chakras are conical-shaped masses of swirling energy. Each chakra has a front and a back. Both the front and the back attach to the spine or the point within the body from which the chakra emanates. In the front, the chakra whirls clockwise. In the back, it whirls counter-clockwise. In general, the front side of the chakric system relates to our conscious self, our day-to-day reality. It contains information and imprints from this life. The back side of the chakric system pertains to our unconscious self, our extended reality. It includes information and imprints from past lives, alternative dimensions, and other worlds.

When we work with the front-side chakras, we gain access to experiences from this life. Contained within each front-side energy center are memories, beliefs, feelings, awarenesses, and needs that affect us right now. Our healing goal is to pinpoint experiences, relationships, and beliefs that adversely affect us. Upon uncovering the causal situation, we then go about processing and clearing it. Clearing a front-side chakra issue usually involves taking an action of some sort, such as thinking new thoughts, adopting new attitudes, or performing in new ways.

When working with the back-side energy centers, we must open to a completely different set of energies. We might unearth experiences from a different time period. We might become aware of a self that is connected to a different dimension. We might tune in to beings from other planets, dimensions, or realities. While we experience our front-side chakras via reality-based memories, feelings, actions, or experiences, we usually experience the back-side chakras through dreams, mystical experiences, inexplicable awarenesses, or unexplainable physical sensations. These back-side chakras contain the data stored in our unconscious or shadow self. Although this data could originate in this-life experiences, it is not limited to that. There is an entire world available to us through our back-side energy system. Therefore, healing or manifesting through our back-side centers can change reality without a response-stimulus, cause-and-effect basis. Our world, beliefs, feelings, processes, and goals may literally rearrange themselves. Such is the power of the unconscious.

	Front Side	Back Side
Relates to:	The conscious self.	The unconscious self.
Ruled by:	Laws of the physical universe.	Limitlessness of alternative realities.
Regulates:	Our day-to-day realities.	Our extended realities.
Manifests by:	Following commonplace procedures.	Connecting to spiritual/cross-dimensional beings and energies.
Contains:	Information about our current life; imprints from this life's decisions, needs, and experiences.	Information about our past lives; imprints from past or alternative decisions, needs, and life experiences.
Heals by:	Allowing us to interface with the tangible world; helping us "do it different."	Allowing the intangible world to change reality for us.

Benefits of the Back Side

Working with the back side chakric system can be extremely beneficial for many reasons. First, while our front side relates to our conscious issues, the back side relates to our unconscious issues. We can work and work and work on our conscious issues, but never uncover the roots of our concerns, which frequently lay in our unconscious. If we can heal the physical, mental, emotional, or spiritual issues hidden in or caused by our unconscious, our conscious reality will respond accordingly.

A second reason for working with the back side is that it opens us to alternative realities rather than just apparent ones. The front side of each chakra connects to the tangible, that which is regulated by the everyday world, whereas the back side of each chakra links us to dimensions and energies that stretch far beyond the day-to-day world. Energy poured through our front sides must obey the laws of the physical universe. If you want to lift a box, you will have to pick up the box. Energy applied through the back chakras is non-conforming. The back-side chakras, each in its own way, can literally bend or shape reality according to non-physical principles. If you want to lift a box by applying back-side principles, anything can happen. Someone else may come along and lift up the box. A sudden earthquake may shift the box for you. The box may just move itself. You never know.

The third reason it is important to work with the chakric back side is that so few people do it. By and large, most metaphysical healing communities overlook a significant aspect of human nature by ignoring one half of the human energy system—the back side, the hidden, occult, shadow side. The back is the side of us that contains our denied feelings, awarenesses, powers, dreams, premonitions, and beliefs. It is the side that hides our repressed memories, unacknowledged knowledge, long-held secrets, and unrealized desires. Because we have hidden these aspects of our nature in the dark for so long, they frighten us. All that is unknown haunts us, which in turn, gives us more reason to deny our shadow side. The problem is that the more we ignore the unconscious truths which align with our back-side energy centers, the more noise and trouble these repressed aspects of ourselves make. Isn't it better to face these demons head-on? We can do this by working with our chakric back sides.

The Power of the Back Side

Time and time again, I have been impressed by the power of these back-side chakras. I have seen clients clear significant emotional issues, heal long-term physical problems, and become aware of long-buried memories, all because we were working on their back-side energy centers rather than their front-side energy centers.

I remember one client in particular. Jamie was struggling with chronic back pain and low-performance issues. Try as she might, she could never get her career going. She was also one step shy of agreeing to surgery to correct her history of back disorders. We used guided imagery, transpersonal psychology, and regression work to walk her into and through each of her back-side chakras. Within each, she uncovered and talked to an aspect of herself that had been repressed since childhood. As she brought these personality aspects to the surface, she asked if they could think of a way to meet their needs, a way that wouldn't result in back pain or poverty. They did, and Jamie's pain disappeared during the session. I encouraged her to go home and continue to do guided meditation and affirmation work with her back-side chakras. I didn't hear from her for another six months, at which point she called and raved, "My back pain never did come back! I kept going through the back chakras, just like you said, and the most interesting things happened!" Jamie went on to recount an unexpected job promotion, an opportunity to attend a select seminar, a fantastic new beau, and a great deal she had just received from an insurance company. She was experiencing the power of the unconscious, which although it can cause all kinds of problems, can also introduce many unexpected, miraculous solutions.

Not every experience with the chakric back side results in such dramatic change. However, the inherent power of these units is underscored for me every time I introduce them to students. After providing information regarding the individual and joint functions of the back-side chakras, I typically pair up students to exchange healings. During these exchanges, students help each other explore the feelings, awarenesses, needs, and problems in each other's energy systems and lives. Without exception, students inform me that the energies felt, healings received, and information gathered is far more powerful from the back side than the front side.

Personally, I believe the front and back sides are equally important and powerful. The difference is that the back sides have been lying dormant, unrecognized, and untouched for so long. The first time someone works with them, it is comparable to opening the door of a long-caged tiger. Any tiger worth its salt is going to leap forth, fierce and ferocious.

So far, I have explained the nature of the seven in-body and the five out-of-body chakras, in addition to the twenty higher plane energy points. As I introduce the seven back-side, in-body chakras, I want to note that there are back sides to the other centers. However, because so little is known about these other twenty-five energy centers, trying to discuss the parallel, but opposite sides of these centers would only add more layers of confusion.

Functions of the Back-Side Chakras

Just like the front-side chakras, the back-side chakras are specific in function. Each has a physical, mental, emotional, and spiritual purpose. Each also interconnects with the others. True health exists when each independent back-side chakra (as well as each front-side one) functions as a healthy individual unit and operates in a consistent manner with the other centers. While much research must still be done in regard to these back-side chakras, understanding and working with them is a critical component to creating a healthy, balanced, and happy life.

The First Twelve Chakras

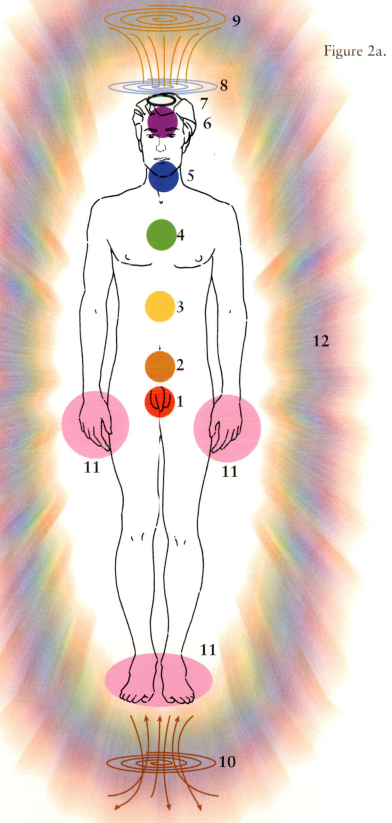

Figure 2a.

Figure 3a.

Your Twenty Spiritual Energy Centers

13	Yin 		23	Knowledge (of Good & Bad) 
14	Yang 		24	Creation Center 
15	Balance of Polarities 		25	Manifestation 
16	Balance of Similarities 		26	Alignment 
17	Harmony 		27	Peace 
18	Freedom & Freewill 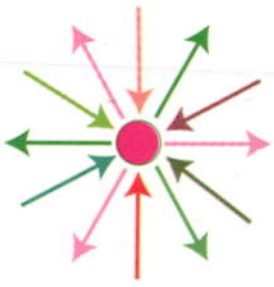		28	Wisdom 
19	Kundalini 		29	Enjoyment 
20	Mastery 		30	Forgiveness 
21	Abundance 		31	Faith 
22	Clarity 		32	Grace 

The 32 Chakras and the Spine

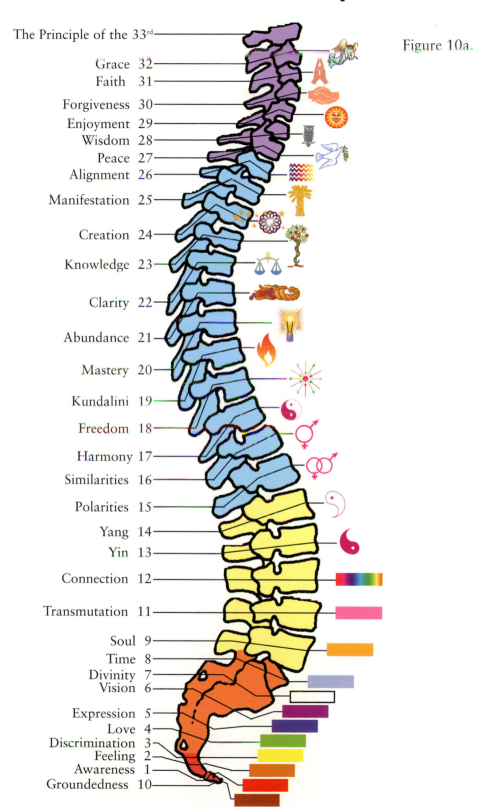

The Principle of the 33rd

Grace 32
Faith 31
Forgiveness 30
Enjoyment 29
Wisdom 28
Peace 27
Alignment 26
Manifestation 25
Creation 24
Knowledge 23
Clarity 22
Abundance 21
Mastery 20
Kundalini 19
Freedom 18
Harmony 17
Similarities 16
Polarities 15
Yang 14
Yin 13
Connection 12
Transmutation 11
Soul 9
Time 8
Divinity 7
Vision 6
Expression 5
Love 4
Discrimination 3
Feeling 2
Awareness 1
Groundedness 10

Figure 10a.

The Layers of the Aura

Figure 6a.

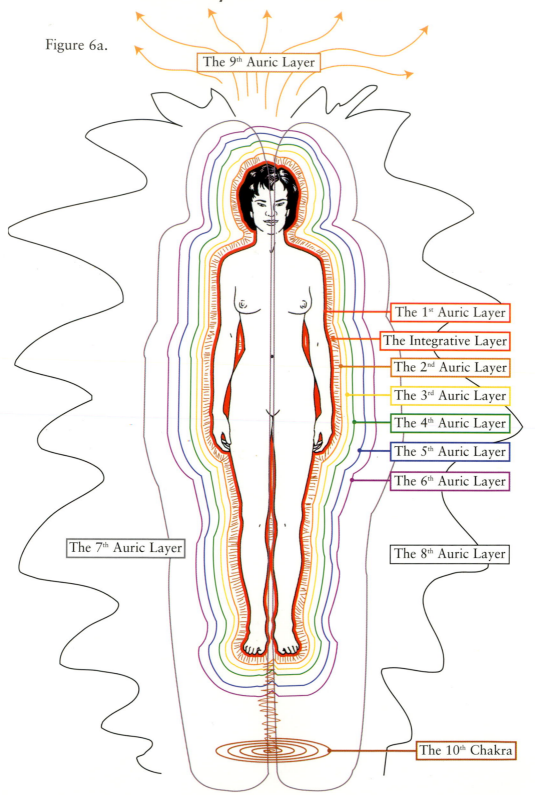

The 9th Auric Layer

The 1st Auric Layer

The Integrative Layer

The 2nd Auric Layer

The 3rd Auric Layer

The 4th Auric Layer

The 5th Auric Layer

The 6th Auric Layer

The 7th Auric Layer

The 8th Auric Layer

The 10th Chakra

Chakra One

The back side of the first chakra is located in a lower frequency dimension. It contains all the beliefs and experiences we have ever held regarding our rights to manifest, create, and flourish on the physical plane. Through this point, we can tap into core belief systems that affect all natures of our being. The energy we ideally want to channel consists of red kundalini energy. We ignite this "life flame" through our first back-side chakra, and open ourselves to our passions, drives, and desires. When this back-side chakra is healed, we can receive all the energies needed to actualize our physical dreams and needs, because we realize that we are physical models of the Divine Source's expression. Here, we can heal our physical issues, including addictions, blood diseases, and inherited problems. Even more important, this center allows us to open to abundance, worthiness, complete health, and a belief in our own sacredness.

Location — Lower frequency dimension. Based in the universal pool of physical matter from which all life springs.

Physical Attributes — Programs DNA. Regulates the body's chemical balance in reaction to beliefs about being deserving and worthy. Coordinates the genetic passage of the collective past. Functions as the access point to the globe of humanity and the human drive for procreation.

Mental Attributes — Holds the key to our beliefs about deserving physical life and well-being. Ideally, it will lead us to the necessary realization that we are a manifestation of Divine Source energy, and we deserve all that our essential self requires for full expression.

Feeling Attributes — Allows universal love energy to enter through the back side of this chakra (which is the basis for the primary feelings shown through the front side of the first chakra). If we disbelieve our own goodness, we will stop up the flow and experience rage, hurt, pain, fear, and more.

Spiritual Attributes — Serves as the physical meeting ground of the sacred. All of life is sacred, from the cellular to the nebulous. Our true essence is breathed into this chakra, where it is shaped for physical experiences.

Healing Applications — The back side of the first chakra is shaped by all of our prior experiences and beliefs, and those of our fellow human beings. We basically want to eliminate the clogs in this chakra, and erase or transform the beliefs that say "I don't deserve a fully happy life." When we become willing to open to the Divine Source's belief system rather than our own, we find a template that allows unlimited amounts of manifestation energy into our first chakra and spinal system. We can apply this raw energy to heal physical, mental, emotional, or spiritual issues.

Symbols — The colors black, red, and white. Cultural death and life symbols, including the scythe, blood, the ankh, the cross, fertility signs, and natural produce such as corn and grain.

Chakra One serves as the foundation for our life experience.

Chakra Two

The back side of the second chakra contains our feelings about ourselves in relation to the holistic universe. The front side contains our feeling bodies, which operate as entities unto themselves. The model or template for these feeling bodies is found in the back chakra. The back side channels feeling frequencies from beyond or outside of us which feed a full feeling or heal incomplete ones. We can psychically see and experientially know each feeling as a whole and complete unit or, conversely, as fragmented and dissociated pieces. Our goal is to weave these frequencies into our feeling bodies, either to complete our incomplete feelings or strip away feelings that are not ours. By opening to the vibrations that we need, we allow ourselves to analyze situations in light of their emotional complexities. This leaves us able to work within the dualities of the physical universe—to understand the good in the bad, the meaning in the meaningless, and the truth within the falsehoods.

Location — Originates in the lower back area.

Physical Attributes — Holds the templates of the front side's feeling bodies. Feeling bodies are material bodies. All physical issues relate, at least at some level, to our feeling bodies. Problems such emotionalism, stress, compulsions, relationship ills, creative blocks, and small back pains can be symptoms of a second chakra back side that is not completely open or that is unprotected. This back-side center can also transform feelings into energy, powers, beliefs, colors, and tones. We can heal our feelings by working with beliefs, colors, tones, and the like.

Mental Attributes — Receives the healing and adaptation energy needed to cope with life's changes. Blocks in the back side prevent us from receiving this energy. Judging the acceptability of certain feelings and denying expression of these feelings causes blocks in the back side of the chakra or in the center meeting point between the front and back sides.

Feeling Attributes — Serves as our feelings template. If we consider all feelings to be equal and good, our feeling bodies will be whole and complete. These feelings can then encourage or discourage, construct or destruct, solidify or change our behaviors so that we can adapt to life's natural rhythms and natural crises. The back side of this energy center will therefore be open to the vibrations and energies necessary for creativity and experience. In addition, it will enable us to obtain and acknowledge the supernatural help necessary to flow with the twists and turns of life.

Spiritual Attributes — Gives the soul the support and fluidity necessary to adapt and thrive in life. The back side of the second chakra is in turn affected by our soul's beliefs about life's meaning and meaninglessness, hope and hopelessness, good and bad, emptiness and existence, the self and the All, and other dualities of existence as they are experienced on the physical plane.

Healing Applications — The back side of Chakra Two is a prime starting point for healing emotional distress; birth, rebirth, and reproductive concerns; co-dependency tendencies; general compulsions; small back pain; and our reactions to life's just and unjust occurrences. Here, we can open to the energies necessary to soothe and heal feelings like rejection, disillusionment, apathy, resentments, and feelings that result from death and loss, grief and pain. When we bring our feelings into balance, giving away those that are not ours and accepting those that are, we open to the power of creation itself. We allow ourselves to manifest the mana that sustains us through life's ups and downs.

Symbols — Cross-cultural forms indicative of feelings, emotions, release, and rebirth, including the moon, water, the Jewish mikveh cleansing pool, natural cycles and the seasons, a naked woman on a crescent moon with her hand on her abdomen.

Chakra Two serves as our feeling template.

Chakra Three

The back side of Chakra Three is really an intellectual template. Through this side of the chakra we gain knowledge of things seen and unseen and, based upon our belief systems, tap into the energies we need to make effective life decisions. If the front side assists us in expressing our will in the world, our back side opens to the drive for achievement. Here, we can heal judgments, falsehoods and incorrect assumptions and allow our drive for success (however we define success) to work for us rather than against us.

Location — Middle of the back.

Physical Attributes — Connects into the metabolic center of the body; affects our general energy level and drive. Decreased life energy, confusion, inability to focus or concentrate, and any physical condition mirroring these symptoms might relate to this center. We need to remember that decision-making, goal-setting, and goal achievement require intellectual energy, which is a material energy.

Mental Attributes — Serves as the intellectual template through which all judgments are processed, accepted, changed, or rejected. Through the back side of the third chakra, thought forms are patterned, brought forward, altered. Beliefs regarding success, assertion of will and drive, and our relationship with the external world are directly attributable to this chakra.

Feeling Attributes — Leads us to totally accept ourselves, our purposes, and our drives. Depending upon the health of this chakra's back side, the highest possible feelings achievable in this area include acceptance, peace, and faith. When the back side of this chakra is completely open and healthy, we would not participate in violence or war, because the basis for war is prejudice and fear. When acting out of self-confidence and authenticity, there is simply no room for violence.

Spiritual Attributes — Gives us knowledge of the seen and unseen, and, provided we have faith in our abilities, gives us the ideas necessary to set and implement our goals. Spiritual doubt is erased. Our soul serves as our spiritual director, supporting us with the concepts and impetus necessary to put ourselves forth in the world.

Healing Applications — It would be wise to work on this center anytime we experience energy issues, whether they be physical, mental, or emotional. Blocks in this center stem from doubt, which is really a lack of faith in our own higher good and goals. Here, we can address and heal judgments, prejudices, incorrect assumptions, painful behaviors, and success issues. One way to approach this healing process is to remember how the first three chakras work together. We add the raw emotions of the first chakra to the intellectual awarenesses of the third to create the emotions located in the second chakra. By changing the directives entering through our third chakra's back side, we can change our feelings and perceptions about the world itself.

Symbols — Typical symbols will relate to the intellect and learning endeavors, including the sun, a book, and words.

Chakra Three serves as our intellectual template.

Chakra Four

The back side of Chakra Four serves as a portal to the wonderful playground of our soul. All of us, even people who consider themselves to be "old souls," in truth have souls that are childlike. No matter what our age, our soul is youthful, because we are all children of the Divine Source. As children, our soul's job is to explore, learn, develop, test, try, and have fun. The back side of our heart, when unstopped, opens us to our spirit's true desires. Most of these desires are childlike in nature and include fantasies like going skinny-dipping, basking in the sun, eating ice cream, or lazing around the pool.

Through this aspect of the heart chakra, we can merge our personhood completely with the divine light of the universe. It is the great space the Divine Source, the Master Planner, has built for simple pleasures. In this space, love is conditional. The condition is free expression of our total being.

Location — Upper back.

Physical Attributes — Serves as the entry point for all physical actions we feel called to do. The physical focus of these desires synchronizes with our heartbeat. Beat, rest, beat, rest—do, be, do, be. Obviously, any heart-related issues would indicate an imbalance in the back side of the heart chakra, as would resistance to following our true calling or desires.

Mental Attributes — Receives love without judgment, and serves as an access point for mental energies that are pure and simple. Through the back side of the heart chakra, we can reach the type of support we longed to get as a child. Here, the conditional belief system of the lower chakras meets the unconditional system of the upper chakras. Our conditional needs, which boil down to the simple requirement to be and express our true self, merges with the unconditional love and support of the universe.

Feeling Attributes — Connects our physically based essence, and attaches to our Divine Source-based essence. This chakra back side needs to be fully connected to the Divine Source. The feelings experienced through a fully open and healed heart-chakra back side will be related to unqualified love and encouragement for being.

Spiritual Attributes — Keeps us continually open to the needs of our soul as it progresses in its growth and development. The back side of this chakra connects to the Divine Source and our Divine Source self. Here, we experience the call of the child we are. Upon experiencing the power of the back side of the heart chakra, one of my students said, "A soul pauses here and is born, waiting to be born again."

Healing Applications — All heart, circulatory, and blood issues could relate to this center. We could also examine the back side of this chakra if we are experiencing constrictions of any sort; dealing with childhood abuse issues; or disbelieving in our own purity and innocence. Often, this center will speak to us through dreams, out-of-body experiences, or guides such as angels who seek to steer us toward our true self and true purpose.

Symbols — Signs regarding the back side of this chakra may be very personal, consisting of images we hold dear and important. General symbols would include any portraits of the heart, butterflies, hummingbirds, or anything childlike and innocent.

Chakra Four is the seat of our heart's desires.

Chakra Five

No one would know that you exist without the back side of the fifth chakra. Here, our truths are made known to us. As we express these truths, others learn about them, too. The back side of the fifth chakra is the center through which we channel thoughts, ideas, and concepts from other beings, other dimensions, and other aspects of ourselves. We receive information through the back of the neck, then pass it along through our conscious, vocal front side. Here, we own what guidance we want and reject that which does not apply to us. In a way, this chakra is the fate center. We constantly select, then voice that which we want to create, versus that which we do not.

Location — Back of the neck.

Physical Attributes — Serves as an access point or a doorway. If we leave our doors wide open, anything can come in and probably will. All sorts of people and beings can set up shop, potentially causing all sorts of problems. Without filters, we may receive guidance from people or beings who don't mean us well. Opening to guidance from twisted sources can leave us vulnerable to making decisions that could cause financial, relationship, and physical distress. Problems with it can create a wide range of material issues, from money problems to throat cancer. On the other hand, being open yet wise with regard to information and guidance can help us create the life that we want.

Mental Attributes — Channels thoughts, ideas, and concepts from other beings and other parts of ourselves. The beliefs of others in our current life, beliefs from previous existences, and beliefs from outside sources can frequently become lodged within the back side of this chakra. One of the most common problems in this chakra is the presence of cords, energetic contracts between ourselves and other beings. Because they are so common, I now always check for cords in the back of the neck. Usually, I find a big chunk of Mom's beliefs entering through the left side of the client's neck and another legacy from Dad planted in the right side. It is important to weed through these old beliefs or old tapes in order to gain control of this center.

Feeling Attributes — Serves as an entry point for any and all feelings; brings us our own or other's guidance as to what reality will make us feel good. Through techniques such as guided imagery, we can exit through this chakra and seek guidance in relation to our feelings. Often, we must rely upon our feeling-based reaction to the guidance received through this back chakra to sift through the information that fits from that which does not.

Spiritual Attributes — Serves as an access point for outside spirits and messages from our spiritual self. Full transmediums use this point as a gateway to leave their bodies and allow other beings to enter. We can achieve as much clarity by remaining in our bodies and listening to the guidance coming in through the back side of this chakra. After all, it is really our soul we want to completely incorporate, not another's. A general rule of thumb when healing or applying this chakra is to speak what we know and release resistance to learning what we must know. Ultimately, what we want to channel through this half of the chakra are words from our Divine Source self. If we concentrate on those words, we cannot go wrong.

Healing Applications — As the major entry point for old tapes, this chakric back side can give us access to ideas for healing just about anything. Through this chakra, we experience the similarities between healing and manifesting. To heal a problem, we must usually open to a new idea and then say what we are willing to do differently. Once we state our intention, we open ourselves to manifesting something new. This chakra back side is also the center to check for unusual problems such as spirit possession or demonic influence.

Symbols — Any which relate to spinning, such as a loom, spinning wheel, or spider. Through the back side of this chakra, we collect the raw material needed to spin our own truths, and therefore, spin our own realities.

Chakra Five serves as the center of self-directed fate.

Chakra Six

Considered the sight chakra, the back side of the sixth chakra reflects all our potentials, while the front side envisions our one, truest path. The meeting point between the front and back of the sixth chakra—the pituitary gland— serves as a prism that receives all our potential visions and evaluates them according to our highest purpose. Our life's strategic plan can be on or off. If our central sixth chakra belief systems are self-affirming, our visions of self will be constructive. If our central sixth chakra belief system is self-destructive, our self-image will be negative, and our goals will be the same.

This chakra is a path chakra. A fully healed sixth chakra back side helps us visualize not only what could happen, but what will happen if we stay true to form. During my teaching sessions, I explain this back-side chakra to students a bit poetically:

> *no one knows*
> *but you and me*
> *where my path shall lead.*
> *take my hand*
> *the light is mine*
> *thy light divine*
> *is me.*
> *to the temple*
> *of perfect self*
> *we create the sight*
> *and the path unfolds;*
> *who i am,*
> *God's child*
> *shall delight*
> *in following only*
> *the sights of light.*

Location — Back of the head.

Physical Attributes — Affects both our inner and outer vision. As the center for creative visualization, what we envision becomes materialized in physical reality in this chakra. People often experience the healing or opening of this chakra first as a white-light experience. Upon viewing the intense white light, their lives are never the same. What happens is that they are opening to the path that the Divine Source and their own Divine Source self visualizes for them. If they commit to following it, life truly isn't ever the same.

Mental Attributes — Shows us the beliefs we hold about our true potential. When we are blind to our divine nature, our visions may be immature, too low or too high, or even invisible. Extreme self-negativity can leave us so in the dark that we are susceptible to brainwashing or cult influence. When we lack a clear picture of self, we might adopt others' visions for our life rather than our own. The converse is also true. By affirming our Divine Source self, we automatically receive and select visions that will enable us to reach our highest potential.

Feeling Attributes — Influences and reflects how we feel about ourselves. The more open the back side of this chakra is, the better we feel about ourselves. Lack of self-acceptance, poor self-image, and the like are often directly attributable to a partially shut-down sixth chakra back side. Feelings of low self-worth can shut down this chakra; an inhibited back sixth chakra can also produce depressive feelings. Conversely, the better we feel about ourselves, the more responsive this chakra will be to producing positive feelings.

Spiritual Attributes — Shows our soul what it has created and what it wants to create. When our soul can fully accept the journey already undertaken and open to a higher guiding light, it can not only envision its desires, but be drawn to opportunities that will manifest them.

Healing Applications — Here, we can address problems with low self-image or body-image concerns; confusion about our path, choices, and potential futures; and a general disbelief in a future. During any death and dying process, including those involving transformations or loss, there is typically a necessary and predictable shutting down in this area. We lose sight of clarity as our self-perceptions and choices rearrange.

Symbols — All visual images; story images regarding a river, a path, or a journey; representations of light including the sun, rainbows, and prisms.

Chakra Six is the seat of self-creation.

Chakra Seven
The back side of the seventh chakra is simultaneously located nowhere and everywhere. Here we open to and realize the divine spark of consciousness.

The back side is the access point by which we can connect with all beings of the Divine Source, whether they are physically alive or not. Here is the lifeline to all existence and the truth of our own existence. Through this backside chakra, we channel gold kundalini, the lifeblood of our spiritual existence. One of my clients shared this poem after being introduced to this side of her seventh chakra:

> Oh song of my soul
> sing sweetly to me,
> raise my voice in harmony
> to join the chorus of souls
> singing around me.

Location — The higher planes, where all dimensions/time zones become one.

Physical Attributes — Has no physical attributes because of its complete non-judgmentalism. While problems in the front side can manifest as physical concerns, the back side cannot physically affect us. However, opening to energies available through this back side chakra can lead to physical healing. Any sense of disharmony or incompleteness in our lives could indicate an injured seventh chakra back side.

Mental Attributes — Opens us to the divine spark of consciousness and the universe's positive beliefs about ourselves. When we believe that we are unworthy or when we fear losing our individuality to the greater All, we can close down the back of the seventh chakra. To keep this portal open, we must be willing to change these beliefs or let them be transformed.

Feeling Attributes — Brings us a feeling of being "perfectly still" or "one of bliss" (as described by my students time and time again). The feeling is comparable to that which we experience when praying, meditating, or praising at our own personal place of worship.

Spiritual Attributes — Brings us to the realization that all spirits are equal. Our individuality remains intact, yet we realize that unity (rather than disunity) is of key importance. Most people describe the state of awareness achieved at this level as feeling "at home."

Healing Application — Any and all healers and healing journeyers would benefit from the peace and stillness experienced at this level. At its most basic level, working with the back side of this chakra opens us to a fundamental shift in consciousness. Because its access point to the body is located in the mind, working with the energies available in this chakra back side can dramatically alter our perceptions and thinking.

Symbols — Any symbol of completion or wholeness—the white light, the circle, the spiral, the halo.

Chakra Seven is the seat of wholeness.

Synopsis of Back-Side Chakra Functions

Chakra	Mental Belief	Feeling Component	Physical Process	Spiritual Perceptions
One	Core beliefs about worthiness of life and all that life has to offer.	Access point to energies that determine our primary feelings or reactions to others' feelings.	Seat of our genetic and human collective gene pools.	Place where we can realize that we are a model of God's expression in the physical.
Two	Beliefs about feelings. Are they okay or not? Must I carry others' feelings or not?	Home of our feeling-body templates and access point to energies that feed, support, and heal our feelings.	Source of fluidity necessary to keep system open and adaptable.	Point for acknowledging the dualities of life; contains the assistance the soul needs to experience wholeness through duality.
Three	Beliefs about success and opportunity; center of judgments in a global sense; area for decision-making; intellectual template for goal-setting and success.	Relates to feelings about success and self-acceptance.	Channels the universal energy needed to accomplish goals.	Key area relating to faith and trust in contrast to doubt and fear.
Four	Beliefs regarding our innocence and purity; deservedness of simple desires and needs.	Opens us to activities and needs that will create feelings of love and good will.	Opens us to relationships and dreams that enable us to manifest what we really want.	Place where unconditional love achieves a balance with conditional, reality-based laws.

Five	Contains planted, guided, or self-designed truths.	Regulated by feelings; we must open to what feels right and reject what doesn't feel right.	May contain the germ of many physical diseases; access point to gain guidance for dealing with physical problems or concerns.	Often seen as the "seat of the soul" because it provides us with guidance from and for our soul self (ideally guided by the Divine Source).
Six	Accessible visions and paths relating to the collection of beliefs about self-image.	Following our correct vision assures feelings of high self-worth.	Our visions and choices ultimately create the physical reality we manifest.	By seeing ourselves through the eyes of the Divine Source. we open to the truest visions for self.
Seven	Beliefs only exist at the actual physical access point; these relate to the relationship between knowing the self as an individual versus the self as a member of the whole; there are no beliefs at this level, only the state of acceptance.	Here, we can experience the feeling of completion and harmony, the point from which we need to make all our evaluations; the ultimate feeling to achieve at this level is gratitude.	As we become more open to being part of the whole, our brain patterns, and therefore our physical well-being, can shift toward perfect health.	Place where all souls gather and support the individual's purpose in the grand scheme of things.

The Back Sides in Action

Face it—we're human. Most of us won't live to see the day when all our chakras, especially our back-side chakras, are fully functioning.

The good news is that we don't have to wait. Every time we open or heal one of our back-side chakras, even partially, we create change within the remaining chakras, both back and front.

Every chakra interrelates. For example, the first chakra channels energy that keeps us alive and secure. Its back side funnels material from the sea of matter. The mid-point connection passes this energy through to our front side, which determines our action. The amount of available energy and its direction are regulated by our belief systems. Do we believe that we deserve abundance and love, or are we constricted by beliefs imprinted during our in-utero existence? Do these beliefs insist that we are not wanted, that we do not deserve to have our needs met? The amount of openness or constriction experienced through this overall chakra will be translated into our second chakra. If we screen the energies taken in through our first chakra back side, we inhibit the in-body energies available to our second chakra feeling bodies. Therefore, it will be difficult for us to process the energies taken in through the second chakra back side, which will in turn, further damage our feeling bodies.

Let's track an issue through our back-side and front-side system. Pretend that you meet someone with whom you would like to have a relationship. You meet a man or woman at a party and feel attracted. Through the back-side first chakra, you receive the energy needed to fuel your attraction and desire. If you are completely open to these feelings, this back-side energy feeds your front-side behavior. You take action—you approach this person.

This action kicks energy up to the second chakra, stimulating certain feeling bodies. First, you strike chords with the feeling of excitement. The back side of this chakra kicks in energy to both fuel and temper this excitement. It may, for instance, need to heal your trust feeling, which, based on past experience, is being stimulated toward mistrust. Another feeling, trust in self, combines with your excitement. Because the front side of the second chakra is a personal, receptive chakra (rather than an outward movement one), the front-side reaction is openness to this person.

This energy of openness surges then into the third chakra. The back side provides ideas about how to interact with your object of desire. You sift and weigh these ideas, filtering them through the acquired and innate belief systems which separate the front- and back-side chakras. Eventually, you decide that it is okay to move forward; you trust that you will successfully present yourself.

Having decided to interact, your energy moves upward into the heart. Your back-side soul and heart fantasies enter through the back side of the fourth chakra. How do you sense yourself interfacing with this person? Again, you are working in a personal, receptive chakra. You sense out this person's reaction to you. Your energy adjusts to your heart-felt sense of potentials, then sends your energy up toward the fifth chakra.

Now you are standing in front of this person. It is time to say something. Through the back side of this chakra, you gather guidance from yourself and perhaps other guides about what to say. If this chakra is clear, this guidance will be appropriate. If you hook into old tapes, you could screw it up. Given that you are relatively healed and receptive, you put all the senses, feelings, and guidance into words that project outward. You speak to the person. One of your heart's desires has been to go skiing, so you ask this person if he or she likes to ski.

He or she responds, "Yes!" Your energy surges into the sixth chakra. Through the back of the sixth, we see all of the possible visions that could be produced here. Do we picture downhill or cross-country skiing? A rustic cabin in the Rockies or a chalet in the Swiss Alps? These visions filter through your programmed images of self, finally determining which one to settle upon. All chakras below this one are now activated, so you can decide how to proceed. Will you concentrate on your heart and help make this person and yourself feel comfortable with each other? Will you continue to converse, connecting with words? Will you take further action, employing more of your first chakra?

Whatever you do ideally will be chosen and regulated by your last in-body chakra, the seventh, which is seeking purpose and unity. The back of this chakra attaches not only to the body of spirits eternally surrounding you, but to the higher spirit of the person you are facing. You know that if you allow full expression based on your higher sense of self, whatever you choose to do or say will be on purpose for you and the potential relationship.

Of course, this scenario is a very simplified form of how the chakric back side and front side interact. Misperceptions, judgments, repressed desires, denied feelings, others' issues and energies are not just stored in the revolving point between the front sides and back sides. They can also be found within the auric body, within the soul, and just about anywhere else. If we keep in mind that the back side functions according to our unconscious programming and the front side according to our conscious programming, we can get a pretty clear picture of how we process energy and make decisions.

Most importantly, we can hold onto the fact that all of us have been given the opportunity to experience life, not to avoid it. We are continually given the choices, chances, and means we need to clarify, heal, and transform.

Detecting the Chakras

The front and back sides of the chakras meet in the spine, with the exception of the seventh chakra, which links into the cranium. Physical tools can measure the presence of all these chakras. Scientific and medical communities are testing the presence of these chakras through sound, color, and effect.

You can find your own chakras with a pendulum. A pendulum is made by putting a weight, such as a stone or a ring, on a chain or cord. A pendulum held over the chakric area will begin to swing with the whirling of the chakra itself on the front or the back (figure 5a).

With this method, you can see the flow of all of your in-body chakras, except the back side of the first and the seventh chakras. The back side of Chakra One is located in a lower dimension. You cannot place it with a pendulum; most people cannot even see it psychically. The back side of Chakra Seven opens to a higher dimension, which vibrates too quickly to be found using physical techniques. In fact, this chakra isn't really even located in a physical place. Because it connects us to our higher self and the higher selves of others, it is outside of the time/space continuum. The only way to know or understand the back sides of Chakras One or Seven is to experience them.

Figure 5a.

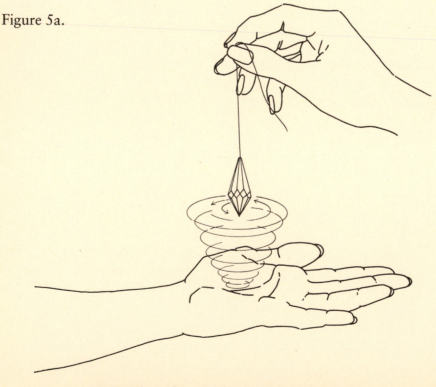

Detecting the chakras with a pendulum.

EXERCISE
Working With Your In-Body Chakras

Ask a partner to help you with this exercise.

A. Laying on your stomach, have your partner to guide you into a meditative state. Allow him or her to place a hand on each back-side chakra area. Concentrate on one area at a time.

As you feel each point, respond to the following questions:

- What can I receive by opening or healing this chakra?

- What is preventing this chakra from fully functioning?

B. Then ask this individual chakra to act as if it is healed. Experience what you would feel like if it really was healed there. Share your observations with your partner.

Chapter Six

The You Around You: Your Energy Field

All physical matter is in constant motion. The molecules in our desks and clothes are always vibrating. The energy particles in the air we breathe and water we drink are in constant flux. The cells in our skin, glands, brain, and eyes—as well as ourselves in relation to our job, car, relationships, and other concerns—are eternally performing the "duty dance with death," as Kurt Vonnegut likes to define life.

Life is movement. Life is a dancing. This constant dynamism produces constant change. Even if we were able to cry out, "Hold it!" and convince all matter to stop its unending waltz, we would not be able to create still-ness. Long after an object has stopped moving, it continues to vibrate, to adapt to the change it has just made. I am reminded of an observation my kindergarten-age son made during a field trip to a nature park. He and his fellow classmates raved for days about a dead salamander they had come across. "Mommy, it was still moving!" he shared in awe. "Even though its guts had been plucked out!"

Every component of our energy field is constantly in flux. Our first chakra pulsates to its own rhythms while our second chakra keeps time to its own beat. Particles from physical and psychic matter dart here and there. Our feelings bounce off our thoughts, which in turn, react to our needs. With all of these different tunes and fluctuations, it is a wonder we can inter-act as an intact entity at all, but we can.

The Aura

One of the reasons that we hold together as an intact entity is because emanating from us and surrounding us is an energy field, typically called the **aura**. Every animate object has an aura (and some people believe inanimate objects also have them). An aura has been described as everything from a light emitting from the body, to a force field, to a universal energy field. Whichever the case, the aura is an esoteric body composed of material energy. The aura is as much a revolving door as our chakras.

The auric body itself comprises many planes. Some auric planes vibrate at a high frequency, and are consequently responsive to our spiritual needs. Some auric planes vibrate at a low frequency, and are therefore responsible for our material needs. These lower frequency ones are the most easily seen or felt outside of our physical body. In reference to Einstein's theory of relativity, Barbara Ann Brennan feels matter and energy are interchangeable and that "matter is simply slowed down or crystallized energy" (Brennan, 24).

Both the lower and higher auric planes interact with their opposites. In many ways, the true job of the lower frequency layers is to convert spiritual mana to physical matter; the function of the higher frequency layers is to transmute physical matter into spiritual energy.

Many psychics differentiate the esoteric bodies this way: the aura is on the outside of the body; the chakras are on the inside. Though this theory can conceptually help us, it does not tell us the entire story. Nature doesn't really differentiate between the insides and outsides of things. The truth is, the chakras are holistic units that tie into, interact with, and help form the auric layers. These auric layers are also holistic units. The aura as a whole includes the chakras and every other aspect of our being. It is also a sub-unit of our energetic self because its major functions enable us to interact with our external environment and the physical, mental, emotional, and spiritual dimensions that are constantly at play with our being. (See figure 6a, color pages.)

The Aura as a Matrix

Rather than consider the aura to be bands or layers of energy, it is more appropriate to think of it as a matrix system. The lines on the matrix intersect to form a grid. This grid could be seen as a completely different energy body, one which incorporates our physical body while locking into points within our physical body. It could also be seen as an extension or sub-unit of a much larger grid, the grid of energy that connects everyone in humanity to each other, to nature, and to the universe itself.

When we remember that we are constantly fluctuating, as is every aspect of our being and those of everyone and everything else, we may start to wonder why we don't just blow apart from all that change.

"All that change" is precisely why we have an aura. This energy field establishes our individual entity while linking us to greater forces. It provides form and substance while helping us remain flexible and adaptable. The matrix lines composing the auric body work like a dot-to-dot puzzle, connecting this sub-atomic particle to that organ; that organ to our brain; our brain to our skin; our skin to climactic conditions; the immediate environment to the sun; the sun to its planetary brothers and sisters. The aura works like a skein to protect us from being over-influenced by the change outside of us. It also works like a computer to regulate our energy system, so that we can respond to the change around us. Our aura notices what is happening millions of miles away and what is occurring in the tiniest particles of our cells.

The Four Roles of the Aura

Usually, our auric energy matrix or field performs its roles automatically. However, we would all benefit from a conscious understanding of our aura and the four major types of roles it performs:

- Predictive.
- Adaptive.
- Responsive.
- Protective.

The **predictive** response of the aura relates to its ability to pick up on possible problems or opportunities. By noting the **adaptive** functions of the aura, we can take note of what affects us and make decisions about how to shape change and thus fit in. Through the **responsive** nature of the aura, we locate and address disease, mental problems, inappropriate belief systems, overextended or denied feelings, family-of-origin issues, relationship ills, career concerns, and spiritual misperceptions. By working with the **protective** role of the aura, we can better learn to take care of ourselves.

The work I've done with chronic fatigue sufferers best illustrates all four roles of the aura. Using intuitive vision, I can spot chronic fatigue sufferers by their aura, because they almost have none. On the average, auras of healthy individuals can spread two to six feet out from the body. The aura of a person with chronic fatigue is plastered next to his or her skin. In these individuals, I typically see a thin, red band on, in, or right on top of the skin, then a thin band of white, then a thicker (two- to three-inch) band of dark black on top (figure 6b). This black band seems to work like a black hole. It absorbs external energy, but holds it fast, providing no stimulation or sustenance to the physical self. The white band, I've come to believe, represents a serious misunderstanding about spirituality. This misunderstanding, I've found, has almost always been carried forth from a past life or from a current-life ancestor, and replayed in early childhood. The red band is the victim's life force

Figure 6b.

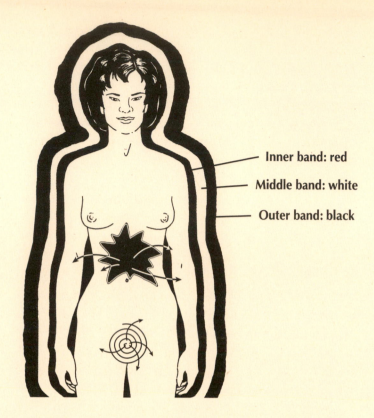

Inner band: red

Middle band: white

Outer band: black

Aura of a person suffering from chronic fatigue syndrome.

energy. For some reason, life has been perceived as too painful to allow this energy to flow through the body.

Chronic fatigue sufferers lack the auric protection they need to combat stress because their entire auric field becomes constricted to the three bands of energy. Whereas persons with healthy auras would repel negativity and allow toxins to be carried out through the various auric layers, the black layer of a chronic fatigue sufferer absorbs all negativity, holding it as would a black hole. In a healthy system, red energy is primarily retained inside one's body, boosting the physical stamina and response ability. Chronic fatigue sufferers, as an attempt to protect or armor themselves, paint the outsides of themselves with this red energy. They are therefore unable to summon inner strength when needed.

A normal aura also provides for adaptability and flexibility. With chronic fatigue, the auric layering is rigid, so that external or internal stressors cannot flow around. The chronic fatigue victim finds him/herself constantly doing energetic battle and therefore, constantly exhausted. Finally, the chronic fatigue sufferer lacks the auric gift of predicting. The healthy aura encompasses the self and can foretell future possibilities because certain of its layers stretch into other dimensions. Other layers dip into the chakras, our reservoirs of experience, to pull up the wisdom needed to make adjustments based on potential events. Chronic fatigue sufferers, being confined to a very narrow shell, simply cannot sense these future potentials. Hence, they become exhausted by life's series of unexpected twists. (See the Appendix for how the energy bodies appear when various medical conditions are present.)

Obviously, having a healthy aura is important, and allowing it to fulfill all four roles is vital. So what exactly is this aura, and how is it constructed?

The Auric Layers

The aura is a matrix that interlocks us into the larger matrix(es) of our inner and outer environments. An energy field, the aura comprises various units, usually called auric layers, which interlace with the chakras, energy points, and the body itself. Each of these layers or matrix units has a physical, mental, emotional, and spiritual dimension and purpose. Understanding each of these layers can assist us in living the lives we want to live.

There are many esoteric names associated with the auric layers. There are also many auric experts and auric systems, which lead to disagreement about how many layers of auric bands there are. There have also been many esoteric names associated with the auric layers. The ideas perpetuated by this system will be in line with others, but will differ because I will present each layer in a simplified fashion, emphasizing the connection between the auric layer and the chakra most associated with it.

I believe there are nine basic layers or matrix patterns in the auric system, two somewhat intangible layers atop these, and a twelfth layer, which is equivalent to our twelfth chakra. When working with clients, I typically work with the nine basic auric layers. To describe these first nine layers, I simply use numbers, then provide a label consistent with other metaphysical systems.

First Auric Layer

I associate the first auric layer with the first chakra; therefore, its functions are similar to those of the first chakra. It protects, identifies, and solidifies our physical awareness.

Most metaphysicians think the primal auric layer is affiliated with the etheric body, which they envision right next to the skin. I believe the first auric layer is the skin. Any time one of my clients is dealing with basic security or safety issues, protection and boundary issues, life and death issues, or skin or appearance issues, I work with the first auric layer or encourage this person to work with someone who, directly or indirectly, does the same. This professional group can include chiropractors, medical doctors, acupuncturists, hands-on healers, massage therapists, personal trainers or other exercise specialists, or anyone who interacts with the body.

Our skin both holds our insides on our insides and keeps our outsides on our outsides. It also regulates the interaction between these two. The energetic matrix associated with this auric layer has a similar function. It creates a form in which to house our spirit while we are on this plane, and helps us reflect the truth of our spirit to the world. It does the latter by helping our skin register our life experiences, reflect our feelings, and hold physical space.

Remember that the aura is not separate from the body. This association is most clearly illustrated by the workings of the first auric layer. The first auric layer is the skin and aspects of the physical body. I see the matrix pattern that connects to the front side of the chakra as the same as our physical skin. The matrix pattern associated with the back side of the chakra attaches or loops into a lower frequency of matter, from which it draws material energy to sustain the boundaries necessary for everyday living and life itself.

Considering the skin to be an auric layer was relevant to my work with a psoriasis patient. His psoriasis was all over his body, and he had tried all available medical and clinical therapeutic approaches. In providing him with insight, the only image I could get was that of an infant who longed to be held by his mother. He confirmed that, to his knowledge, his mother had seldom held him, and that even now she never hugged him. I believe that lacking this protective nurturing from the maternal role model, my client's first auric layer had failed to receive a template it needed.

Moody and often emotional, my client fit the thin-skinned reactive profile. His skin got better every time he began to direct his issues and feelings toward this childhood issue. Unfortunately, just when his skin condition had almost cleared, he decided he didn't need to face these issues any more and instead began focusing on past romantic experiences. His skin condition immediately flared up again.

Location — The skin (figure 6c).

Physical Attributes — Regulates all physical requirements for the skin, the largest organ in the body. All issues or diseases affecting the skin or our basic physical survival needs may indicate a first chakra and first auric layer concern. These include career and money issues, and other security-related functions.

Mental Attributes — May reflect beliefs about one's deservedness, safety, identity, sexuality, and other issues.

Feeling Attributes — Registers primal feelings on the skin and through concrete, first-chakra-related realities such as the bodily needs for housing, relationships, and sustenance. These feelings include anger, hurt, rage, terror, joy, pain, guilt, and shame. Physical anomalies such as acne, psoriasis, and shingles may indicate a first-chakra issue (often emotionally based) reflected on this first auric layer.

Spiritual Attributes — Links to our concrete reality through the front side of the first chakra. The back side of the first chakra connects into the first auric

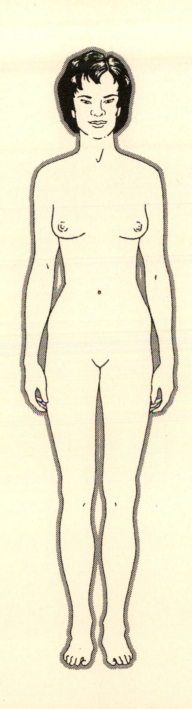

The first auric layer (the skin).

matrix and draws forth our hidden or learned beliefs about the Divine Source and our relationship to it. If we can allow our first auric matrix to also link with a spiritual template, our immediate life concerns would be greatly enhanced.

Healing Applications — It is wise to remember that the first chakra contains our basic programming, including those of our family-of-origin belief system. Skin diseases or problems may have a root cause in our family system. Problems in the material world, a rash of life and death issues, security and safety concerns, or sexuality questions and issues may suggest the same. These events may also indicate that the auric matrix connected to the back side of our first chakra is being affected by fundamental spiritual beliefs. While we can use negative symptoms to assist us in locating causal issues and addressing them, we can also take a preventative approach. By being willing to honestly search, own, and transform our core identity and beliefs, the auric field can encourage success, health, and happiness because it connects to the physical and material universes.

Another key situation that can affect or be healed through the first layer concerns childhood abuse issues. Emotional, physical, spiritual, or mental victimization or damage may be reflected in the skin or through a person's physical appearance (with problems such as weight issues or slovenliness). Remember, though, that this auric layer has a non-material as well as material matrix pattern. Abuse patterns may also be aurically reflected in external ways such as lifestyle, choice of clothing, career and money, and other aspects of survival.

Second Auric Layer

The second auric matrix is the feeling body. This matrix field connects our internal feeling reality with the events, experiences, or people on the outside of us that are encouraging or triggering our feeling states.

Most esoteric experts call this second layer the emotional body. We might be playing a semantics game, but I think it is critical to define emotion. Emotions are produced when a thought form joins with a feeling body or part of a feeling body. Other cultures hold this belief, such as the Hawaiian kahuna culture, described by Serge King. "To the kahunas, emotion is more than just feeling; it is the movement of mana (energy) in the body accompanied by a specific thought" (King, 63).

A **thought form** is just that—an idea, concept, or original thought. By themselves, thought forms are pure energies that leave our psyches once they have registered. A **feeling body**, on the other hand, is an amoeba-like form. Each form encapsulates one feeling. We should be born with intact feeling bodies.

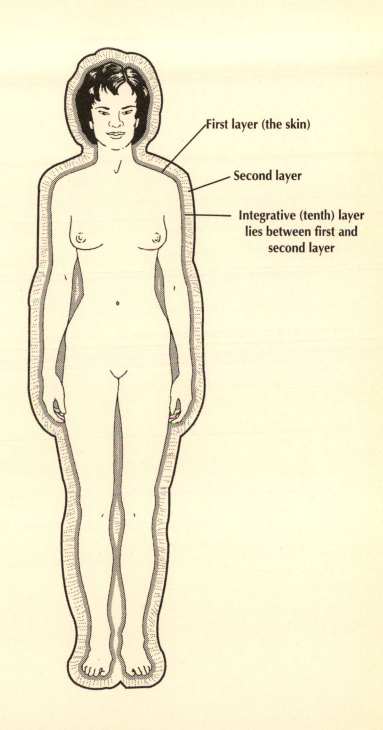

First layer (the skin)

Second layer

Integrative (tenth) layer
lies between first and
second layer

The second auric layer.

I began working with feeling bodies by spending time with a healer in Japan. He had approached me on the street and tapped my abdomen. My husband and guide were not around; I was pregnant and felt rather scared and vulnerable. The man proceeded to form a small circle with his thumb and index finger, all the while tapping my stomach. With one circle came a smile; another would be accompanied by a frown. Yet another with eyes big in fright. After a time, I began to understand—he was talking about my baby's feelings. Gradually, I began to be able to see or picture these feeling bodies. Since then, I have seen many of my students and clients work with this idea to their advantage.

At its purest, the second auric matrix is innocent of thought forms, which are often related to judgments, beliefs, and prejudices. The colors or reflections of our feelings can and should be expressed through this auric body. I know many healers and psychics who examine this auric layer to assess their client's emotional state. Carol Dryer, a Los Angeles-based psychic, says that she can tell a client's reaction by how the colors in the auric field change. She says, "For instance, if their field becomes foggy, I know they're not understanding what I'm telling them" (Talbot, 192).

In general, the job of this auric layer is to both protect us from externals that could harm our feelings, and to register external realities by awakening or deadening certain feelings.

I often compare the second auric matrix with a musical composition. Our little feeling bodies lay latent within us, each looking like a colored note. When we perceive a threat, the auric feeling layer intersecting with our front-side chakra strikes the fear feeling. To assist our response, the second auric layer may then strike a different note within our back-side second chakra, bringing in energies that will help us reestablish an equilibrium within our system. This auric layers play the notes that need to be played, inside and outside of us, to maintain our composition of self, to creatively and emotionally express ourselves in ways consistent with our basic nature.

There are often so many holes, unfelt feelings, feelings that are not ours, or other anomalies in our system that this second auric layer has a difficult time functioning.

Location — Roughly follows the contour of the body, intersecting in the front and the back with each chakra and bulging around the second chakra. The color of this layer varies from person to person and depends on the composition of our basic nature and our programming. When healed, this auric field tends to be fluid and watery, and shimmers when we are happy and content (figure 6d).

Physical Attributes — Links us to the energies that stoke our feelings and those that carry away the waste products. Feelings fuel us. They are likened to the gas that feeds the line, providing energy for appropriate response and action.

Feelings also tell us what is happening in our lives. Anger can empower us; sadness can point to the causes of loss. If our chakras, behavior, and auric field are doing their jobs, we will feel "in the flow" and energized. If they're not, all sorts of physical problems can abound, namely, those associated with the second chakra. I also examine my own or a client's second chakra layers if there are difficulties with co-dependency, stress-related illnesses, poor relationships, and creativity issues such as writer's block.

Mental Attributes — Nearly everyone carries misperceptions about the validity or "okayness" of certain feelings. These prejudices can warp the feeling auric field, leaving us susceptible to imbalances and negative situations, or just plain confused and lacking in energy. Affirming feelings in ourselves and others keeps the second auric field in shape and operational.

Feeling Attributes — Connects to each and every feeling that we have ever had or every feeling that lies dormant within us. It feeds and heals our feeling bodies and protects us from feelings that are not ours. Holes in this auric layer can leave us vulnerable to damage by others' feelings or cause us to hold onto feelings that enter us. Judgments about feelings can cause us to repress our feelings. Built-up feelings form walls in the second auric field. We think these walls protect us, but they really prevent us from allowing our feelings to protect us.

Spiritual Attributes — Keeps us alive and connected to our honest reactions, because feelings express our truths and cleanse our auric field.

Healing Applications — Many people are aware of the link between feelings and illness. Stored, denied, or stuffed feelings and awarenesses build up within the physical body. Discolorations, abnormal bulges, or a misshapen appearance in the second field can indicate either an over-abundance or under-representation of certain feelings. These problems may help diagnose a current physical anomaly or predict a potential one. Abusive situations can also greatly affect this auric field. Sexual, verbal, physical, or emotional abuse or neglect often injures or tears the second auric field.

Sometimes, an intuitively sensitive person can help determine potential abuse issues by reading the second auric field. A safer approach is to actually work with problems apparent in this field through techniques such as hands-on-healing, allowing clients to recall, remember, or diagnose their own issues. Therapists and other mental health professionals often consider their jobs to be related to feelings. They can help clients label and understand their feelings, clear blocked feelings, release feelings that are not theirs, and renew and lighten the second auric layer. The effectiveness of their work usually depends upon the breadth of involvement they have reached with their own feelings.

Third Auric Layer

Most commonly called the mental body, the third auric layer relates to the third chakra. Its form is much more defined than the feeling auric layer. Psychically, the matrix lines are usually quite apparent.

The patterns within our third auric matrix are determined by our unique inborn and acquired intellectual abilities and gifts; our educational experience; and our innate and modeled judgments and prejudices. The mental auric body actually expands outward from our third chakra. It culminates as a wall or mind field around us. This personal mind field links with the mind fields of others, creating a holistic network of learnings that stretches beyond our current time/space continuum. This may explain the "hundredth monkey" effect. It seems that behaviors or understandings will suddenly become commonplace when enough animals or people start doing or thinking similar patterns. Perhaps this syndrome occurs when enough individuals connect via the third auric layer. Through this auric field, we can tap into a cross-dimensional body of knowledge that can feed our body, mind, and soul with the ideas necessary to generate well-being and success.

Grasping the idea that we have a mind—not just a brain—is important. Through our third chakra and its associated auric layer, we can tap into constructs and data as needed. It also calls for a redefinition of self—we are much more than we appear on the physical surface. Deepak Chopra, a noted holistic physician, describes the self as "our conscious intelligence," and explains that "intelligence is not simply in the head." Chopra says that the "expression" of intelligence occurs at the cellular level, with the hormonal systems and antibodies that regulate the body's essential functions. "Although these expressions of intelligence can be located, intelligence itself cannot. It permeates each level of its expression; it is all-pervasive in us and universal in nature. Intelligence is mind...and its scope embraces the Cosmos" (Chopra, Deepak. *Creating Health*. Boston: Houghton Mifflin Company, 1987, 83–84, 109).

Typically, the mental auric layer is yellowish, although its colorations, brightness, and patterns change from circumstance to circumstance. For instance, certain strands of the third auric matrix glow more when someone is thinking hard. Likewise, there will be a tendency for this layer to strengthen when in use.

During my travels, I have noticed significant differences in the general color of this auric field from culture to culture. Many Caucasian American, Northern European, and Jewish cultures appear to have predominantly yellow third auric layers. Yellow is the color of rationality, thinking, and clarity, attributes of value to these nationalities. The mind field in several Indian and Pakistani nations has a bluish or sometimes purplish tinge. In Peru, the shamans I met glowed with bright reds and greens. While watching North American Indian ceremonies, I detected more turquoise, gold, white, or

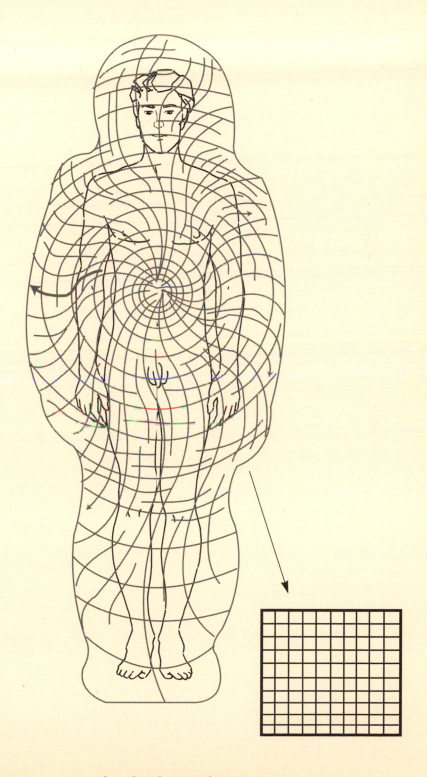

The third auric layer.

muddy red, depending on the tribes. In all cases, shades of these colors lingered long afterward. In Japan, I detected particles of silver. Different ethnic groups, different cultures probably tap into different points of consciousness in the group mind. Learning how to communicate with consciousness points, through reading, learning, and travel, can only expand our own awarenesses.

When we are sleeping, the front aspect of the matrix almost seems to switch off, and the back part begins to glow. When sleeping, our mind begins reaching into our unconscious learnings. We are tapping into that universal body of knowledge and learning. The auric field connecting to the back-side third chakra feeds the back sides of all our chakras, helping to clear misperceptions and reveal necessary information. Some of the ideas that we get while sleeping come from the openness we might experience while our conscious reality is on hold.

Location — Emanates primarily from the front and back side of the third chakra. It looks like a matrix or network pattern running atop and through the second auric layer, connecting to the cross-dimensional mind field around us (figure 6e).

Physical Attributes — Assists in opening us to energy, ideas, concepts, and notions that affect our physical lives, specifically our digestive and metabolic systems. Because of the connection between learning, thinking, and success, this auric field can provide us with the ideas and clarity we need to be successful at work and play.

Mental Attributes — Potentially links us to infinite storages and processes of data, information, and concepts. This auric layer is the primary point of operation. By psychically observing this field, we can see how extensive our subject's knowledge base is and determine his or her comfort level with receiving learning and information. Prejudices, biases, and misperceptions will show up in this auric layer as torn matrix points, discolorations on or in-between matrix lines, incomplete patterning, and other such anomalies.

Feeling Attributes — Actually interconnects with the first auric layer through the second auric layer. This intersplicing with the feeling auric layer contributes to the creation of an emotion, which is a thought plus a feeling. When a thought and a feeling are joined, we are propelled into motion—e-motion.

Spiritual Attributes — Helps us open ourselves to structures, ideas, explanations, and assistance for achieving our soul purpose. "You are what you think" may not be completely true, but our thoughts do define our concepts and images of life.

Healing Applications — By working with the third auric layer, we can isolate thought processes and beliefs that are harming us. After diagnosing them, we can change them. Likewise, we can work with the first, second, and third layers simultaneously to break emotions into their subcomponents, helping us change self-destructive behaviors, mental patterns, and overwhelming feelings. This auric layer can also be used to diagnose and work with intellectual problems or learning difficulties. We can also deliberately tap into the back-side auric layer in order to find the answers to informational questions that we have.

Fourth Auric Layer

I concur with most other metaphysicians' view that this heart-associated auric layer is the astral body. Our astral body links us to the astral plane, which is a dimension upon which many guiding spirits and earth student spirits dwell. In *Women's Psychic Lives*, Diane Stein says that our physical body and etheric (aura) body is connected by a "silver cord." During astral projection, she says, "the dense physical and psychic bodies separate, sending the etheric…'flying' while the body remains at home. The silver cord stretches infinite distances, connecting the physical…to…psychic bodies" (Stein, 28). Via the silver cord, this plane is the most frequently visited by our souls when we are children, undergoing transition, or sleeping. These out-of-body experiences often increase during times of greatest need, when we require help beyond the physical. Through this auric field, we return home for advice, help, and nurturing. Through our astral body, we can also visit with people who are in-body (alive). Physical distance has no bearing in this plane, only time does. Here, we can meet up with a long-deceased relative or a potential future life partner, work through a few of our issues, or receive whatever learnings we need.

When I was young, I actively engaged in relationships with positive beings through this astral plane. Guardians, angels, and teachers were very real to me. I still remember one of the more critical of these experiences, which occurred when I was twenty-one. In a vision/dream, I was being reviewed by a panel for my abilities to materialize objects. They stuck me in an empty room and told me to fill it with objects. I tried, then cried.

When the "reviewers" came in, I became angry. I asked them how they could give me this test when I'd never received instructions. Staring at me, they said they would consider that point. I then awoke from my dream. A few days later, I received a book in the mail from nowhere; it was about manifesting. I was suddenly swamped by flyers on subjects such as "Creating Your Own Happiness."

Typically, this field surrounds our entire physical body. Through the back side, it connects us to the Divine Source. Through the front side, it connects us to people with whom we are in relationships. The malleable nature of this energetic layer is one of the reasons it often contains, holds, or forms cords or contractual agreements between people.

Figure 6f.

Relationships to spirits, ancestors, etc. "Divine Source Energy."

Relationships and interactions with living people we know.

1'

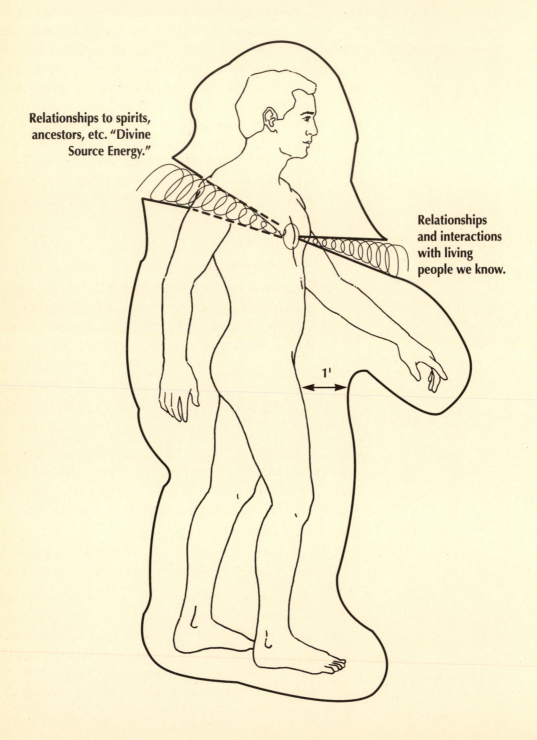

The fourth auric layer.

A healthy fourth auric layer can have many different colors, widths, and shapes reflected within it. I most often see it with a rose glow, though it can frequently reflect silver, blue, or green. We tend to see rose when we are feeling loving, blue when we are in a place of understanding, and silver when we are in communication with guides. This layer will tend to be about a foot in width, though the presence or absence of loved ones, love itself, or cords will greatly affect its dimensions. Of course, our natural disposition will shape this layer to suit our personality and our needs.

During sleep or deep meditation, this auric layer can open and invite us to experience the astral plane. When we leave our bodies at night or through astral projection, we are simply following the matrix lines connecting us to our astral-based self, held by the silver cord. Much learning and healing can occur during these visits. I remember a very clear dream in which I became connected to an Indian shaman in the Southwest. For several evenings, I held conversations with him around his fire. He looked, seemed, and felt very real to me. Finally, I asked him why we needed to be connected. He said he had known me before and had a piece of my soul he needed to return. I accepted it back and the visits stopped.

We can astral project for other reasons. Two or three times, I have been drawn out of my body. Once, I was thrown into a mouse and physically experienced that way of being. I formed a similar relationship with an eagle. Another time, I actually experienced having my etheric self turn into a white jaguar.

Many of my clients—nice, normal, mainstream people—relay similar stories to me. One woman called me at 4:00 A.M., terrified because for three hours she had been taken into one animal after another. Another woman called because her recently deceased father had just visited her. One man called after he had suddenly projected himself into a friend's room and said "Hi." His friend had just called and asked him what he'd been doing in her bedroom. These critical experiences can provide learning and insight, but we must be careful. The astral plane can also open us to malicious and evil energies and beings. That is why I insist that clients first learn how to protect themselves, then connect to the Divine Source, before further explorations in this realm.

All of these experiences indicate only one thing: we are revolving doors. We are more than that which we are trained to perceive or to believe.

Location — Lies atop the mental auric layer, surrounding the physical body with an approximately one-foot thick glow. Through the back-side heart chakra, it connects in a stream of energy to the Divine Source; through the front side, it interacts with our environment and with our relationships (figure 6f).

Physical Attributes — Can help us pinpoint past, current, or projected cardiovascular issues; can also provide further information or healings regarding general physical issues. Interestingly, it is easiest to read the physical aspects of this auric field when the subject is "heartily" exercising in or out of bed. (This may account for the reason so many love partners get a feeling about their mate's potential health problems.)

Mental Attributes — Can clue us into our ideas about relationships and our beliefs regarding deservedness. If we could connect more fully to the Divine Source through the back-side planes, our physical and relationship realities would shift, primarily because we would be feeding ourselves with love and messages about deserving love.

Feeling Attributes — Connects our lower astral bodies with our higher ones, thus melding physically-oriented feelings and awarenesses with spiritually adept feelings and awarenesses. Through our feelings, which indicate our highest needs and desires, the fourth auric layer provides us the opportunity to experience and manifest all we dream about.

Spiritual Attributes — Invites our soul to meet with other souls on the astral plane. Here, we learn from each other, exchange data and information, and work through our life's lesson plans. Ultimately, we allow Divine Source energy to support us.

Healing Applications — Through this auric layer, we can diagnosis current or potential heart problems, and relationship issues (past, present, or future). Awareness of our heart's desires can also be picked up in the fourth auric field. Issues may also be addressed by working with this field or through visiting the astral plane.

This is the layer on which cords are easiest to perceive. All cords have a negative impact on us, because they limit current relationships or recreate relationship patterns. They also dampen the awareness of and realizations about how to achieve our heart's desires.

Fifth Auric Layer

The fifth auric layer could also be called the parallel field. This field opens to all planes and dimensions, but in a rather interesting way. It reverses a parallel dimension's form and shape, projecting it into us through a mirror rather than as a straight-forward image. Our fifth chakra, working in tangent with other chakras, must reverse this image so we can understand it.

The front-side, more physically apparent aspect of the fifth auric field has a hard, smooth surface and lies more or less on top of the fourth auric layer. It works somewhat like a convex lens. Images, forms, ideas, and messages from other planes, transferred via the back-side aspect of the fifth auric layer, are reversed when entering the third dimension. They then hit the front-side lens or screen of the more tangible aspect of the fifth auric layer

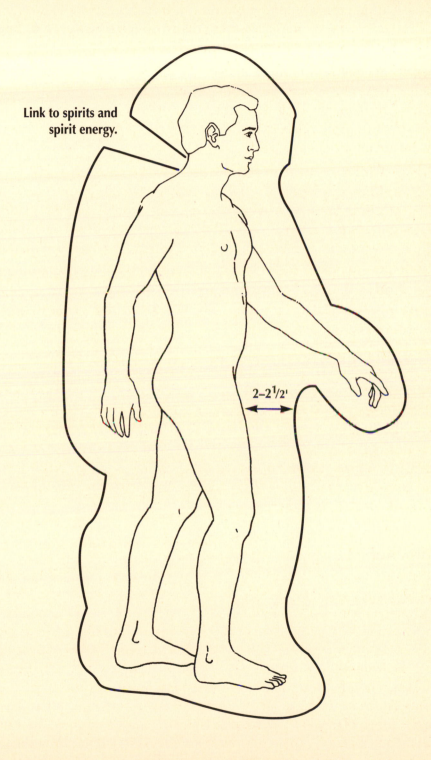

Link to spirits and spirit energy.

$2–2\tfrac{1}{2}'$

The fifth auric layer.

and are integrated within our system. We can receive both information and healing energy through this method.

Though the fifth auric layer opens us to other dimensions, we must remember that at some level we reside within these other planes. We could interpret the guidance transposed through the parallel auric layer to be from other beings and planes. It is also likely that this data comes from another aspect of ourselves. These alternative selves co-exist in parallel realities and can reflect choices not taken, generations not born, planets not conceived in our reality. We can gain much wisdom about our current choices and their possible consequences by using the fifth auric layer as an access point.

Location — Begins about two to two-and-one-half feet out from our body. It links into parallel universes, skimming along the grid points of all other dimensions (figure 6g).

Physical Attributes — Can potentially re-create that which has been created in another plane or dimension. This auric field links to these possibilities and to beings with wisdom representing them. Because the basic connecting chakra is the fifth, it is commonly believed that the fifth chakra is the manifesting chakra or sometimes, the place the soul connects to the body. By working with the parallel auric layer, we gain access the data and energies available to acknowledge or speak the truths of our being and wishes, a very important step in manifesting the physical. Because we can also tap into negative spirits, we need to apply spiritual safeguards as protection.

Mental Attributes — Connects us to the realms of possibilities so that we can select which beliefs, truths, and realities most authentically reflect us. Because there are a thousand ways to state one truth, "Which is the right one for me?" is an important question, and this layer helps us answer it. Otherwise, we may experience consequences of self or other judgments, critical messages, or demonic/negative manipulations.

Feeling Attributes — Can open to us parallel opportunities and realities, different ways to feel and to express. We can reach into this field to receive options in these regards. We can often dissolve feeling blocks and problems by working with this auric field.

Spiritual Attributes — Allows the soul to explore its options. It can test the waters before making decisions, or experience the outcome of the choices it has made.

Healing Applications — Becoming conscious of this auric layer, specifically of its two-fold nature, can help us become conscious of our decisions and their potential outcomes. Through this layer we can also gain access to the worlds or actions that created our current conditions. The opportunities for change and transformation are limitless.

Sixth Auric Layer

This auric layer is composed almost exclusively of light, earning it the label "celestial body" from other metaphysicians. I call it the light-body auric field, because its matrix patterns are spun of actual light fibers. In *The Holographic Universe*, Michael Talbot writes that many religious traditions believe that a spiritually advanced individual often will have an aura so bright that it is visible to the naked eye. He suggests that this belief is why saints and holy beings are depicted with halos around their head. He also makes note of a Sufi mystic, Hazrat Inayat Khan, who died in 1927, who "is said to have sometimes given off so much light that people could actually read by it" (Talbot, 165).

This auric layer meshes together the more-structured fifth auric field and the less-formed seventh auric field. It combines the necessities of choice and consequence with the truth of universal love and support. When working with this energy layer, we are tapping into higher truths for creating images that can be actualized in physical reality.

I became highly sensitized to this auric layer while working with shamans and healers in Peru, the Yucatan, and Costa Rica. At certain times, I could clearly see with my physical eyes the strands of this layer. While the strands obviously connected these healers to the ceremonial participants or to their patients at hand, I could also see them extending far away—countries away—to subjects who had requested healing. I would later relay my pictures of whom they had been healing from such a distance, only to find out, by a photo or offered description, that my visions had been accurate.

Many other tribal cultures I have studied, including the American Indian culture and cultures in Brazil, Bolivia, Siberia, and Hawaii, stress the importance of vision, the importance of seeing what is true, versus what is not. We can examine reality for its truth by scanning along the sixth auric layer.

Location — Appears to be a glow of light about three feet or so around the body, because the matrix pattern is so interlaced and fine. In many people, this energy is concentrated around the head; ideally, it should be spread out around the entire physical body and appear spiky, with strands of light connecting it to visible and invisible realities (figure 6h).

Physical Attributes — Enables physical manifesting and healing when we achieve a link between the light body auric layer and the white light of the Divine Source.

Mental Attributes — Reflects thoughts and thought patterns we hold about ourselves. These thoughts are more like attitudes than they are separate thoughts, and they reflect the achieved level of self-acceptance. When deciphering the meaning of the various discolorations, smudge spots, holes, or lackluster images, it is helpful to request a psychic picture for clarity.

Figure 6h.

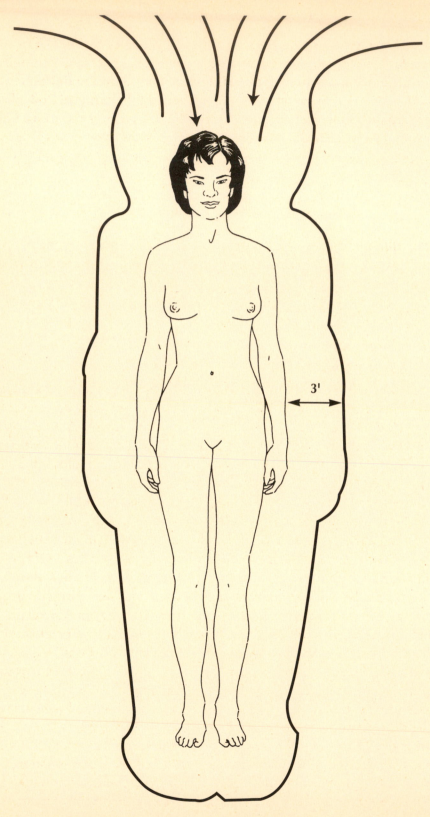

3'

The sixth auric layer.

Feeling Attributes — Attaches us to a higher order of feelings than those encapsulated in our physical bodies, which operate almost like separate, ruling identities. When searching for this level of connection to the higher feeling bodies, we follow the strands of light beyond the physical body. When healthy connections exist, I visualize the higher feelings as egg-like fluid beings, and the sixth auric layer folding into them like waves of cloth.

Spiritual Attributes — Gives us access to the higher qualities of feelings, thoughts, and manifesting possibilities. Energies received through this auric matrix feed all aspects of ourselves, including (and some might say, especially), our soul.

Healing Applications — The light-body auric field is an interesting one with which to work. One fantastic healing application is to first conduct healing work on this aura, as if preparing a template for the desired change, then to pull this template down into the physical. This field can also be examined for problems that might suggest a disturbed state of self-acceptance.

Seventh Auric Layer

This auric field is usually considered to be the last one framing the physical body. Also called the ketheric auric layer, to most people it appears in egg form, extending about three and one-half feet beyond the physical self. In *The Holographic Universe*, Talbot mentions several ancient traditions that experienced this field, including the Kabbalah, a Jewish mystical philosophy, which called this emanation *nefish*. The Kabbalah "teaches that an egg-shaped bubble of iridescence surrounds every human body" (Talbot, 165).

This auric layer also penetrates the tenth or grounding chakra, assuring that our spiritual connections to the outer world are grounded in the material.

I work with this auric layer in three major ways. The first is more psychological, if not mystical. Connected to the ketheric realm, this auric layer avails us of the actual or symbolic self associated with our spiritual purpose. I can best explain this notion by speaking of the *kachina*, an American Indian demi-god. Each of the hundreds of kachina gods are associated with a particular cause or truth; they are literally "agents of the gods"—gods with human traits. One, for instance, may bring spring rains. Another represents the truth of love and harmony. Often, I explain that when working with the seventh auric layer, I am helping clients view their kachina self—the self who left the Divine Source with a purpose or truth to carry forth.

In classes, I have helped participants surf the seventh auric layer in order to link with this ketheric or kachina self—the self who best illustrates our spiritual nature on this plane. The idea is that if we could better understand the self with the spirit abilities and gifts, we could each better integrate those gifts into everyday life.

Figure 6i.

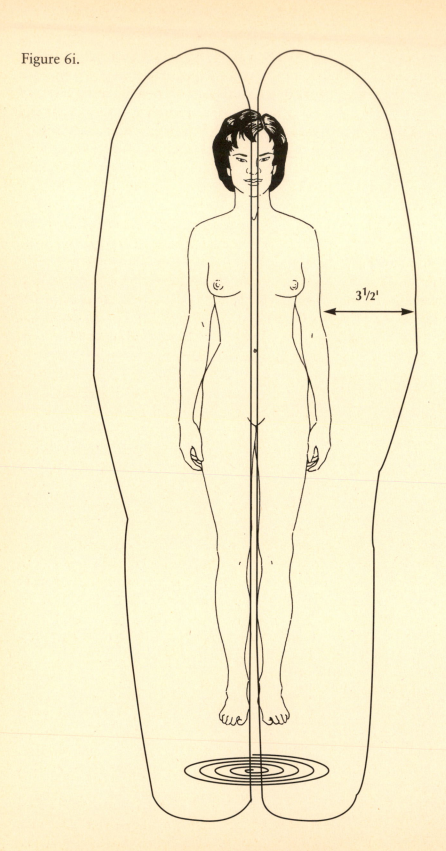

$3^1/2'$

The seventh auric layer.

Class members are often astonished at the findings. During one particular class, one somewhat meek and mild participant received vision that she was a bold speaker who could receive, through the seventh auric layer, all the words she needed to convey her messages. Another, a very classically educated and rather proper woman, pictured herself as a bear, able to channel great warrior power through the seventh auric layer in order to build her own business. Yet another rather bold personality was a soft and gentle healer. Each of the figures presented/actualized during this exercise embodied gifts that these participants had known were present, but had been too frightened or embarrassed to use. During the next few weeks, participants reported changes in their character; these alterations complied with the learnings from the exercise.

One of my other applications for seventh auric layer work regards healing. I sometimes scan the seventh auric layer to preview potential cancer or other serious diseases, and to check on the conditions of current major illnesses. Of course, these types of psychic scans are questionable at best; however, I believe that as we become more and more disillusioned with what technology can provide we will be increasingly forced to trust our own intuition or gut senses in regard to our personal health. We will also increase our reliance on helping each other with our various intuitive gifts.

Given that, I believe that many cancers enter the auric field before they show up in the body. In our society, the seventh auric layer is the easiest of the outer layers to read. It is also one of the most vulnerable, because spirituality is so little respected (and this energy layer is ultimately related to spirituality). Often, this layer is pierced or damaged by the conditions which cause cancer long before these conditions actually manifest.

In general, I have found, as have many of my colleagues, that cancer is often a disease related to repression of feelings, especially anger and fear. Repression of anger, an important protective feeling, can suggest a judgment against power. For instance, if we were abused or witnessed the violent use of anger, we might conclude that use of power is bad and hurts people (like it hurt us). Likewise, most of our spiritual disciplines reinforce this negative opinion of anger and righteousness—a good person is a meek person.

Now, power is just directed energy. Energy, like anger, can be used to cause harm or to assure safety. Our immune system, sense of safety, and well-being in the world are founded upon our ability to realize and direct energy for protection and manifesting. If we don't know how to properly fight disease, abusive or poorly intentioned people, criticism, and the like, we certainly cannot fight off the thousands of viruses and conditions that cause cancer and other major diseases.

Almost all the cancer patients with whom I have worked fit the above description. They hold judgments against anger, although they are often inwardly frothing with it, and they have spiritual beliefs that argue against power. Logically, these beliefs will repress the performance of both the emotional auric layer and the seventh auric layer. I can frequently see a hole in the seventh auric layer of people who already have cancer. Usually, this hole or mottled spot lines up perpendicular to the actualized cancer. To me, actualized cancer appears in the body as a dark spot with red and white dots or hazy shapes around it or as a funny bluish color. However, potential cancer often starts as a hole in the seventh auric layer, then bleeds through underneath auric layers. The closer the damage to the physical body, the more complete the manifestation of the condition. (Although sometimes, the integrative auric layer will hold a major disease for several years before it actually dumps it into the physical body.)

I think back to a client with breast cancer in her history. She was experiencing a great deal of pain in one of her breasts, as well as fibrous tissue. We saw a hole in her seventh chakra, but the line of darkness did not penetrate to her breast. I didn't think she had cancer, but it seemed she could at some point develop it. Medical professionals verified that she did not have cancer, as far as they could tell. She did, however, take precautions, such as changing her diet, working through her emotional issues, boosting her immune and endocrine systems, and addressing her spiritual dissatisfactions. Her fibrous condition disappeared as did the pain. (See the Appendix for an illustration of the aura of a person with breast cancer.)

A third important application of seventh auric layer work is sometimes seen as a bit morbid, but if ethically applied, it can be extremely helpful. This application is connected to the death and dying process. In the best of all possible worlds, most individuals prepare for death during a five- to seven-year time span, meaning that their souls begin to disengage and prepare for the passing about five to seven years before their body dies. This idea has, interestingly enough, been confirmed for me through corporate consulting work I have done for an elder residence. Workers there have said that they can often tell when someone is going to die and that the process typically lasts about seven years.

Though this ending process is actually quite complicated, I will say that the thickness and whiteness/brilliance of the seventh auric layer changes the closer someone is to death. In general, as the soul prepares to leave, the seventh auric layer thins out. More spiritual energy is therefore directed to and through it, thereby lightening the tone of this layer. As this occurs, there is a subsequent stripping away and penetrability of the underneath layers. With less auric protection, a person's body becomes increasingly susceptible to illness and disease. Thus, health deteriorates, even as the spiritual nature of the person potentially strengthens.

The seventh auric field extends into both the conscious and unconscious planes, as does the first auric field. It affects the pineal gland and the cerebral cortex, thus broadening the scope and abilities of our thinking processes. It carries forward from there to link into all major avatar entities (ascended human beings) and figures, and to link into Shamballah, the mystical, high-frequency heaven located on earth (a place I have sometimes seen in very powerful visions, but have yet to fully actualize). Through the back side, this layer connects us to the spiritual aspect of absolutely everything and everyone, and is ruled only by one principle: we are one.

This aura interlocks with all others, gluing itself into the spine. In this way, it constantly delivers spiritual mana to our physical self.

Location — Typically seen as an egg shape around the physical body. It also extends to avatars and "Shamballah," a mystical city symbolizing heaven on earth, and links us to every other being who has achieved a complete and humble love for the Divine Source (figure 6i).

Physical Attributes — Affects our entire existence, because it is intricately tied to both the brain and the spine, which regulate all of life's functions. Training ourselves to feel, see, or hear this auric layer can greatly speed both diagnosis and information gathering.

Mental Attributes — Enables us to tie into correct thought processes, and to seek advice from the ancients and the avatars for earthly concerns and from the saints for spiritual matters—all positive interactions if they guide us toward the Divine Source.

Feeling Attributes — Is the place where feelings meld together like a rainbow melting into one great white light. The resultant feeling is more an awareness of bliss than a single noteworthy emotion.

Spiritual Attributes — Is the place where all is spirit, whether it categorically relates to the physical, mental, emotional, or other.

Healing Application — It would be wise to investigate how to personally tap into this auric field. Because it connects our physical self to all of life and all that is good about life, its potential for drawing healing and abundance to us is immeasurable.

Because the next two auric fields, along with the integrative field, affect the physical, mental, emotional, and spiritual so completely, I will provide only broad descriptions of these energy bodies. Much of this information comes from my own work, and so can only be substantiated experientially.

Eighth Auric Layer

The eighth auric layer relates to the eighth chakra, which concerns itself with past, present, and future time and all our experiences within time. This energy field connects in through the top of our head, then spreads around our body, attaching to the primary and secondary chakras, front and back.

It keeps us both plugged into the moment and provides the present time with a context.

I see the actual appearance of this layer as a lattice work of moon-colored strands backed by a void or black energy. We could press on any of the points within this matrix and re-experience something that we or those close to us have gone through or might go through. This implies that we could use this auric layer for prediction, memory recall, and transformation in regard to both the past and the future. When working with the auric field, it is important to not get too detailed when trying to recall history or predict the future. This energy field, more than any other, is a complete system unto itself. It tells the story of who we are right now. Too much tampering with the evidence will shift the present, perhaps in ways we don't foresee and may not want.

There are four very interesting applications for sub-components of this energy field. I have done considerable work with these as a practitioner and a teacher and will share a few of the outcomes.

The first application of this auric layer pertains to our **white zone** memory. The white zone is that area or state in which we exist just prior to entering a lifetime. Regression into or recall of the major decisions we made about this lifetime can be extremely enlightening and assist us in changing negative agreements that are not in our current best interest. I believe Dr. Joel Whitton, professor of psychiatry at the University of Toronto Medical School, has been regressing individuals into this white zone in his research on reincarnation. He finds that when people were in this "between-life realm, they entered an unusual state of consciousness in which they were acutely self-aware and had a heightened moral and ethical sense." Dr. Whitton calls this "metaconsciousness." He says, "Carefully or haphazardly, we choose our earthly circumstances. The message of metaconsciousness is that the life situation of every human being is neither random nor inappropriate" (Talbot, 215–217).

The white zone is typically reached through guided meditation, shamanic journeying, trance, or regression work. I most frequently guide clients into the white zone when they simply can't get over or beyond a certain event, relationship, or problem. One woman, for example, had obsessed about a prior boyfriend for years. Traditional psycho-therapy had simply not been helpful at all. I guided her back into the white zone, where she recalled writing a soul contract with this man. A **soul contract** is an agreement between souls about how they will interrelate in the upcoming incarnation. This particular soul contract called for a marriage between my client and her ex-boyfriend. However, at the critical destiny point, the crack in time at which during their soul negotiations they had agreed to marry, he had reneged. I helped my client dissolve the original soul contract as was her right because the other party had broken it. She called a week later, in ecstasy, psychologically free of him for the first time.

I also worked with a client who was having difficulties relating to her mother. By regressing into the white zone, she discovered that her father had married the wrong woman. She had decided to enter this life through her ties with her father. As she had not karmically needed her mother, she had never bonded with her. This new information helped my client make peace with her feelings and lower her expectations regarding a mother/daughter relationship, actually improving her relationship with her mother.

Another interesting application of the white zone relates to a client with chronic fatigue. He was extremely psychic. In fact, during our first or second session together, he automatically brought himself into the white zone before I even told him there was one. There, he recalled a past-life trauma and a decision his soul made before this life—it would punish itself by closing off his body from the flow of life energy. This young man, by conducting past-life regressions, made new decisions. When last I heard from him, he had regained enough energy to work full-time.

A second application of the eighth layer involves the Akashic records, the accounting of all we have ever done, been, said, or experienced throughout all of time. By riding the waves of our eighth auric field, we can not only tap into these records, but replay them. Unlike some intuitive consultants, I do not automatically relay or bring people into past lives to address current concerns. I encourage people to only search these distant times when under extreme pressure, to search for a causal issue they already think lies in the past or to address problems that can't be solved by looking at this life's events. Sometimes seeing a pattern being played out in another setting (a past life) with different players will give a client the perspective he or she needs to break a pattern.

I have a few reasons for advising caution with this type of regression. Unless we are fully prepared to acknowledge all that we currently are—good and bad, light and dark—we are not ready to know about all that we have ever done. We must continue to move toward forgiveness and gratefulness. Learning about how great we used to be can overshadow our current concerns. Learning about how bad we once were can make us feel worse about ourselves. The bottom line is that we are here to deal with the present. We are here to understand the family in which we have been born, to learn about this life's purpose, and to carry out this life's tasks. We don't want to get lost in the past only to forget about the gift of life we are currently holding.

I have, of course, helped people with a lot of past-life issues. Phobias often relate to the past. During the course of two to three months, one of my clients, who had participated in years of psychoanalysis, cleared himself of several obsessive/compulsive disorders by remembering past lives. These disorders included compulsive hand-washing and a fixation on being punished for being evil. The critical lifetime involved purging himself for something unclean he had done during biblical times.

I've seen many women clear their fears of success by remembering lifetimes in which they had been killed or tortured for speaking their truths or for being powerful. One, a doctor, had actually reached a point where she was afraid to practice medicine. She unearthed a time when, as a healer, she had been stoned for making a mistake.

Physical issues can also relate to past-life phenomena. I was healed of an allergy to nuts due to remembering a past lifetime set in the 1300s. During that time, I believe my parents had tried to starve me. I had existed solely on what I could salvage, nuts providing the staple of the diet. My sensitivity to nuts disappeared after that session.

The third eighth auric layer application is one I've only recently begun to apply. It concerns a "place" I call the **black zone**. During the past few years, I've started to work with a lot of dying or critically ill individuals, often visiting hospitals or hospices to do this work. I also work with a lot of people who have lost loved ones. Consistently, I have found that upon dying, most souls spend some time in a space that, while involving a life review, encourages more than that. Often, the newly dead will linger on the earth plane, and some get stuck. These souls are usually called ghosts, beings who consciously or unconsciously choose to remain on this plane in a form similar to that created for the just-finished lifetime. However, all souls invariably and inevitably are guided to the black zone. Here, a life review may be conducted or completed. Then souls are encouraged to heal those parts which need further healing or to claim fragments of themselves which, in any lifetime, have been splintered. If this process is required, a soul contract is drawn up. It is similar to that created during the white-zone stages, but pertains to the experience in-between lives, which we call death.

My only confirmation of this zone is that, when I have tuned into it for clients, I have been able to consistently tell them facts about their loved ones I couldn't have known. I have also had dying people relate things to me that imply that there is in fact a place to which they are going. I have also guided students into their own black zone to do healing work. Most have reported this as extremely powerful and real.

A fourth application of the eight chakra layer is informational. Through the eighth auric field, we can tap into others' eighth chakras. By working with ethical spirit guides, a good healer/facilitator, or by employing good boundaries, it is possible to query others for assistance through the eighth auric field. I often do this for clients, then provide intuitive assessments. I do, however, prefer to help clients seek their own information. I have my own set of biases and screens, and though I work hard to protect clients from them, I am obviously vulnerable to seeing or interpreting data through my own lenses.

Ninth Auric Layer

This auric layer relates to the ninth chakra. It actually occupies a very small, almost nonexistent, space on the physical plane. I see it almost as a pinprick located above the head. It need not occupy much space because it operates under the laws of limitlessness and abundance and can, I believe, motivate energy to move beyond the speed of light.

Working with this auric layer entails guiding oneself or being guided into this small portal. Having a facilitator is very helpful. Short of that, you can work with guides and visualize that you are attached to a lifeline of sorts by which you can haul yourself back to this reality. You are not really in any danger because you are descending into a part of yourself. However, you may learn some surprising things about yourself.

Most people experience a world of wonders on the other side of this portal. The actual ninth auric field is both a boundary for and the content of the world of our soul, the heaven we are trying to achieve on this planet or any other for that matter. It can be beneficial to travel here to meditate, to peruse ideas, to problem solve, or to heal. This aspect of ourselves is so peaceful, it is a wonder we don't journey here more often.

My journeys here often connect me to a feeling rather than a place. Some might call this place heaven, nirvana, Shamballah. It opens me to the experience of metatonia—a state of bliss and enlightenment—for which we so often search.

I believe that this field is the one to which Barbara Ann Brennan refers in *Hands of Light* when she describes the cosmic fields which "relate to who we are beyond this lifetime." She also describes the delivery of miraculous healings through this auric layer. "As I watch guides working from this level, it appears to me as if they simply remove a whole side of a person's energy bodies (and all fields with it) and put in a new set...," she says. "This...has the effect of healing the patient very rapidly" (Brennan, 230, 233). Obviously, this auric layer has tremendous impact.

The Integrative Auric Layer

The integrative auric layer is an extremely important auric field, as it relates to the tenth chakra. Many people call it the etheric body and see it as the layer next to the skin (see figure 6d). To me, this auric layer, which does lay next to the skin, plugs into both the tenth chakra and the ground. It is the auric layer of form. When we feel secure, this layer can extend up to three feet away from our skin. When we are feeling threatened, it may cling skintight.

I sometimes think that this integrative layer is a traveling path for the double that so many sorcerers and shamans speak of, that second self able to separate from the physical body. Carlos Castenada, trained by the Yaqui Indian don Juan, experienced this doubling. These out-of-body experiences are not unknown to Westerners either. Many of us can relate to feelings of separating from our bodies, jerking away during the night, suddenly feeling we are somewhere else. According to researcher Charles Tate, there are five features related to out-of-body experiences:

1. A floating feeling.

2. Seeing one's own body.

3. Suddenly being at a place of which you just thought.

4. The belief of having a non-physical body.

5. Absolute certainty that the experience was not a dream.

(Kalweit, Holger. *Dreamtime and Inner Space: The World of the Shaman*. Boston: Shambhala Publications, Inc., 1984, 53.)

The integrative layer can serve as a pathway between the physical world and the spiritual world. Sometimes, this layer itself can form the double that travels.

I have also found that this auric layer, programmed by our genetic and soul heritage, can be read or probed for primal and soul-based information. This layer incorporates all the experiences we have had in-body, whether in this life or any other. This practical data is registered in the physical matter that composes half of our energy body system. Also keyed in are the energy imprints relating to our soul purpose and path. This auric layer actually integrates our physical matter (prana) with spiritual matter (mana). It connects our chakric energy centers with our spiritual energy points. In addition, this energy body provides our physical, emotional, and mental aspects with a blueprint for growth, development, and change. So many hands-on-healers work with the etheric body, because altering it can make both physical and spiritual change.

Other Auric Layers

There is a lot of research that could substantiate the existence of the these ten auric layers, including studies at UCLA, Duke University, German and Russian government research, and probably a great deal of unpublished American government research. There are also phenomenon like Kirlian photography, a type of photography that takes pictures of auric layers. As each auric layer ultimately connects to a different dimension, modern physics could even be stretched to imagine the existence of these auric layers. The modern, scientifically based string theory can "prove" that there are ten dimensions. Of course, there are also thousands of years worth of mystical and practical experiences that could sustain the idea that auras exist. However, there is little data to support my theory that there are two auric layers on top of these major ten layers.

I do believe that there are eleventh and twelfth auric layers. The eleventh, in my work, is simply an extension of the eleventh chakra. It differs in that it is not limited to the space around the hands and feet; rather, it extends beyond, touching the energy of the top twenty spiritual energy points, among other spaces.

I came up with this theory while working with the eleventh chakra in healing. One of my clients had carpal tunnel syndrome. We tried and tried to clear it with "regular" intuitive or spiritual healing methods, to no avail. Then I had her flow out on her eleventh chakra. She pictured waving energy that washed out of this plane and connected to other feelings. To my surprise, these feelings were conceptual states—the same ones represented in the top twenty spiritual chakras. She could palpably feel the wavy energy from these chakras through her hands and feet. Her carpal tunnel became significantly better when she worked with the Creativity point (Point 24). (I believe, though, that the connection between this chakra and her syndrome was unique to her and the causal reasons for her condition.)

Over time, I have assisted clients with becoming more directive regarding what energy they are bringing in and out of their feet and hands. When grounding, I often have them work with what I now call this eleventh auric layer, pulling energy up from the very depths of the earth or the very tips of the heavens. Sometimes, the aftershock is so great, some clients have a difficult time moving afterward! Remember, the eleventh chakra and therefore the eleventh auric layer, is about transmutation—our bodies will physically experience that which we are pulling in.

I also believe that there is a twelfth auric layer; in fact, I see this layer as the glue for the twelfth chakra. As you recall, the twelfth chakra is a collection of secondary chakra points. Though these points connect outside the body through a series of psychically apparent fibers, I perceive another body around these fibers. This glowing energy looks like a vibrating mesh of atoms that form a net cast far, far beyond our human sphere. I have sometimes worked with this net, which I call the twelfth auric layer, to call spiritual energy in for people with serious and traumatic conditions, such as post-accident victims. I almost always see an instant relaxation in the body, for though this auric layer, you can work on all the secondary chakras at once.

For example, I witnessed a seminar participant (who had a history of near-fatal injuries) hit her head and nearly die. Surrounded by a group, she received a lot of spiritual attention. For my part, I could see her soul leaving. It had already unplugged from her chest and was trying to release its connection to the silver cord, one of the secondary chakra points. It was also cutting into the mesh that I consider to the be twelfth auric layer. I instantly knew that if her soul completed its "surgical warfare" with this aura, this woman would be dead.

Telling her soul that this was not its time to leave (seldom am I that intrusive, but in this case, it felt appropriate), I forced the twelfth auric layer closed again and yanked her back into her body along the silver cord. Against all odds, this woman recovered very quickly.

Working With the Aura

There are so many ways to work with the aura, we could devote an entire book to this topic alone. I'll discuss a few of the ways that I approach the aura.

When working with auric fields, I first select an intuitive technique. Do I want to visualize the aura (and the chakras)? Do I want to use my intuitive auditory skills and listen to information about them? Do I want to apply my feeling-based or kinesthetic abilities to interact with them? Do I want to incorporate all three approaches?

Having selected an approach, I then decide if I want to picture the overall auric body or immediately center on individual layers. Generally, I check out the overall field as I scan the chakras, then I isolate a few particular layers. (Sometimes, I scan the overall field by examining each layer, one at a time. When I do this, I usually begin with the integrative layer and move upward and outward toward the ninth.) I used this method, for instance, with a woman who was worrying about whether she had breast cancer or not. I first clarified three points with her:

1. To work with me, she needed to continue working with her medical doctor.

2. I was not going to diagnose in any way, only share senses and pictures, and help her get the same type of information.

3. I would not judge the course nor the outcome of her disease process as good or bad, but I would encourage her to open fully to the Divine Source during our interactions.

I relayed my pictures to her after doing a complete scan of the aura and chakras, then centering in on two chakras and two auric fields. The discolorations in the auric field around her breast and abdomen were in the second and seventh fields. As we discussed these discolorations, the emotional and spiritual causes of her problems became obvious. Among other things, her father had told her that her mother's death was her fault, at which time the breast problems had started. We did quite a bit more probing and work, but my client's breast pain disappeared and her medical test results were normal. Of course, we can't prove that our work cured her, but I tend to agree with the sentiments expressed by Ywahoo in *Voices of Our Ancestors*. "As you look at yourself, you are recognizing a vibration of life. Removing some of the obstructing thought forms is a result of meditation. See the effect of your consciousness on the stream of life. *Choose to manifest wholesome thoughts*." (Emphasis mine.) (Ywahoo, 75.)

If I am using visual techniques, as I did with the above-mentioned client, I typically search for discolorations, abnormal shapes, bulges or weak spots, frays, or funny colors. The presence of any of these details points to a current or potential problem. I use my mind as much as my intuition when doing diagnostic work on the aura. I recall what this aura layer is about, and I begin to tick off possible problems in my head. If I am working with someone, I may ask them pertinent questions. I may even have them picture their own aura and tell me what they see.

When using auditory intuition, I ask questions of guides or of my own intuition regarding the health or needs of a particular auric band. Typical questions may include:

1. What is the overall condition of this auric layer?

2. Are there any problems I/we need to know about?

3. What are they about?

4. What are the consequences of healing this issue?

5. What are the consequences of leaving it the way that it is?

6. How can we best work with any difficulties?

When using my kinesthetic senses, I may work many different ways. With hands-on healing or therapeutic-touch techniques, I may feel for hot or cold spots or for irregularities in the energy field or on the skin. Usually, heat means that there is too much energy in one spot, which could reflect the presence of stored or unfelt feelings or an unprocessed belief or issue. It might be a collection point or drop off for another's issues or feelings. Heat found during a scan means something different than heat felt during an energy exchange. When doing a healing, my hands often grow hot as an indication that I am sending energy into the client.

A cold spot usually indicates an absence of feeling, awareness, or consciousness. It might also reflect a hole in the auric field. Holes can cause the dissipation or loss of energy, and also leave one susceptible to the energies of others. When my hands are cold during a healing, however, energy is being released or pulled out. Often, clients who let go of powerful feelings, beliefs, memories, or misperceptions become extremely cold. They may get the chills for up to an hour, or experience hot and cold flashes for days. One of my clients had a longtime knee injury that operations couldn't fix. Her knee actually moved (permanently) three inches immediately after a session, and she experienced these types of flashes for two to three days. The physical healing of her knee also released many long-stored energies and emotions.

Yet another kinesthetic technique involves using the straight intuitive ability to sense out or tune into the auric field. We all have the ability to sense out issues, feelings, abnormalities, or sensitivities in ourselves and in others. The key to applying this ability is to trust our perceptions and to encourage others to do the same. Sometimes, tuning in requires that I allow myself to feel my client's issues or symptoms as my own. I have been trained in several countries in shamanism, so I am fairly comfortable with this method; however, I caution most people against it. It is not your job to take on your clients', friends', or relatives' problems or issues. If you find that you naturally involve yourself this way, I encourage you to immediately learn about boundaries and protection, and get training from someone who understands the issues and ethics involved in this healing style.

While visualizing the auric layers, I may also ask questions of myself, my client, our guides, or the Divine Source. If I sense an abnormality when scanning with my hands, I may guide my client into that part of his or her body, requesting that they visualize the problem or a representation of it. There are countless ways to blend kinesthetic, visual, and auditory intuition. I usually integrate all three approaches. I have found it more than worthwhile to practice using all three separately and individually, so that I am capable and confident, able to draw on all my abilities when they are called for to manage this investigative process.

Ultimately, the productivity of a scan or a healing directly correlates to how willing I am to open to (and get out of the way for) the Divine Source. I see myself simply as a vehicle or channel for divine healing. As a human, I constantly work like a hollow bone, an imperfect vehicle which must be stripped to be a conduit for love. As a healer who must remain non-judgmental regarding my clients' particular and individual beliefs and processes, I ask that they receive the highest form of guidance possible at that time. The bottom line is that all the techniques, teachings, and knowledge in the world matter little compared to our attitude.

Healing Auric Problems

We can also use any of these styles to actually make alterations to the auric field. Visualization is a powerful tool. If there is a cord, for instance, we can first visualize it, then use guided imagery to understand the nature of the relationship connection. Finally, we can use visual techniques to remove the cord and heal the remaining hole. Visualization, in the form of guided meditation, trance, regression, and hypnotherapy work, is extremely useful. It enables us to guide ourselves or another person into the heart of the issue.

Auditory skills assist us in calling on internal and external sources of wisdom. I often facilitate a discussion between a client and a part of themselves. I may have them talk to that hole in the aura or speak to the person whose issues they are holding. I also speak with my own and the client's guides during most healing processes and encourage my clients to do the same. Frequently, I ask these invisible guides to actually conduct a healing for me; for myself, I call on angelic beings or Christ. Others may call on their own traditions.

There are innumerable kinesthetic healing techniques. They include channeling energy into someone or removing energy from his or her field. These techniques might involve soothing the energy field or zapping it with a needed bolt of energy. Usually, I integrate all three approaches. When doing this, I commonly seek answers to the following questions:

1. Are there any immediate or potential physical concerns?

2. Are there any belief systems or patterns negatively affecting this auric layer?

3. Are there any feelings that need to be freed, expressed, or claimed?

4. Is the soul trying to say something to me through this auric layer?

5. Are there any guides attached to this auric layer that have a message for me?

6. Are there any positive, current, or potential life experiences this auric layer is blocking or trying to draw to me?

7. Are there any inherent family-of-origin issues that are negatively affecting this auric field?

8. Are there any relationships affecting this auric layer, negatively or positively? What do I need to do about it?

9. Is there anything I can do to help this auric field right now?

Responses to these questions will usually tell me what I need to do.

In general, I have found that the technique used is the least important part of any healing procedure, whether we are working with the aura or any other part of the energy system. Keeping our own and our clients' best interests uppermost in our minds is the most important part of any healing. Holding good intent protects both them and us from any potential damage.

The Other Dimension: The Middle Energetic Layer

There is another systemic layer that lies interspliced between the our chakric and auric systems. I use it to provide clients with a description of their soul imprint or personality characteristics. Learning how to perceive this layer can help you provide yourself and others with critical input for relationship or career decisions. We are, after all, happiest when a relationship or job involves all of our being, not just part. This layer can give you snap-shots of the traits you need to have to become fully engaged on a personal or professional level.

I read this middle layer just as I do a television screen. First, I check out a client's auric bodies, then scan the chakras. I then move my inner eye to a space between the two and blank out the aura and chakras. Now I am at the middle energetic layer.

Typically, I experience this layer with my inner vision and in color. Since I have not read about this technique or this layer in any other sources, I can tell you only that for me and my students this visual approach seems to be the clearest way to reach into this layer. I often use and teach auditory and kinesthetic means of interpreting the data, but right now I will concentrate on the visual.

Basically, I read the middle energy layer by looking at the energy layers on top of the chakras. It is actually a series of layers, each a different color. The colors themselves and the width of their bands are usually different than those of the chakras themselves.

Let me give an example. When scanning one client, I saw a swirl of purple around her feet, a piling of blue on her thighs and abdomen, a pink band in front of her heart, and an orange band going around her head.

From this picture, I determined factors about her basic personality. I informed this person that, according to my system, I would guess that she is most comfortable when she is in a state of change or transformation or associated with people who are. She may want to work in a field that helps people undergo transformational processes. (I received actual pictures of possibilities, but they followed after I'd noted this general information.) I drew these conclusions from the purple around her feet. I know that purple, as defined by my description of the sixth chakra, relates to transformation and intuitive vision. The feet relate to the tenth or the grounding chakra. Anything relating to the feet or that underneath the feet has to do with where that person places themselves in day-to-day reality. As I continued with the session, I suggested that this client is naturally a compassionate and understanding person, and that her emotional state is probably quite affected by others. I also suggested that she consider applying her compassion in a professional capacity, then I expanded upon this information.

These latter comments I made because I knew the following. Blue relates to the fifth chakra and has to do with understanding and learning. Thighs relate to inherited functions; my client probably inherited a great deal of compassion and understanding from her family. The blue over the first chakra tells me that she would be good at professions involving some sort of emotional clarifying and compassion, and that in major relationships, communication would be a primary need. The blue over her second chakra told me that she needs to have her feelings understood.

I went on with this assessment, making sure that I checked for validity with her, and that I gave her practical applications of this general information. Although I gave her a number of career suggestions, I was careful to not tell her what she should do. At the time, she was employed as a loan officer in the banking industry. Given our assessment, that profession didn't seem to fit, but it was important that she reach this conclusion for herself.

One year later, she returned—ecstatic! She had just completed her application for a master's degree in divinity, concentrating on spiritual counseling.

She had connected her compassionate nature and association with transformation with spiritual work. Rarely have I seen such a glow on someone's face. Each other client who has experienced this technique has been amazed at its applicability and helpfulness.

Colors, Body Parts, and Their Meanings

The following is a brief synopsis of the colors and body parts as they apply to the magnetic layer. I would encourage you to try to read them and see how accurate you can be.

Colors and Their Meanings

Red	Life, passion, energy, motivation linked to providing basic needs for self or others.
Orange	Creativity, feelings, attracted to that which is newly emerging.
Yellow	Intellectual, mental, indicates organizational, categorical, management skills.
Green	Healing skills; likes to see people or projects moving from point A to point B.
Blue	Compassion, understanding, communicable; likes learning and understanding.
Purple	Deeply intuitive, humanly spiritual, color of transformation.
White	Relates to principles, concepts, and purpose.
Silver	Transmission; can transmit data from one point to another.
Gold	Color of universal love.
Pink	Color of human love—combines white of spirit/purpose with red which protects/provides life.
Brown	Earthy and earth-bound; indicates a connection to nature or natural processes.
Black	Can indicate a strong ability, hidden power, or a need or skill in protecting oneself or others; may also cover a hidden or understood ability that needs to come forth.

Body Parts and Their Significance

Feet	Relate to grounding; where one would prosper in regard to living environment; type of work atmosphere needed.
Knees	Concerns style of mobility; how person changes and shifts with life's ups and downs.

Thighs	Relates to inherited traits and tendencies; masculine and feminine programming; and stored, unprocessed emotions about masculine and feminine nature.
Hips	Relates to first chakra issues; look here to understand fundamental career and job needs/skills/industries.
Abdomen	Relates to second chakra issues; this area can provide insight into person's basic feeling nature and creative gifts.
Stomach	Relates to third chakra; indicates person's mental gifts and success drives.
Heart	Relates to relationship needs, behaviors, and personality.
Thymus	Relates to the connection between someone and their spiritual identity, and beliefs about the right to be strong and safe.
Throat	Relates to person's communication style and abilities.
Face	How someone sees the world; what they need to see when they wake up in the morning.
Forehead	Relates to someone's sense of body and self-image; his or her goals and predictions for the future.
Top of Head	Relates to important and innate principles; what is important to this person.

In general, issues in the right side of the body concern stereotypically male regards—action, behavior, relationship with the world. Issues in the left side of the body relate to stereotypical female concerns—receptivity, emotions, guidance, and relationship with the inner self.

EXERCISES
Reading Auras

I. Reading Your Own Aura

    A. Take a piece of paper and some crayons or colored pencils. Draw a body shape on the paper. This shape is you. After bringing yourself into a meditative state, pinpoint an issue you are having in your body. Are you having pain anywhere? Do you have fear in your gut? Is there a place you feel shut-down? Make an "X" in the corresponding chakra.

    B. Now decide to which auric layer that chakra, and therefore that issue, relates. Draw this aura on your sheet. Now pretend you're the intuitive doctor. What color or discolorations are in this layer? What needs to be changed? As you draw, be creative.

C. When you are done drawing, see if you can picture this aura in your head. Play around with it. See if you can make changes. Do you feel any shifts in or around you?

D. What have you learned about yourself?

II. Reading Someone Else's Aura

There are three ways to read another person's aura: visually, verbally, and kinesthetically.

A. **Visual** — Ask your partner to stand next to a blank wall. Turn off all room lights except one; if possible, illuminate or back-light your partner with this light. Focus your eyes on the outside of your partner's form, then blur your focus. Look for shapes, energy bands, colors, or any representative visuals. Record your observations and interpret them for your partner, asking for validation on what fits and what does not.

B. **Verbal** — Ask your partner to share a problem, concern, or question. Take a few moments for reflection and ask your intuitive mind to tell you what auric layer is most affected by this issue or which one holds the key or solution. Write down or verbally share information that comes to mind. Continue to question your intuition to find out additional information.

C. **Kinesthetic** — Ask your partner to lie down. Rub your hands together until you feel energy flowing between them. Run them along the outside of the person's body, checking for hot or cold spots, funny feelings, emotional reactions, bumps, or indentations of the energy body. See if you can distinguish one auric layer from another, differentiating them based on their frequency and your partner's reactions.

III. Reading a Partner's Personality Imprint

Working with any of the methods above, scan for the personality layer rather than the chakras or auric layers. Share your reactions and reasoning with your partner.

Chapter Seven

Getting Into the Flow:
Rays of Energy

Rays are universal energies that are available to us all. Tapping into them is a perk for being human, because they can assist us with anything and everything that meets, greets, or beats on us during our life journey.

Some metaphysicians theorize that each ray is linked to a particular figure or being. Metaphysicians following the group called the Great White Brotherhood believe in this type of link. According to them, there are seven rays and seven advanced beings who act as guardians and administrators of each ray.

I do believe that humankind is gifted with much advanced guidance and that humans are supported by the energy of rays. I feel the use of any and all of the rays is available to each of us. We may choose to go through a gatekeeper or not. However, in my practice, I haven't found any practical reasons to associate a universal ray with one and only one being.

The other application of rays that has found favor is assigning rays a role in figuring out our basic personality. Jack Schwarz, a recent proponent of this theory, believes that we can figure out our basic personality or purpose based on which rays enter our bodies. Alice Bailey, an early "theosophist" and contemporary of C. W. Leadbeater, also worked with rays in this way.

There is a popular metaphysical belief that each soul is attuned to a certain ray and uses its energies to complete its purpose. I make amendments to this belief. We very well might use certain rays more than others, either because we are more comfortable with a particular energy, or because we need a certain ray to balance ourselves. However, I do not believe it is true that a soul runs on only one or two rays. Each person has a unique personality. Our souls, which seek balance and completion, will need certain energies at one time and other energies at another time. The Cherokee tradition seems to support this view, as Ywahoo says in *Voices of Our Ancestors*, "Each of us at some point in our life is radiating and resonating according to those different rays" (Ywahoo, 108). While we might draw more consistently on one energy source or ray than others, it would only be because it suits our soul purpose. We do not, however, revise our soul purpose according to an incoming ray. I find that we merely use power from it, as we do from other sources.

My statement may make more sense if I explain my view of the rays. A ray is a stream of consciousness, and the most complete rays are emitted right from the Divine Source. These rays vibrate at rates that are safe, powerful, and uplifting. The rays are more than simple bands of light that splay forth as do the sun's rays. In my view, they flow in a circular pattern, moving outward from the Divine Source to us, then back to it.

One of the most important paradoxes to understand in relation to rays is that a ray, or stream of Divine Source consciousness, never actually leaves the Divine Source. Rays feed our Divine Source self, the aspect of ourselves which knows it is one with the Divine Source and has never left it. Our human self is intimately linked to this Divine Source self. In fact, it is a reflection, or some would say, a projection of it.

It is as if part of ourselves created a dream-world called Life in which to explore, play, and learn. It then projected itself into this playground and began to experiment with different beliefs, feelings, and other modalities. The in-life self has never really been any different than the Divine Source-based self; it is just an extension of it. The Divine Source self is always anchoring our human self. However, for various reasons, most selves began to believe that there was a split. I think this belief stems from a sense of guilt for wanting to experiment in the first place. This chasm of guilt and shame is what we must bridge to evolve our human self, not to some unknown point of achievement, but back to the realization that it is and always has been within the Divine Source.

I think that rays feed the Divine Source self. They provide the knowing, learned part of ourselves with the rich nutrients that are necessary to maintain and strengthen our essence. As an in-body person, we must realize that our Divine Source self is our human self. The job of the rays is to loop us back into the fold, to help us remember our Divine Source self.

I perceive six major rays and a seventh energy stream that interact with our inner Divine Source self. I see each of these major six rays entering at a particular point in the body and exiting through another. When they enter and exit, they do so from both sides of the body. Of course, this statement in itself is a paradox, for each of the rays really move from the inside of our body to the outside. Establishing a conscious relationship with each of these energies is easier if we first concentrate on these entry and exit points.

Many of you probably realize that I reduced the typical number of the rays from seven to six. I perceive the seventh ray to be the Divine Source self. After opening to the first six rays, we must see and acknowledge ourselves as children of the Divine Source. Conversely, if we were to realize ourselves as part of the Divine Source right now, we wouldn't need to understand the other rays.

The Six Major Rays

Ray	Entry Point	Exit Point
First	Coccyx	Pineal gland
Second	Third eye/forehead	Abdomen
Third	Stomach area	Throat
Fourth	Front of heart	Back of heart
Fifth	Eighth chakra	Tenth chakra
Sixth	Divine Source self	Ninth chakra

The qualities of the rays themselves are similar to those mentioned in other texts. Here's a synopsis.

First Ray

Key Aspect — Will power.

Entry Point Significance — Establishes the Divine Source self's existence on a physical level.

Exit Point Significance — Reconnects the human self's existence to the Divine Source.

Second Ray

Key Aspect — Love and kindness.

Entry Point Significance — Allows human self to see self through the eyes of the Divine Source a lens of infinite kindness and love.

Exit Point Significance — Returns our feeling states, both the difficult and positive, to the Divine Source for healing and completion.

Third Ray

Key Aspect — Intelligence.

Entry Point Significance — Brings Divine Source ideas to human self for consideration (allowing human self to consider what to activate or not).

Exit Point Significance — Returns decisions, consequences, or learnings back to the Divine Source.

Fourth Ray

Key Aspect — Unity.

Entry Point Significance — Reinforces the fact that the Divine Source will bring heart's desires to the human self through concrete reality.

Exit Point Significance — Reflects harmonies and disharmonies back to the Divine Source for reflection and healing.

Fifth Ray

Key Aspect — Knowledge.

Entry Point Significance — Awakens all past and potential future knowledge of the human self and other human selves, making this knowledge available for everyday use.

Exit Point Significance — Grounds this knowledge into the human self's current material reality.

Sixth Ray

Key Aspect — Idealism.

Entry Point Significance — Grants the human self the clean and pure unconditional acceptance, love, and principled support that only the Divine Source self can provide.

Exit Point Significance — After awakening the soul's essential nature, loops back into the Divine Source self, closing the circle between the two.

Seventh (Final) Ray

I don't consider this energy to be a ray. Rather, it is an awareness that comes when we realize that we are in the Divine Source, that we are nourished by the white light that is, contains, and includes everything.

Working With the Rays

We can choose to work deliberately or unconsciously with the rays. In a deliberate approach, we assess what is missing in our lives or what type of energy might be helpful. For instance, one of my clients, James, was experiencing financial problems. Because he was already deeply interested in the concept of rays, I asked him to begin working with First Ray energy. While money issues could reflect any of the rays, I knew that baseline security issues originate in the first chakra, and that the First Ray enters through the first chakra. I also know that money is tied to the grander issue of purpose, being on our right career path. My decision was underscored by the fact that the First Ray exits at the pineal gland or seventh chakra, which pertains to purpose. Finally, the First Ray has to do with will power. Break this term down, and we have "will" plus "power"—what we want plus the power to achieve it. Thus, I blended my rationality with my own intuition to make a suggestion to James.

For his part, James meditated on the First Ray and his Divine Source connection three times a day, imagining the ray entering through the coccyx and exiting through the pineal gland. He focused on each twist and turn undertaken by this ray. During the course of two months, he worked through several issues pertaining to money, including beliefs that he didn't deserve any, confusion about how to make it, and anger toward his father, who focused solely on money.

With James, I did something a bit different. About one month into our work, I suggested that he begin to concurrently use the Abundance energy point, which sped up his progress in actively working through his issues. Within two months, he had taken a new, better-paying job. Within six months, he was well on his way to saving enough money for a down payment on a house.

Certain issues may also call for mixing the rays. When playing chemist, it is helpful to spend some time figuring out all sides of an issue before dabbling. Let's say you have pinpointed the First Ray for your money issues, but sense that you need something more. A little bit of thinking may help you remember that you didn't have troublesome money issues until you got divorced. Knowing that the heart (fourth) chakra deals with relationships, you may try on the idea that the Fourth Ray may also hold healing for you.

I underwent a rather unusual experience with the rays shortly after separating from my husband. As the one forced to move, I found myself with $500, two futons, and a small child. I went to bed one night asking that the Divine Source send me whatever ray energy I needed to help me get on my feet. I will never forget that night.

At first, I was aware of red energy, that of the First Ray. A voice in my head said, "This may hurt." That was an understatement. The sharpness of the pain, the creak of bones moving—I was terrified, not sure what monster I had unleashed. At that moment, I was a firm believer in the old maxim of the cure being worse than the illness. On rolled the evening, with each color illuminating different aspects of my personality and altering me in different ways. I experienced the presence of beings, but more than one to a ray. I found them comforting and reassuring.

Within a year and a half, I was living in a comfortable suburb, had bought land outside of the city, paid all my debts, and had 700 clients. I believe a lot of it had to do with the ray clearing and some prior and subsequent work I did with the higher energy centers (plus the old-fashioned Puritan work ethic).

Methods for Ray Work

There are several methods for working with the rays. A psychically visual person may tune into themselves or another person, and scan for the presence and absence of the rays. Psychics often interpret the colors of the rays this the following way:

Ray	Color
First	Red or rose.
Second	Orange or lavender (as different from violet or deep purple).
Third	Yellow or lime-green.
Fourth	Green or pink.
Fifth	Silver or black and white.
Sixth	Gold or purple.
Integrative	White.

Besides searching for missing or incomplete ray connections, it can be helpful to determine which rays we are most heavily drawing upon. This information can tell us about our own or another's current, primary needs. If we are tapping into a lot of Second Ray energy, chances are that we are, at least at the moment, concentrating on feelings and the expression of them in our life. If we are pulling in Third and Fourth Ray energy, we are using intellectual and relationship energy. Perhaps we are considering how our ideas about a relationship stack up against the reality of a certain relationship.

Because the list of possibilities and their interpretations are endless, it is important to trust our intuitive senses in regard to our usage of the rays. If someone tells us we are a Third Ray person, and we don't think so, we don't need to accept that information as valid. If we perceive a lot of Third Ray energy in ourselves, however, we have options about how to use this knowledge. We can seek to further understand our familiarity with the Third Ray, the ray of intelligence. Perhaps we can challenge ourselves to make even more use of our brightness, or to establish new ways to relay it.

Using Ray Energy

There are many ways to actually tap into or pull in ray energy. The first method is probably the easiest, but the most difficult to describe. We simply pull it in. We ask for it, sense the ray's presence, and bring it into our bodies. If you take this approach, remember to check both the entrance and exit points. Are they clear and unclogged? Are the rays flowing completely through these points, or are some of them getting stuck? We know that we have succeeded when we feel different.

Another method is the visual approach. We can psychically scan the entry and exit points and search for the rays. We want to check for colors and discolorations, the strength and intensity of the rays entering and exiting, and if the ray is trying to illuminate anything for us.

Another scanning method involves the auditory approach. We can always ask our own self or a guide to simply explain to us what is happening with the rays. We can listen for responses or write them down.

Good questions to ask about any specific ray can include:

1. Can I locate the ray in or around me?

2. Is the ray entering the entrance point?

3. If not, why? Is the entrance point blocked? With what? An emotional, physical, mental, or spiritual issue? What do I need to do or believe to open up this entrance point?

4. What effect is the ray having inside my body?

5. Is there anything I need to do or know to use this ray so it better serves my needs?

6. Is the ray exiting my body?

7. If not, why? Is the exit point blocked? With what? What do I need to do or believe to open up this exit point?

8. How does the ray look (or feel) when it leaves my body?

9. Is it appropriate that it looks (or feels) like this? If not, what do I need to do or know?

10. Does the ray loop back completely to the Divine Source? If not, how am I preventing its full return?

11. Are all my rays in balance? If yes, how can I assure they will remain that way? If no, what must I do or know to bring them into balance?

If we were to distill this information and all other ray information down to its bare bones, we would eventually arrive at this conclusion: rays are there to help us love ourselves better. If we are willing to love ourselves, we will automatically reach for the right star.

EXERCISES
Working With Your Rays

I. Select a scanning method and search your own field for the rays. Draw or document your findings (include a picture of a body). Then, guiding yourself into a meditative state, ask yourself the scanning questions outlined at the end of this chapter. Record your answers. What do they tell you about your current state of affairs?

II. Select one ray to work with for a week. Every morning and evening, picture or feel this ray coming into your body, emerging from the exit point, and connecting you to the Divine Source. At the end of the week, evaluate what happened in relation to that ray's primary focus.

III. The following set of questions is designed to help you figure out which ray(s) you are currently using the most. Knowing this information can give you clues about the professional or personal focus you may need to keep at this time.

    A. What color seems to best explain your personality at this time?

        1. Red.

        2. Orange.

        3. Yellow.

        4. Green.

        5. Silver.

        6. Gold.

        7. White.

    B. What would best describe your nature under the following conditions?

    When working....

        1. Forceful: It's important to get things done.

        2. Considerate: What matters is doing things in a good way.

        3. Pondering: It's important to consider options so as to make the best decision.

4. Team-oriented: The best work is done when each person is doing his or her best.

5. Learned: Knowledge—knowing what to know—will reflect in the final outcome.

6. Idealistic: You can't reach the stars unless you set out for the stars.

7. On-purpose: If I stay connected to my Divine Source, what I do will be perfect.

In relationships....

1. Powerful: Let's be real with each other.

2. Kind: I believe in loving my neighbor as myself.

3. Thoughtful and Intentional: There are consequences to actions; let's think things through.

4. Harmonious: It's important that we operate as a unit, supporting each other.

5. Understanding: If we know where each other is coming from and why, we will get along.

6. Connected: We are striving to be one.

7. Accepting: People are who and what they are supposed to be—at all times.

At leisure....

1. Physical and self-determining: I like to keep moving.

2. Reflective: This is the time to achieve a higher understanding of matters.

3. Studious: I need time for research, study, and thinking if I am to be at my best when it counts.

4. Open: By staying open to and following my desires, I become a better person.

5. Curious: I want to learn everything there is to learn.

6. Dedicated: When I'm doing something, I want to do it as well as I can, even if it's play.

7. No different: Always, I am being myself, held in the Divine Source.

C. What qualities do you use most in your daily life?

1. Determination.

2. Consideration of others.

3. Reason.

4. Compassion and harmony.

5. Understanding, relating what you know.

6. Adherence to beliefs.

7. Conscious awareness.

D. The following is a list of famous people and a quality that helped make them great. If you had to choose a hero/ine from this list, who would you choose?

1. Mickey Mantle (baseball great): He took a natural talent and pushed himself to make it better.

2. Mother Teresa (humanitarian): She shares love regardless of someone's race, color, age, or creed.

3. Albert Einstein (physics master-mind): He was a brilliant man who strived to interrelate science and spirituality.

4. Martin Luther King, Jr. (civil rights leader): He told us we were all the same and lived that principle.

5. Madame Marie Curie (scientist): She tirelessly dedicated herself to research and to sharing this knowledge to help humanity.

6. St. Clare or St. Francis of Assisi (religious-order leaders): Both believed that people were capable of living a spiritual life, and they taught others how to do that.

7. Spiritual prophets: Those people whose lives and work led others to connect with the Divine Source.

To decipher:

Count the number of times you selected each letter. Use the following chart to graph how many times you choose each ray.

1 = First Ray	**5** = Fifth Ray
2 = Second Ray	**6** = Sixth Ray
3 = Third Ray	**7** = Integrative Ray
4 = Fourth Ray	

Most of us draw on one or perhaps two rays more often than the others. Use the following breakdown to determine what you tend to do:

Five choices in one ray group — You are a strong proponent of this ray. Probably, your soul purpose relies on a solid application of the energy available to you from this ray. Your friends would probably describe you as someone with the personality qualities most often relegated to this ray. Knowing this, draw on the strengths of this Divine Source energy, but stay open to the fact that other people may see life a different way. You will need to form partnerships with others in some endeavors to assure balance in your projects and life.

Four choices in one ray group — You strongly adhere to the traits inherent in this ray, drawing on them and probably expressing them to achieve your goals. While not as strident as someone with five choices in your ray group, you need to be careful to respect others' methods and insights. Using the ray that won the single vote can alleviate the intensity of the other four rays and add balance to your personality.

Three choices in one ray group; two in another — You probably draw equally on two different types of ray energy, marking you as fairly adaptable and balanced. In your work, you tend to apply qualities from both categories. You are the ideal bridge person—someone who can help glue two seemingly different points-of-view or approaches together. Having two strong suits can sometimes be difficult. The jewel in the center is this: when stuck in a particular issue, you can switch your approach to the problem. For instance, if you can't figure your way out of a dilemma via one of your tendencies, flip into a different "ray" of thinking.

An array of ray choices — If no strong inclination emerges, you are more of a generalist than a specialist. In relationship, you could easily learn to see more than one point-of-view, and might need to be careful to represent your own strongest viewpoints. Sometimes, it's important to be one way more than another; take care not to be wishy-washy. As a natural peacemaker and mediator, use your gifts wisely and thoughtfully.

Chapter Eight

The Guardian Principles

All major religions, sciences, industries, medical approaches, and disciplines are ruled by established **principles** or guidelines. Principles may be drawn from any number of sources. Some are concluded from practical experience, such as the notion of gravity developed by Newton. Some are created from empirical investigation, such as the laws of thermodynamics. Some are delivered from on high, such as the Ten Commandments or the teachings of the Buddha. Some stem from plain old common sense, such as the wisdom found in old wives' tales. Whatever their origin, all principles have one thing in common: they define the culture which creates them or adapts to them.

Principles are important. They provide continuity and define boundaries, thereby assuring a level of safety. They can unite people under a common intent, thus furthering a cause or movement. They also set standards, encourage research, and help people understand each other. Principles accomplish many higher ends.

Principles can also be used toward less desirable ends. They can separate people, for instance. The caste system in India is upheld by religious principles that divide the deserving from the undeserving, leaving the latter hungry, sick, and unfulfilled. The principles applied by the Nazi regime directly resulted in the deaths of millions of people who didn't fit the "divinely inspired" Aryan regulations. Many Americans' ancestors were chased out of their birth nations because of principle; unable to ascribe to the rules of the time, they chose different standards, and were either forced to leave their birth nations or chose to do so to escape further persecution.

Besides causing rifts between people, rigid principles can also limit the growth and development of ideas, science, progress, change, and goodness.

Throughout history, certain religious beliefs prevented or delayed the development of science. Imagine where society would now be if Copernicus' theory that the earth is round would have been accepted by his peers instead of left dormant for several years. Ironically, scientific standards themselves have been used to prohibit personal development. We now see such a situation where some American governmental and business institutions are trying to stop people from using color therapy, herbal tonics, and hands-on healing. Even the use of vitamins has come under fire in recent years.

Principles are often misapplied. The fault usually doesn't lie with the principles themselves, but rather in the perception and application of them. People are people. When we hold misperceptions, such as the belief that others are out to get us or that we have to lie to get ahead, we might twist the truth to escape perceived threats or the dangers of self-disclosure. When considering the existence of principles, we must pay close attention to the applications of them. It is not enough to say, "The world would work better if everyone loved each other." We should consider how to personally apply this principle in an ethical way.

There are many universal principles governing our planet, our nations, our states, our businesses, our family, and our daily lives. Many of these principles cross ethnic, socio-economic, geographical, and political boundaries. Many peoples hold several principles in common. Even my son, upon hearing the Golden Rule for the first time at age five, could relate to it. In his own words, "That means if I give Bobby a toy, he will have to give one back!" Principles such as "Love they neighbor as thyself" show up in most cultures one way or another. The idea that "God is love" is commonly shared by many religious groups.

If so many of our principles are the same, then why do we all seem so different? There are several possible answers to this question. Although we may share similar principles with another person or group, we may differ on our interpretations of common principles, we may apply common principles differently, or we may also hold dissimilar principles that cause conflicting understandings of our common principles. Yet despite these problems, humanity continues to create and uphold principles. We create them because we need them.

When working with the human energy system, we are faced with a comparable need for principles. The question is, what are the principles under which we can work with the full human energy system? Under that question lies an even more important one: how can we ethically work with this system? How are we to assure ourselves that this information doesn't become fodder for misapplication and unethical practices? We have a myriad of facts, systems, and treatments that can be applied in our esoteric, spiritual relationships and everyday lives. We are not trying to build yet another reason to criticize or judge ourselves or others. I am not trying to build yet another system that results in manipulation or fantasy.

As I've noted, principles can be derived from several origins. We could create a whole set of principles to regulate work with our human energy system, and inevitably, anyone working with this information will do so. What we really need is a set of guidelines under which to develop our own individual values and principles. We need guidelines that are principled, but which are also universal in nature. We need guidelines that don't exclude anyone, yet imply ethical standards. We need guidelines that validate everyone's point-of-view, but do not imply that one set of experiences is better than others. We need guidelines that are steps rather than rules. These guidelines, in turn, must encourage us to reach for our highest set of principles, in concept and application.

The following guidelines are the ones I have developed for myself. I believe that they are universal in origin, but need to be personally shaped and applied. They are suggestions, not rules. They conform to most doctrines, sets of principles, concepts, and ideals, yet have a practical application. I offer them as a set of guidelines to follow when working with your own or another's human energy system. They have been developed to specifically apply to the human energy system, because they align to the holistic nature of the centers themselves. While they are practical, they are also conceptual. I would encourage you to use them or at least create your own guidelines, always keeping in mind that their applicability is contingent upon your intent. These principles can help us all open the revolving doors between the material and spiritual within each of us and within humanity as a whole.

Principles for the Human Energy Process

Principle One

The human energy system is designed for two activities—healing and manifesting. Ultimately, we are:

1. **Seeking to heal that which is preventing us from manifesting our heart's desires.**

2. **Seeking to manifest that which we require to heal damage to our true selves.**

Our heart's desires come from our essence. Our essence is both the spiritual and physical manifestation of what the Divine Source wants for us. Our essence desires to be its full self on the physical and all other planes. The human energy system, because it works like a revolving door between the spiritual and the physical, is the optimum vehicle for both healing the issues preventing full self-expression and the manifestion of our essence's true desires.

Principle Two

Healing and manifesting are one and the same activity.

On the physical plane, healing occurs when we channel, change, or rearrange matter. Healing allows us to fully manifest ourselves. Manifesting involves channeling, changing, or rearranging spiritual energy. It allows us to heal damages to our true selves. When we are involved in a healing process, we are either trying to repair damage in order to return to a more complete state, or we are opening to changes in order to achieve a desired new state. To accomplish healing, we must learn how to manifest; to manifest, we must be willing to heal whatever is in the way of having what we want. Both processes share the same end. They assist us in knowing and actualizing our true selves.

Principle Three

True healing, and therefore true manifesting, depends on being willing to change.

This concept sounds simple, and it is. Our resistance, however, sometimes makes its application difficult. For instance, if we require healing or are living in a state of need, at some level, we are resisting the manifestation of our desires. We might be doing this for any number of reasons. We don't believe we really deserve the things we want. We aren't finished learning from the current experience. We want something different than we think we do, or we are just plain scared to take a chance. Perhaps we don't want to get hurt or be let down again.

Change is a frightening concept to most of us. Even when our minds seem comfortable with the idea, sometimes our feelings or bodies resist. When we fight our resistance, our resistance fights back. What we must do then is become willing to change. Short of that, we can become willing to become willing to change. When we stop fighting our resistance, we open the revolving doors to different opportunities for healing or manifesting.

Principle Four

To change, we must be willing to let go.

To let go is to surrender. To achieve our heart's desires, we must let go of everything that is not a heart's desire or anything that does not align with the Divine Source. We must be willing to release everything that is not of, from, or for our essence. We must surrender to the Divine Source all that is not of us.

Principle Five

**Letting go requires a full acceptance of our current state, a willingness
to love ourselves completely, and a willingness to be loved completely.**

We can only let go of something we fully accept. For reasons known or unknown to us, we often resist the healing or manifesting of our heart's desires. We must accept the wisdom of our hidden knowledge; we need to accept the resistance. Only from a place of self-love can we allow change, and thus, risk loving ourselves more. Because we are turning our resistance over to the Divine Source, we must also be willing to allow the Divine Source to help us or to love us. Letting go symbolizes the state of perfect self-love.

Principle Six

**The norm is what we perceive it to be. If we change our standards,
the norm changes as well.**

Our current state of existence is always the state we consider normal. Illness, money limitations, career or relationship dissatisfactions, and other uncomfortable states come from our standards and really reflect that which we find normal. The job of our physical energy system is to maintain our standards. The job of our spiritually based energy system is to help us create the reality of our optimum or essential standards. If we allow our essence to establish our physical, mental, emotional, or mental standards, our energy system will change its idea of normal. We will then heal and manifest our heart's desires.

Principle Seven

**The more we align our healing and manifesting standards with those
of the Divine Source and our Divine Source self, the happier we will be.**

The Divine Source and our essence or Divine Source self are composed of pure love energy. Everything of the Divine Source seeks pure self-expression. When we are being and acting from our total selves, we are self-fulfilled and happy.

Applying the Principles

These principles are meant to be the fodder for guidelines that individuals or groups define for themselves. They are not principles unto themselves. Just about any system of principles could apply to them, including the Twelve-Step principles, religious doctrines, even the Hippocratic oath.

Even though these guidelines sound conceptual, I apply them in practical matters. One way that I do this for myself or clients is to go through each guideline one-by-one. For instance:

Principle One:	What is the heart desire I am working on right now?
Principle Two:	What do I need to heal in order to manifest what I want, and what do I need to manifest in order to heal what is in my way?
Principle Three:	Am I truly willing to change what is preventing my success, or allow the Divine Source to change me?
Principle Four:	Am I truly willing to let go of what is preventing my success?
Principle Five:	Am I willing to love myself exactly as I am, to love myself enough to change, and to be loved enough to get the help that I need?
Principle Six:	Am I willing to change my perceptions of normal so that they include fully living in/with the desired change?
Principle Seven:	Am I willing to be happy (in relation to this issue)?

We can walk just about any issue through these seven principles. We can even use this model to diagnose what is really going on with us.

Another way that I use these questions is to fully incorporate my seven in-body chakras into the process. I bring my awareness into my first chakra and ask myself the first question, then I bring myself into the second chakra to ask the second question, and so on. You will notice that each principle reflects the basic nature of the chakra of the same number. Through this method, we gain a complete understanding of our issue with its healing and manifesting repercussions, and open our entire bodies to the change process. This opening greatly speeds up our healing/manifesting process.

These principles boil down to this: we are our essence—our Divine Source self—and deserve to have our lives reflect this truth. That means that our physical, mental, emotional, and spiritual realities can be in alignment with our heart's desires. We can be happy.

We will explore these principles in more depth in relation to our physical, mental, emotional, and spiritual well-being throughout the rest of this book. The following exercise will help you practice these principles in a concrete fashion.

EXERCISE
Practicing the Principles

I guide my classes through this exercise and encourage you to have a companion do the same for you.

A. Bring yourself into a meditative state. Pinpoint an important issue or problem. Take a few moments and let yourself experience all your senations about this issue. How do you perceive this issue in your body? How does it affect your life? How does it affect the lives of those around you? How long have you been aware of this issue?

B. You are now going to spend a few minutes reflecting on this issue. Create a bubble of red, attach it to your first energy center, and enter this world of red. Ask yourself the question pertaining to the first guideline: What is the heart desire I am working on right now?

Remind yourself that underneath your problem lies a desire, a dream, or a need. What is it? As you see or sense what is lacking or missing, ask yourself what you are striving to achieve. While surrounded by this red color, let your body experience what it would be like to have what you want.

C. Now create an orange bubble. Attach it to your second chakra. Enter this world and respond to the question relating to the second guideline: What do I need to heal in order to manifest what I want, and what do I need to manifest in order to heal what is in my way?

As you ponder this question, let your creativity run wild. Picture pictures, think thoughts, imagine stories that provide insight.

D. Next fashion a yellow bubble and connect it to your third chakra. Here, ask the question: am I truly willing to change what is preventing my success?

Don't answer too quickly. Are you really willing to change what is preventing the achievement of your heart's desire, to heal or manifest that which you need? Only move forward when you sense that you could, whole-heartedly, respond with a "yes."

E. Now there is a green bubble connected to your heart. Enter it and ask yourself the following question: am I truly willing to let go of that which is preventing my success?

Let yourself pause and feel your reactions to this idea. Are there any fears? Inhibitions? Questions? Be honest. Then dig deeper. Are you really happy hanging on to this problem and everything associated with it? If you can say and feel a "no," you are probably willing to let go.

F. Now you form a blue bubble and attach it to your throat. Inside this bubble, ask yourself the next series of questions: am I willing to love myself exactly as I am, to love myself enough to change, and to be loved enough to get the help that I need?

Here we must speak our truth. We must stake a claim for ourselves. Discuss resistance with yourself; ask the blue color to help you find the truth in any negative judgments you hold about yourself and to release the negativity. When you can say that you are a fully deserving person, move on.

G. You approach a shining purple bubble emanating from your forehead. This purple bubble is the center of your self-image. Ask yourself: am I willing to change my perceptions of normal so they include fully living in/with the desired change?

Allow yourself to picture your current self-image. It is this self who is creating your current reality. Does this person look satisfied? Happy? Like he or she feels good about themselves? If not, seek another level of understanding. What does the self under this self look like? Where is the self with the low self-image? Feel your compassion toward this figure and ask how he or she would like to appear. Would that individual be willing to accept a new standard for him- or herself, and therefore for his or her reality?

Actually visualize the change process upon this aspect of yourself. See yourself altering your perceptions by changing the image. Then move on.

H. You enter a white bubble floating from the top of your head and ask the question: am I willing to be happy (in relation to this issue)?

At this level, you may open yourself up to feeling and experience what happiness is like in relation to this issue. Bathe yourself in the white light. Surround your issue, your image of it, your feelings about it, in white light. Then ask the Divine Source to transform the issue and the energy of it. When you feel complete and whole, return to your heart.

I. At the heart level, pull the colors from the bubbles back into their respective energy centers. Leave behind everything you are ready to release—all the false beliefs, low self-images, dark spots, and discolorations. When you are ready, release these bubbles into the atmosphere, asking the Divine Source to break them down to their substance and recycle the energy.

J. Breathe deeply and return to a conscious state.

Chapter Nine

The Spirit's Design

So far, I have outlined the basic components of our energy system, and established the patterns of development and guidelines by which they operate. It is now time to flesh out the practical healing and manifesting applications of this system. You would think we ought to begin with a physical orientation, because most of our concerns are physical. Most of our worries focus on jobs, money, homes, relationships, health, and belongings. We often believe that if we alter our physical reality or just do something different we can improve our total well-being.

Although this approach is logical, we are exploring dimensions that present us with additional possibilities. There are two ways to make change. First, we can alter physical energy, and we frequently do. Because we are revolving doors, altering physical energy will change first our physical reality, then our spiritual reality. The Twelve-Step programs are based on this theory. If we quit drinking, stop smoking, cease obsessing, our belief systems and feelings will clear. We will be able to better reach our spiritual self and our higher power.

However, because we are revolving doors, the opposite is true as well. If we affect our spiritual self or energies, our physical, mental, and emotional selves will react. The catch is, the subsequent reactions are not equal to the physical change. They are greater—drastically greater. Our spiritual self and system do not have to rely on physical laws, such as time, cause and effect, and stimulus/response.

The foundation of all my human energy system guidelines is the knowledge that there is a Divine Source and that we have/are a Divine Source self.

All energy emanates from the Divine Source, which means that all the matter that forms our universe, our houses, our physical bodies, and even our feelings comes from the Divine Source. It takes a lot more energy to rearrange matter once it is established and patterned than to appropriately form it in the first place. Think about how difficult it is to lose those last, stubborn ten pounds than to stay at our ideal weight. Think about how much more effort it takes to reupholster a chair than it did to have the factory make the original. Think about how much more difficult it is to have to get well than to stay well. Think about how much easier, in the long run, it would be to first change our spiritual self and allow that change to rearrange the rest of us.

There are many other reasons why working with the higher frequency spiritual energies is the most effective way to heal and manifest. To fully understand this idea, however, we must understand a little bit more about how our human energy system is organized and how it originated.

Why Spiritual Healing Can Affect Change

To best make use of our spiritual bodies, including our spiritual energy points, we need to understand a few basics about the human energy system in relation to spiritual development. All aspects of the human system can be organized into three major physical components of self: the body, the mind, and the soul.

My description of our generic spiritual development is echoed by Zachary Lansdowne, who says, "The viewpoint here is that the soul exists prior to physical incarnation and then acquires a personality of the mental, emotional, and physical bodies" (Lansdowne, 5). Like Lansdowne, I believe the soul is that aspect of us that has been around the longest. In effect, our soul body is the framework for the spark of the Divine Source that we are. It is the self that was projected from the Divine Source when our Divine Source self decided to experiment with physical reality.

Every soul carries a mission, a purpose. This purpose is related to what the Divine Source self wanted to learn or experience on the physical plane. Every soul has a different purpose, because every Divine Source self is unique. One soul's purpose may be to learn how to be happy; another may desire to be of service and to heal.

At some point in our soul's development, it added a consciousness or an awareness of being. The soul learned that it is an "I am." This self-consciousness created a second aspect of our self—our mind. The mind aspect of ourselves expresses through and records within it learning, teaching, and knowledge. Our mind is that part of ourselves that performs comparisons and contrasts. Our individual mind holds the beliefs and intellectual understandings that we have gleaned through all our soul's experiences. Its job is to help guide us through reason, to make the choices that will allow us to accomplish our soul's overall purpose. To guide us, our mind holds our individual knowledge, but also connects into the mind bodies of all other beings. Jung called this vast network the "collective unconscious."

Unfortunately, by the time we develop a somewhat functional soul and mind, our experiences of the physical plane were beginning to tarnish us. We experienced pain and suffering, and did not know what to do about it. Our soul might have confronted difficulties in actualizing our purpose, while our mind may have compared us to others and decided we were wanting. Any number of difficulties might have bogged down our creative and evolutionary processes.

In reaction, we added a body, which helped us to more fully experience the physical plane. Through our body, we were supposed to actualize our soul purpose and heal any blocks we had to fulfilling this mission. The trouble was, our body experienced excruciating pain and blamed itself (and was probably blamed by both the soul and mind in the process). Our unhealthy patterns locked in and became the fodder for many return trips to this physical plane. One life followed another. In each, seeking to dig ourselves out of the trench, our soul carefully prepared its lessons plans before the next de-ascension or incarnation. In *The Holographic Universe*, Michael Talbot describes studies done by Dr. Joel Whitton on regressed subjects. He describes a light-filled place where individuals "no longer possessed the ability to rationalize away any of their faults and misdeeds, and saw themselves with total honesty...when subjects planned their next life, they did so with a sense of moral obligation" (Talbot, 215).

However, our soul consistently forgot one important fact—the body has feelings. It does not like to be hurt or to suffer. Here originated a basic conflict between the soul and the body; the soul would choose lifetime experiences that exposed us to more pain and more difficulties so we could get it right and make amends to those we wronged in previous lives (Talbot, 215). Because it hurt so much, the body would rebel. We have never gotten it right, because getting it right is just too painful and too difficult.

As with our other lives, our current incarnation is an attempt to clear unhealthy patterns and to achieve our soul purpose. Because our body remembers and holds every experience within it, however, the failures, disappointments, abuses, and dysfunctional patterns we experienced before this lifetime have probably been recreated during this lifetime.

Most of us can probably sense that our mind, body, and soul are not unified. They have learned to mistrust each other. Our soul has made decisions that have harmed the body; our body has rejected parts of our soul purpose. Our mind has stored judgments that have solidified self-destructive patterns. The rift between these three aspects of ourselves has grown over time and exists today.

Under this theory, healing involves sewing up the rifts between our body, mind, and soul. Only when these three aspects of ourselves unite can acts such as manifesting be accomplished. Unless all three aspects of ourselves act in concert, the soul will undermine the body, which can undermine the mind, and so on.

Spiritual healing might be one of the only means for accomplishing this healing task, because spiritual healing works with the invisible energy that resides between these disattached aspects. Our essence or Divine Source self, when on the physical plane, is composed of spiritualized matter. We begin to heal the split between our three units when we realize that this essence is the core energy or flame connecting the body, mind, and soul (figure 9a). All three actually reside within our essence or Divine Source self. Whatever their individual issues, they are interconnected by invisible threads of spiritual energy to each other and to the Divine Source. Everything is made of Divine Source energy, including the empty space between our split aspects. Barbara Ann Brennan describes this belief in *Hands Of Light*. "The whole universe appears as a dynamic web of inseparable energy patterns.... Thus we are not separated parts of a whole. We are a Whole" (Brennan, 25).

Essence energy really works two ways. It exists in balled-up form, usually within the heart energy center, ready and waiting to be energized. This inner self, the one I usually call the spirit or essence, is imprinted with information about our essential purpose, essential needs, and essential personality. We could say that our real selves are walled up within our hearts, waiting to break free. Our real selves are waiting for the day that our body, mind, and soul start working together instead of separately.

The other way our essential or spirit self works is by enveloping and surrounding us. It draws us outward. Remember, one of the reasons we are here is to create. We want to evolve, try new things, expand, become more aware. These urges are our essential energy guiding us to a completion not yet achieved on the physical plane.

Spiritual healing involves helping our true spirit break free, which means recognizing that it is already free. Once freed, it can reconnect our body, mind, and soul, so we can work in a harmonious fashion to achieve our purpose. This step brings us into our intermediate and advanced healing stages (figures 9b and 9c). Spiritual healing also involves manifesting our desires, so we can become more than we have ever become. To truly accomplish our purpose, we must be willing to be who we really are, and we must be willing to become who we must become.

Figure 9a.

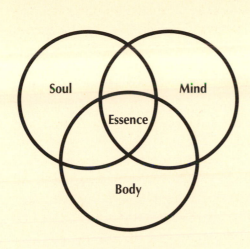

Most soul/mind/body
connections.

Figure 9b.

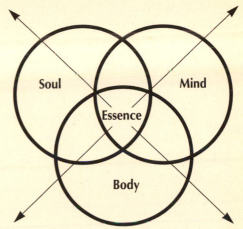

Intermediate healing stage
involving expression
of essence (similar to
living our purpose).

Figure 9c.

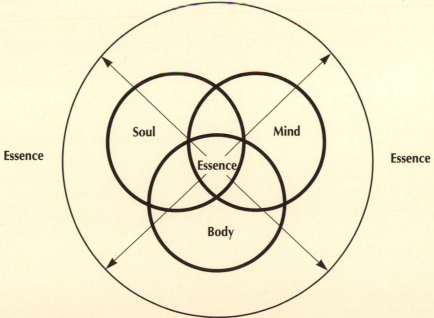

Advanced healing stage.

Work, Magic, and Miracles

Work

To be who we are and to become who we must become can be an arduous task. We all know this, because we all have already worked hard to try and accomplish these goals. One of the reasons we have worked so hard, yet merited so little, is that working hard goes against the spirit's design. Spiritual healing and manifesting our Divine Source self is supposed to be easy. The trouble is, most of us are programmed to make things difficult.

In his book *Illusions*, Richard Bach conveys a story that illustrates our natural attraction toward selecting difficult over easy. Don Shimoda, the Christ-like figure in the book, once asked a group what they would be willing to do in order to be enlightened. "If I told you to become enlightened you needed to work hard, to suffer, to be punished, would you be willing to do it?" he asked. They responded with a chorus of "yes."

"And what if I told you that, in order to be enlightened, you had to be happy?" he asked. The people looked puzzled. Many become angry. If enlightenment was easy and made one happy, it could not work (Bach, Richard. *Illusions: The Adventures of a Reluctant Messiah*. New York: Dell Publishing Company, 1977).

We are each programmed with the hard-work ideal. It is reflected in the American dream, the Puritan work ethic, and the Catholic emphasis on guilt and shame. Every culture has its own set of standards, and most of them perpetuate the notion that to become enlightened, successful, accomplished, or even good enough, you must work hard.

Work is one way to create healing and manifesting. Working requires the generation and movement of physical matter to affect change. Healing by work could involve getting an operation, taking pills, changing our diets, going to a health club. Manifesting by work could involve holding down a job, writing resumes, building the object we want, implementing our strategic plans.

Working hard is very much a front-side, in-body chakra phenomenon. Our (front-side) first chakra enables us to lift, move, carry, and do all of the physical actions so important to creating change. Our second chakra provides us with the feelings that motivate our decisions and actions. Our third chakra generates the ideas behind our hard work. Our fourth chakra makes us establish and work on the relationships that make us productive. Our fifth chakra speaks the words that solidify our viewpoints. Our sixth chakra makes us see the reality we need to change. Our seventh chakra controls our thinking. Our eighth chakra provides us the karma or lesson-filled experiences we need to work through in order to grow. Our ninth chakra feeds us our soul's lesson plans. Our tenth chakra establishes the body through which we are to work.

Work is a part of every change process. Because we are on the physical plane, we simply have to, at one point or another, pick up the phone, go to the doctor, write a letter, eat, sleep, bathe—do what we need to do to heal or manifest. The problem is, we believe so obsessively in the effectiveness of work that we forget or don't even realize that there are two other highly effective vehicles for creating change: magic and miracles.

Magic and Miracles

Magic involves allowing other people to help us. **Miracles** are created when we allow spiritual energy to do it for us. While all three avenues of change—work, magic, and miracles—siphon energy from the spiritual to the physical, work emanates from primarily physical and only incidental spiritual energies. Miracles work almost entirely with the invisible, higher frequency energy. Magic stems from equal shares of spiritual and physical energy. Zachary Lansdowne's outline of magic parallels my suggestion that work plus serendipity produces magic. His "working of magic" includes five steps: intuitively receiving an idea, constructing a clear mental picture, adding emotional desire, adding vitality, and finally putting in dense physical matter (Lansdowne, 84). My explorations of magic are similar, except that I connect them to relationships.

Spiritual healing and manifesting is easier than any other variety because it involves allowing ourselves to become agents for magic and miracles. Magic and miracles are not associated with occult or even religious processes. They are natural forms of creation. We are all gifted with the inner knowledge of and outer rights to them. To allow magic to happen, we must understand that not only are we revolving doors between the material and the spiritual, but that other people are also revolving doors. If we allow ourselves to trust other people, they can become mediums for channeling spiritual energy to us.

As I see it, magic can appear in many forms, but it always comes through other people. It is operating when, out of the blue, a long-lost friend calls up just at the moment we needed to speak to him or her. It occurs when that telemarketer coincidentally shares information that we have been seeking. Magic exists when a friend says exactly what we needed to hear, or our boss gives us an unexpected, but much-needed raise.

Magic may also be present in situations that do not immediately seem to benefit us. I remember three incidents of magical fate regarding my last car. I had asked the Divine Source to help me get rid of my old blue Plymouth, which kept breaking down. I had also requested that somehow, I be able to earn enough from the car to pay for a sizable down payment on a new one (given that I didn't have any extra funds). Within the next month, I was involved in three accidents. In each case, the other party was at fault and no one was hurt; in each case, the only damage was to my car. The final blow totaled the car. My insurers not only took my old blue Plymouth, but paid me enough to buy a brand new vehicle (which, incidentally, has only required $50 in repair bills in three years).

Magic is a spiritual healing force, even though it uses people as delivery vehicles. The key to magic is to trust people. I am not talking about being naive or ignorant; it is important to know who is trustworthy and who is not. The best way to engineer magic is to be clear about the healing or manifesting need, then be open to allowing the Divine Source to work through the appropriate, safe person.

Miracles are obviously connected with the divine. The trouble is, few of us recognize the presence of miracles in our current lives. Unless we open to them, believe in them, and notice them when they occur, we will probably experience few miracles. My theory is that most of us manifest and heal backwards. We make gains from 90 percent work, 9.9 percent magic, and if we are lucky, .1 percent miracles. I think it is supposed to be the other way around—90 percent miracles, 9.9 percent magic and .1 percent work.

The key to opening ourselves to miracles is to appropriately define them. A miracle is any occurrence that furthers us on our path to purpose or completion, and that is engineered by the Divine Source energy. For a miracle to occur, our will must be out of the way. We must stop insisting that our goal must be met a certain way or through a certain person. We cannot afford to believe that our long-term mate must be that great-looking woman or man we met at the last party. We cannot inform the universe that our book must be published by this or that publisher. Remember, people have free will. If you are counting on a certain company to hire you so that through it you can fulfill your goals, you may be seriously disappointed. Because each and every person within that company has free will, they could turn you down, or they may hire you, and you find you hate the job.

If we block our spirit by being attached to the "how," we may not let our spirit design a situation that will really work for us. We can—in fact, we must—state our dreams and desires. However, holding on to a certain path, person, or process only limits the maneuvering ability of our spiritual self, energies, guides, and the Divine Source itself. When we state our needs and then, following our principles, surrender the "how" to the universe, we move into a state of letting go. When we stop trying to make it happen and instead let it happen, we create an enormous potential for miracles.

These miracles or gifts of grace, as some people call them, may appear minuscule or gigantic. I have seen miracles ranging from finding the fifty cents needed for that much-desired can of soda pop, to someone recovering from cancer before my very eyes. Noticing miracles builds our faith in them. The more faith we have, the more miracles we get. Faith is about trusting other people, the Divine Source, and the self that wants to give us what we desire. Seen this way, miracles are something you can train yourself to get.

I had one of my classes try an experiment. The participants were to write down any dreams or wishes they would like manifested within the next month. We then set these lists aside. The next assignment was to forget these goals and concentrate instead on what miracles occurred in their lives during the next month. They were to keep a miracle journal in which to record each day's miracles.

After their first week, most class participants reported similar findings. They were surprised at how many small miracles occurred daily. These miracles ranged from having a squirrel perch near them when they were feeling lonely to having a car break down right in front of the neighborhood service station. Normally, they would not have noticed these miracles. Becoming more conscious allowed them to recognize these slices of reality for what they really were.

I suggested that during the next week they should broaden their horizons by actually requesting a miracle every morning upon rising. They were not yet to determine the nature of the miracle. The list of miracles reported the following week was at least ten times longer than that of the previous week. These miracles included an array of small assistances, but also included some miracles of note. A gust of wind, for instance, drove one woman inside a restaurant right before a gang of kids began shooting down the street.

Finally, we turned back to our lists of dreams and wishes. I asked the miracle makers to review their requests under the following guidelines:

1. Will getting this wish help my body, mind, and soul integrate?

2. Will getting this wish help me to love myself (and others) more?

3. Am I willing to not get this wish if achieving it injures my relationship with the Divine Source/my Divine Source self?

After the participants retooled their wishes, I then walked them through an adaptation of the Universal Guardian Principles. I had them ask themselves as honestly as possible the following:

1. Am I willing to manifest the healing I need in order to have what I desire, and to heal through the manifestation of this desire?

2. Am I willing to change what needs to be changed to allow this desire to come true? (This is the work component of the request.)

3. Am I willing to let go of my images and ideas about how this desire should manifest, and allow it to happen?

4. Am I willing to hold myself in a state of surrender and openness?

5. Am I willing to have my perceptions of myself change so I can further love myself?

6. Am I willing to be happy even before I am graced with this wish?

I didn't see nor hear from the participants for a full two weeks. Was I surprised when they bounded in for our last class session! Their reports were amazing. During the previous two weeks, one woman had been offered a medical practice in a different city, and had accepted it. Her request had been to find a more meaningful work environment in another town. Another had made peace with long-term abuse issues following a series of dreams and revelations. Her request was to heal from her childhood abuse. Another woman had made the decision to quit her job after receiving in the mail an unsolicited information packet about a school. She had wanted career direction. The list went on and on.

We can, of course, devote most of our attention to working hard, to making things happen. We could also allow ourselves to open ourselves to magic, to receiving help from others. We could ask for and expect miracles, miracles that can pour like mana from the sky, tangible, everyday, reality-based miracles. It is up to us.

Perhaps the most important information to remember about spiritual practices is that, ultimately, they are about bettering our quality of life through spiritual assistance. Our body, mind, and soul require integration if we are to fully be our true selves, and to enjoy the lives we have been given. This integrating process is most effectively undertaken when we realize that we are of and from the Divine Source. For this reason, we can knit our wounds and dreams with the fabric of Spirit.

Direct Spiritual Energy Techniques: The Body and Spiritual Healing

We can apply the idea of work, magic, and miracles in direct spiritual energy manipulations. The first and most obvious transmission vehicle for spiritual energies is the physical body itself. When working with the body, we are basically involving ourselves with meeting the body's needs. The primary body needs are:

1. Food.
2. Shelter.
3. Clothing.
4. Air and water.
5. Touch/love.

Spiritual energy can be transmitted through any of these vehicles, to heal problems or manifest desires not only of the body, but also those of the mind and soul.

Food

Food has frequently played a dual physical and spiritual role. Consider how many cultural rules there are regarding food. The Jewish tradition forbids eating pork, the Hindu forbids eating beef, and many Native American tribes prohibit foods that are not sacred. Conversely, there are foods that bestow spiritual power. Ethnic ceremonies are often based on stringent rules regarding what foods to serve. While conducting two weeks of shamanic ceremony in Peru, I was put on an *icaro*, or medicine man's, purification diet. Refraining from salt, sugar, and heavy meats, I was given foods known for creating a healthy body and open psyche. Before participating in Native American sweat lodges, I was instructed to fast. A Costa Rican shaman told me to refrain from all meats and always eat yams before giving a healing. On the other hand, Moroccan magical beliefs involve a concept known as *kimia*, which multiplies food.

Even Caucasian cultures have their spiritual food traditions. Who could imagine an Easter without ham or a Thanksgiving without turkey? It's a standard American practice to pray over food before eating.

I have often had clients address physical concerns spiritualizing their approach to food. This technique is particularly helpful for issues centered on weight, body image, diabetes, or terminal illnesses which affect the appetite or physical body weight. Often, I have encouraged them to choose one of the spiritual energy points as a focus and to assign particular foods with that value.

For instance, I had one client who was significantly overweight. Since childhood, she had eaten to deny her fears. Though I didn't tell her we were working with an actual energy point, I suggested that Faith might help her balance her fears. She worked out ways to eat in faith, saying affirmations such as "I'll always have what I need" and "I can trust that this food will nurture my ability to be strong." She also decided to start eating foods that would put her in touch with her faith in herself rather than food that would "space her out." With time, she began eating less compulsively, lost some weight, and eventually joined an eating disorder program, prepared to address her emotional issues.

Shelter

Since humankind emerged, shelter has been seen as a vehicle for spiritual growth. I have been in sanctuaries all over the world and can testify to their power. There are the Indian *kivas*, underground shelters in which people cleanse, heal, pray, and communicate with ancestors. Japanese monasteries and temples hold energies capable of salving and renewing one's spirit. I have worshiped in Jewish temples, German cathedrals, and Norwegian *staves*. I have walked the grounds of ancient ruins that, after centuries, still speak of the sacred ways. There are the *fogues* in the British Isles, houses of the dead in which prayers were answered. There are the temples in Greece through which oracles channeled prophecies. There are the Mayan caves in which the gods of the underworld connected with the people of the physical world. There are the burial mounds throughout Europe, and the pyramids in Egypt and Central America.

Then there is the most sacred dwelling place of all—the home. I have seen clients, friends, and myself physically benefit by considering the sacred in their surroundings. Gerald, a professor, complained of being too stressed out at work to do his job well. When he brought into his work space objects which he considered spiritual, including rocks and a bear rug, he reported a significant improvement in his work life and attitude. Mary, a mother of three young children, was beside herself with daily stress. She formed a "Mom's Place," a spot in one corner of the family room where she could meditate. When she was there, she was to be left alone. Using it made her stress levels go down. Another client created a sanctuary of plants, beautiful rocks, and a small water fountain to establish a natural sacred space in her home and provide a grounded, peaceful air to her entire home.

Again, I often encourage the connection between the concepts represented by the spiritual energy points and the environment. According to the *feng shui* system, an Asian approach to energy management, whatever you put in the left, back corner of the room will be accentuated in your life. I encourage clients who have abundance issues to hang a representation or symbol of what they want in this corner, such as a picture of a loving relationship or a coin. I have experienced fast and real results from this method and others.

By spiritualizing food and shelter, especially in conjunction with the spiritual energy points, we can encourage both manifesting and healing. In a direct fashion, we can change our diet and improve our immune system. We can eliminate a toxic substance and improve our health. More metaphysically, when we nourish ourselves with food that is spiritual, our physical bodies can transform. When we make our living place an altar space, all that we think and do within our own walls becomes a reflection of peace.

Clothing, Air, and Water

Clothing, air, and water are material substances that can also hold spiritual properties and potentials. I am hard-pressed to find a woman who wouldn't admit that she is what she wears, or at least that her clothes can determine her mood. Apparel and accessories have always been a part of ceremony and meaning, from initiation and funeral rites to weddings and births. Air and water, too, join the elemental forces of fire, earth, and in some cultures, wood and iron, as spiritualized forms of matter. Of course, having decent air and water can affect our health and well-being.

Touch

The most ambiguous need of the body is touch. Though many of us still struggle to believe that touch is a need (which it is), we typically think of touch-related professions when we think of spiritual healing. Hands-on healers use touch as a spiritual transmission vehicle all the time. So do MariEl, Reiki, or Kofutu healers, many of whom use mind symbols to link with spiritual energy. Chiropractors, acupuncturists, shamans, and witch doctors use touch as well. Even AMA-approved medical practitioners rely on touch; notice this next time you get an annual exam.

The most beneficial touch-related healing occurs when the healer, consciously or unconsciously, runs spiritual energy into the physical and back again. I have seen physical, mental, and emotional issues clear up, evaporate, or transform, in response to simple touch techniques. However, to be an effective spiritual healing tool, this touch must be employed as a channel for the Divine Source.

Touch can also be a necessary ingredient for manifesting the needs of the body, as well the mind, soul, and Divine Source self. An artist touches stone to fashion a sculpture. A business person touches the computer to prepare a report. Nearly all of us interact with the physical components of our environment to construct, build, or make the objects, forms, or materials that we need.

Some people worry that touch will cause further injury. Psychiatrists, for instance, are not legally allowed to touch their clients. Often, sexual or physical abuse victims shy away from touch to avoid further traumas. Conversely, I have seen that appropriate touch can legitimately heal emotional and physical wounds. Through hands-on healing, I have helped clients shrink growths, reduce swelling, and eliminate pain. I have seen clients recall painful memories upon pressure-point stimulation, thus allowing themselves to work through their issues.

I remember one of my most bizarre experiences that enabled touch to heal me. I was receiving an acupuncture treatment in Belize, and the healer's room was located on the site of a Mayan ruin. Jenkins, the healer, stuck me full of needles, then lit a tobacco-like substance to help the purification process. He placed this substance between my toes. As I lay there "smoking," I remembered an incident in which I had been burned by a cigarette as a child. As I recalled, relived, and released this experience, I literally felt the subsequent tension in my body lift. It has been gone ever since that day.

I like to remind my students that touch is not only a physical function. Because we are revolving doors, our energy also touches other people. Our auras often interact with each other, as do our chakras. Because our spiritual energy points exist outside of the space/time continuum, they are always interrelating with those of others. Often, I perform healings while seated across the room from a client. In fact, I work on the phone each week with five to ten clients who live in other states. Much to their amazement, I can read their energy as clearly as if they were right next to me, because I can touch the spiritual energy points and work from that level.

Food, shelter, clothing, air, water, and touch fulfill our body's basic needs, but have even more impact if we open to the spiritual values and energies that can be channeled through the body's physical processes.

The Mind and Spiritual Healing

The mind also responds to spiritual energy, and can serve as a vehicle for spiritual healing. When we think of our mind's needs, we think of a different list than that associated with the body. Our mind requires the following:

1. Learning.

2. Stimulation.

3. Thought.

4. Appropriate attitude.

5. Functional beliefs to serve as a framework for the above.

Learning is an obvious human need. As children, we were born with the drive to learn. We only have to look at the intense growth cycles of children to see that, if provided a supportive, stimulating environment and solid learning opportunities, a child will eagerly fulfill this innate drive to grow and learn.

From learning comes thought. As children, we formed ideas, opinions, and constructs as glasses or filters through which to understand the world and our place within it. These thoughts were partly determined by our own internal world and partly from our perceptions of the world around us. The interaction between our internal and external world determined our attitudes. Underneath all of these mind-related components lay our beliefs, our philosophical understandings of ourselves, others, and the universe.

To grow correctly, our maturing mind required an input of information that would lead to health and well-being. It also needed a process for assimilating, interpreting, and disseminating data. While we probably received data and support that were healthy and helpful, most of us were probably also exposed to information and systems that left us feeling bad about ourselves.

Changing this condition in adulthood can be a slow and arduous process. We could undo all that has been done by peeling back the learning layers. Step by step, we could re-analyze, reassess, reassemble, and reformulate every single thought, attitude, idea, or learning we have ever digested and start from scratch. We could also bypass most of this hard work by turning to magic—opening to relationships that will help us from this point on. People such as friends, therapists, and educators often qualify as the magicians in this healing and manifesting process.

Even better, we could open to spiritual data and energies and let the Divine Source energy do the work for us. When we open this way, positive thinking, attitude, and knowledge are ours. We are led to information sources that will meet our needs.

The Soul and Spiritual Healing

The soul is the most obvious vehicle for channeling spiritual energy. In my view, the basic idea behind soul work is that illness or lack stems from discordance within the soul. In *Dreamtime and Inner Space*, Holger Kalweit says that most shaman-based societies believe that "the cause of illnesses reside in the soul body. Healing must therefore concentrate on harmonizing this soul body" (Kalweit, 29).

Many spiritual healers believe that our soul should perform all of our healing or manifesting work for us. Many indigenous cultures work directly with the soul, applying spiritual healing principles. Most of my learning in these cultures relates to shamanism. I have been amazed at the changes that have occurred when I have applied some of the cross-cultural soul techniques I have seen demonstrated. I've been fortunate enough to visit real shamans in other countries, but on a day-to-day basis, however, working with these shamans isn't a possibility. That is why I believe we need to become our own shamans.

Spiritual healing can be about being our own shaman or assisting another person in this capacity. A shaman walks between the physical and spiritual worlds in order to help individuals heal physical and spiritual issues. We can all serve this function if we are willing to talk with the soul—our own or someone else's—and to become its therapist or witness. We must ask the soul what it needs in order to repair itself after trauma, or from the pain of separation from the body, mind, or Divine Source. We might also need to negotiate new working relationships between these various components of self.

I think that most of our souls hold misunderstandings about their places in the universe, doubt their deservedness of material wealth and health, and have mixed feelings about inhabiting a body in the first place. Therefore, I believe that the soul itself needs energy for spiritual healing and manifesting.

Typically, I have found that soul injuries result from trauma, fear, or mistrust. The soul may respond to these traumas in many ways. It may fragment, weakening and debilitating itself. Fragments can remain within the physical self, or become stuck, lost, or glued into past lives, previous experiences, or other realities. When fragments leave the body, the physical self is left unprotected. If a fragment hides within a part of the body, the unfilled part of the body is left unguarded. If a fragment becomes stuck in another time period or in another person or object, the "you" in your current life may feel inexplicably drawn to the time period, person, or object, holding the soul piece.

A trauma can also cause a soul to partially or fully leave the body. I find this often in clients who have been abused. Energetically, I perceive voids in the body or aura. For instance, schizophrenics look void from the neck down. Typically, I see the soul of a schizophrenic as a milky-colored form, attached from the neck up and sometimes broken into two or more distinct shapes over the head. Sometimes the soul remains this way in the body until it is hooked by an experience familiar to that which caused the original trauma. At this point, it often dissociates or completely flies out of the body until calm is restored.

The first step in the shamanistic work of soul healing is determining the current state of the soul. When acting as a shaman for myself or someone else, I usually check to see if the soul is:

1. Stuck in a pocket within the body.

2. Dissociated from the body, perhaps still attached by a cord.

3. Fragmented, with different pieces in different places.

4. Hiding in a past life or childhood experience.

5. Projected into the future.

6. Only partially connected to the body.

7. Fully intact within the body.

When locating a soul, our shaman self may experience the soul in visual form or sense inaudible words. Sometimes communication takes place by writing or by simply experiencing feelings. These same practices can be used to repair or recognize the relationships between the body, mind, soul, and the Divine Source.

Sometimes, I have clients check for the where-abouts of their souls, especially if they are experiencing a lot of fear, indecisiveness, frustration, or working through childhood issues. I clearly recall the impact reported by one woman who found part of her soul dangling by a cord in the universe. Knowing life would be scary, it had refused to enter her body. After she convinced it that she needed it inside her body in order to be better connected to the power of Spirit, she reeled it in. She shook for two or three days, then told me, "I finally began to learn who I was! I've never been so happy or so strong!"

Once the state of the soul is diagnosed, the job of the shaman begins. When the soul is ill, cursed, or unable to operate, the shamans of most indigenous groups respond with soul healing, either for the community or the individuals within it. Sometimes individuals are even healed within the community. This is true in many tribal cultures, such as the Australian aborigines, African Zulus, and African Kung. The latter group, for instance, holds group dances. A dancer dances to reach *kia*, a trance-like state which enables him or her to pull *num*, the boiling snake energy of healing, up their spine. In *Boiling Energy: Community Healing Among the Kalahari Kung*, Richard Katz tells of Kung who can control this energy to "apply the num to healing." They pull *twe* or heal while in the state of kia because they can then "see things you must pull out, like the death thing the god has put in people. You see people properly, just as they are" (Katz, Richard. Boston: Harvard College, 1982, 42). The healers see the soul issues, and sometimes must even leave their bodies to fetch the errant or sick soul. Hence, shamans reflect the part of us that can walk both worlds, something we must all do to achieve true completion.

I often do similar group work for clients. I recently conducted a group shamanic healing for a woman who was suicidal. Within the presence of warm and supportive people, she left her body and searched for her soul, which she found huddled near the Divine Source, too scared to come into her body. She convinced the soul to come into her. The next thing we knew, she jerked violently, and her neck reddened. Previous aches and pains disappeared, as did her desire to die. She has had no suicidal tendencies since then.

Of course, soul healings are more frequently done in private, as our culture is often frightened by magic. One woman attending this group-healing session approached me later for a one-on-one session, saying she felt "too embarrassed" to be so exposed. (I was not surprised; she was a sexual abuse victim.) She felt unable to have a good relationship, make decisions, or even recover from the trauma. When I asked her to look for her soul, she found that it was only partially connected to her body, and on it was a dark spot. Upon seeing this, my client burst into tears, and sobbing, told me she'd never believed that God loved her because she had been "dirtied." Through the session, she began to heal this idea, and her soul returned to her body. Her work in therapy rapidly progressed after this session, and when last I saw her, she said she was finally beginning to think she could live a normal life.

The final step in soul work is to assign the body, mind, and soul a project through which they can iron out their differences. I have given assignments such as reap abundance, build a solid marriage, heal a broken leg, or make a decision. Ultimately, I want these three entities to integrate, meaning that I want the whole to have integrity. I have found that when each of these three aspects feels listened to, heard, noticed, and important, our decisions automatically create our highest good, because they have more integrity.

As these three aspects become more and more blended, it becomes more difficult to distinguish between their voices. At this point, many of my clients report hearing a new voice, one that is often quite wise, or they begin to have white-light experiences, in which they see or feel the amazing power of the Divine Source's white light. Whatever the case, these symptoms mean that the essence is slowly beginning to emerge as the primary self. This is what we want.

Origins of Spiritual Healing Energy

At any point during a spiritual healing or manifesting process, I may encourage a client to work directly with one of the spiritual energy bodies. It is often helpful to focus a spiritual energy point on a particular chakra, ray, principle, auric layer, and, always, the Divine Source, in response to a specific concern. This focus can illuminate the root cause of an issue or concern, and thus shed light on a solution. It can also move us from the level of work to the level of magic and miracles.

These top energy points can be very powerful. Personally, I use great care when I work with them, because I greatly respect their intensity. A few years ago, when I was first experimenting with the thirty-two energy center system, I went through a experience that firmly convinced me of the power latent within these higher energy points.

During the middle of a summer day, I decided to take a walk. There were many people around until I reached a bend near the river close to my home. I was attacked. In the middle of the fray, I desperately called upon the power of the Divine Source through the thirty-second energy point, Grace. My attacker suddenly looked up over the water. Through his eyes, I saw a wicked, horrible-looking woman scolding him. With my own sight, I saw Christ. The man ran off. There was no flesh and blood person in sight. I hobbled home, and when I arrived, a nurse was ringing at my door. She had gotten my name from someone and "coincidentally" decided to stop by to check out my work. As she nursed me, I called the police. There was a squad car in the vicinity. The policeman who arrived told me that he was a healer "on the side" and gave me a "shot" of energy. I worked further with the thirty-second energy point that day, and my wounds, which a doctor had said would take weeks to heal, were gone within two days. While I can't prove that this energy really saved me, this experience alone showed me the power of calling upon spiritual energy.

Spiritual Energy and the Chakras

The greatest impact can be achieved by bringing energy through the top spiritual chakras and energy points into our lower chakras. One of my clients, for instance, was experiencing a work-related problem. All Jay's ideas and actions were met by friction. We began our work by analyzing the issues. He searched his past for patterns, then learned communication skills applicable to his job. Though progress was slow, he was seeing changes. However, we didn't stop there; we moved to the level of magic. He made a serious commitment to asking his soul to open to those around him. On the physical level, he asked them for project input and shared with them in loving ways. His situation drastically improved. As he built bridges, others crossed them. He wanted more, so he tackled the issue from a spiritual perspective. I saw him move to the plane of miracles as soon as he honestly searched for the spiritual energies that would alleviate and heal this situation. He began to check in daily with his intuition. He then chose several spiritual energy points on which to concentrate, and opened himself to the points of Peace, Faith, and Alignment. He received both a raise and a promotion. More important, he felt better about himself.

Another client reported success by tapping into these spiritual points to alleviate a work matter. For years, Dora's relationship with her boss had been strained. She had finally arrived at the conclusion she needed to "get out from under." We perceived that her core resistance was affiliated with her heart; she felt guilty and scared whenever she asserted herself. When she drew Faith and Wisdom into her heart, it seemed to me that the room literally glowed. A week later, she was offered a new position within the company, reporting to a different boss.

Spiritual Energy and the Auric Layers

Working with the auric layers is similar to working with the energy center system. Again, we can do it the hard way by searching for holes, blocks, resistance points. We can become magical about it by seeking assistance and help, and requesting that relationships help us heal the problem areas. We can also move to the level of miracles. Remember, the outer layers of the aura interface with the spiritual, and the inner layers connect with the concrete. By linking the outer with the inner layers, and connecting both with the desire to receive the correct Divine Source information or energies, we can alter our energy systems, and therefore alter situations.

I performed such a feat in Wales. At the time, I was afflicted with a skin disorder. I decided that I was willing to allow the Divine Source energy to help me, so I simply made that statement and let it go. For two days, I was plagued by what I perceived to be fairies. A bridge seemed to disappear, as did two hours of one of my journeys. Out of the blue, my headlights would flash. I would get lost in fog, circling around and around the same point. The situation culminated in a little town called Castletown. There, I linked my first auric layer with the outer auric layer, and using guided imagery, switched the polarities, asking that the two share their understanding with each other.

Suddenly I found I had grown a cyst about an inch and a half long. When I went home, the physicians could not determine what it was. I was about to have the cyst surgically removed, when I realized that if I could trigger its original growth, I could also trigger its reduction. I linked both first and outer auric layers to the Divine Source and switched their polarities back. The cyst disappeared within thirty minutes, as did my initial skin condition.

Spiritual Energy and Rays

Yet another means for spiritual healing is to utilize the powerful energies of the rays. Harnessing the power and influence of these energies can provide us with the energy necessary to clear out the spiritual blocks that prevent our full access to spiritual energies. We have already discussed the various properties of the rays. Suffice it to say that at any time during the day we can request assistance from any one or all of the rays any form of spiritual guidance. The stronger our request, the greater our need, the clearer we are regarding our need, the swifter the response.

These and other methods are available for healing and manifesting. They may all take place by following the Universal Guardian Principles or steps for transformation. What exactly can we heal or manifest through spiritual work? Just good feelings or a better connection to our higher self? No. We can open ourselves to healing and manifesting anything by working with these higher frequency energies—better relationships, a good job, a healthier body, a new home. How about a few good times?

EXERCISE
Keeping a Miracle Journal

A. Write a one-week wish list. Within one week, what would you like to see healed or manifested within your life? Go over the list of questions contained in this chapter to help you define and refine these wishes, so that you know they speak to your highest good. Set these wishes aside.

B. Create a "Miracle Journal" for yourself. Every evening, record the miracles that you saw or felt took place. Every morning, request miracles to help you gain your wishes.

C. At the end of the week, review your wish list and your Miracle Journal. What headway did you make, or what headway was made for you this week? If your wishes have not been completely fulfilled, review them. Are they too broad, too narrow? Do they really describe a heart's desire, or are they just something you think you should want?

D. Go through the Guardian Principles and move to a place of acceptance. Rewrite any wishes that haven't come true and, without putting a time period on them, return to keeping your Miracle Journal until you automatically request, notice, and feel grateful for the miracles present in your life.

Chapter Ten

Working With the Body: The Key Points

When healing or manifesting, one of the most beneficial physical techniques to use is to focus on the spine. All of our fundamental energy bodies connect to the spine. The backs and the fronts of the in-body energy centers link to the spine. The rays enter through spinal contacts, and the auric layers connect to the chakras which align on the spine. The spine tracks with our childhood development issues. The spine is the literal backbone of any and all physical healing.

The spine is also a central point for connecting our physical and spiritual energy bodies. I have uncovered and practiced with a system that does this very well. I call it the **Key Point System**. The idea behind this system is that each of the thirty-two energy centers is linked to a specific vertebra, with an additional energy connecting to the top vertebra.

The basis for the Key Point System is the idea that the spine serves as the staff of life for our entire energy system. The structure of the spine supports this point of view. From a front view, the spine looks like two pyramids joined together at their bases. The upper section is formed by the vertebrae from the second cervical to the last lumbar, and the lower section is formed by the sacrum and coccyx. *Gray's Anatomy* says the upper pyramid is constructed of three smaller pyramids. Physically, the pyramidal structure is one of the most solid on earth. Metaphysically, the pyramid is often considered to be a magical construct, a form through which we are able to channel and ground energies. Our spine makes use of both these physical and metaphysical abilities as it connects matter and spirit. What better unit upon which to work, both for healing and manifesting reasons, than the spine itself?

In general, I believe the energy centers link to the following vertebrae (figure 10a, color pages):

Spinal Area	Vertebra	Related Energy Center
Coccygeal	Fourth (lowest)	Tenth Chakra
	Third	First Chakra
	Second	Second Chakra
	First	Third Chakra
Sacral	Fifth	Fourth Chakra
	Fourth	Fifth Chakra
	Third	Sixth Chakra
	Second	Seventh Chakra
	First	Eighth Chakra
Lumbar	Fifth	Ninth Chakra
	Fourth	Eleventh Chakra
	Third	Twelfth Chakra
	Second	Point 13
	First	Point 14
Thoracic	Twelfth	Point 15
	Eleventh	Point 16
	Tenth	Point 17
	Ninth	Point 18
	Eighth	Point 19
	Seventh	Point 20
	Sixth	Point 21
	Fifth	Point 22
	Fourth	Point 23
	Third	Point 24
	Second	Point 25
	First	Point 26
Cervical	Seventh	Point 27
	Sixth	Point 28
	Fifth	Point 29
	Fourth	Point 30
	Third	Point 31
	Second	Point 32
	First	Principle of the 33rd

We can work the spine in a general or abstract fashion, such as laying hands on the in-body chakric areas or concentrating on the particular vertebra to clear a specific issue. We can also work on a vertebrae group, and thus affect a certain type of issue. To better understand this system and therefore our entire human energy system, we need to comprehend each vertebrae group.

The Coccygeal Vertebrae

These four vertebrae form within us at an early age, differentiating while we are still within the womb. When we are young, the coccygeal vertebrae and the sacral vertebrae consist of nine separate pieces. When we become an adult, these bones unite to form two larger bones, five of which enter the sacrum and four which form the coccyx itself (figure 10b).

The coccyx is the most rudimentary part of our spine. It is composed of four segments or vertebrae, the first or top piece being the largest and the last or fourth being the smallest. The coccyx, commonly called the tailbone, performs critical physical and metaphysical functions. Most biologists assign it the function of providing us balance and protection. Metaphysically, I believe it relates to our most basic self and is associated with our reproductive capacities.

The tail end of the vertebrae, the first coccygeal vertebra, relates to our tenth chakra. It grounds us into this reality and serves as the access point for the red kundalini energy.

Kundalini itself, in this system, is associated with a higher spiritual energy center. Through the nineteenth spiritual energy center of Kundalini, we receive the undiluted form of raw life energy. Kundalini or snake energy is an available and necessary component of all developmental life stages. It jump starts us upon conception, and it keeps us alive during our early years. It awakens our sexuality, and it energizes our body to achieve our purpose. Through the tenth (and first) chakras, we receive one aspect of the total kundalini—the red kundalini, which feeds our material self.

Men and women process red kundalini differently, even though the entry point of this energy is the same for both. I have found that the male energy system is usually geared toward first-chakra achievement. As they mature, most men center their identity in achievements related to physical will, which includes sexual, material, and physical prowess. Typically, the call to transcend this first chakra focus occurs after the completion of grounding, which happens from ages thirty-five to forty-two during the tenth-chakra concentration. I believe this transcendence is completed in men when the first chakra cycles back again at age fifty-six.

This Western society first chakra bias partially stems from cultural prejudices, but it is also incorporated within souls that choose to be male. First chakra energy is extremely important; it builds families, cities, and countries.

Figure 10b.

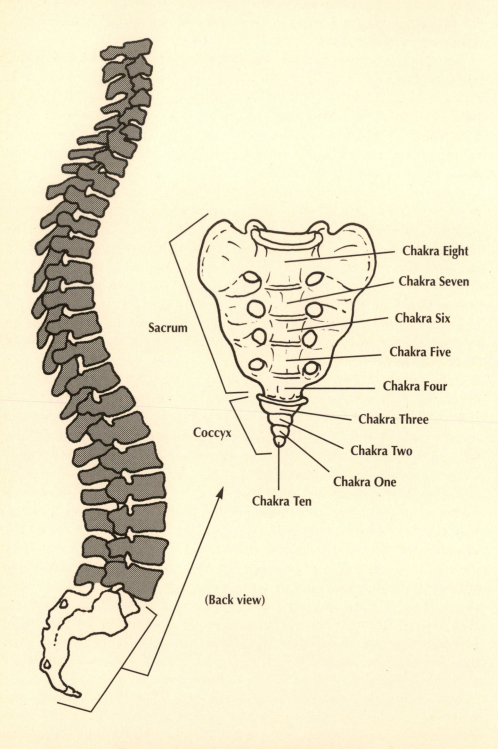

Sacrum

Coccyx

Chakra Eight

Chakra Seven

Chakra Six

Chakra Five

Chakra Four

Chakra Three

Chakra Two

Chakra One

Chakra Ten

(Back view)

**The coccygeal and sacral vertebrae,
and their chakric connections.**

It also lends itself to violence and abusive behaviors. Time and time again, my male clients aged forty-plus talk about how scared they are of maturing, for to mature, they will have to face their own feelings of being hurt, or worse, of hurting someone.

I think it is this fear, combined with cultural and familial blocks, that cause so many mystics to bemoan the dangers of allowing the kundalini to rise. In fact, there is a widespread idea that if not properly controlled, kundalini initiation can injure the psyche or soul, or even kill someone. Leadbeater sternly advises that "no one should experiment with it (kundalini) without definite instruction from a teacher…for the dangers connected with it are very real and terribly serious" (Leadbeater, 81–83).

This belief makes sense if we remember that the majority of these mystics are men, and that they are speaking to men. Therefore, most warnings relate to men's experiences of the kundalini awakening. As kundalini passes through the tenth chakra and into the base of the coccyx, it stimulates the entire first chakra region. Any unresolved primal, maternal, sexual, or success issues become stimulated, and the effect can be explosive in first-chakra-centered individuals.

Ultimately, men need to move their center of power and kundalini processing from the coccyx to the third chakra, which is regulated by the dorsal (thoracic) region. This shift would involve processing kundalini in the eighth dorsal vertebra, through which spiritual, not just physical, kundalini may be channeled. (The eighth dorsal or thoracic vertebra is the lock-in point for the Kundalini spiritual energy center.) This transference would also enable men to positively address any ego or low self-esteem issues stored in their third chakra. Through the appropriate use of kundalini power, true personal power can be realized.

I have been present with men who have tapped into their kundalini. In fact, I witnessed three such awakenings in one day. Each man literally went berserk with the rising of the energy. As a woman, I felt frightened by their intense screaming, sexual innuendoes, and shaking. As a healer, I forced them to carry the snake energy straight into their third chakras, where I assisted them with opening to the Kundalini energy point. I then guided them to a different form of kundalini—the golden kundalini—which was accessible through their seventh chakra. (See the "Cervical Vertebrae" section in this chapter.) Essentially, I helped them loop the red and golden kundalinis together. Immediately, these men calmed down. During the next few weeks, they reported increased energy, awareness of gifts and goals, and a new sense of calm.

Women can also tap into red kundalini through their base coccyx vertebrae, but many women fail to ever completely open to this energy. This is partly due to strong societal judgments about women's sexuality and cultural conditioning that represses women's drive for material success. Religious views that emphasize that women's basic nature is evil certainly do not help matters. When a woman does allow her red kundalini to enter, I have found that she needs to use this energy differently than a man does. If she doesn't, she runs a risk experienced by one of my clients.

A young mother of three, Beth had for years represented herself as a stereotypical good girl. Her husband, a successful lawyer, spent very little time at home, and she was lonely. Two events precipitated the opening of her kundalini. First, she began recalling sexual-abuse memories. After two years working with me and a licensed professional, she began to feel more whole in relation to these traumas. She continually expressed to me, her friends, and her husband an increased desire for companionship, but her husband paid no attention. Then she met a motorcycle racer, and every single sexual cell in her body sprang to life. The kundalini was rising, but driving her crazy. She went so far as to leave in the middle of the night one time to seek this man hundreds of miles away.

A male approach to this rise in kundalini would not have helped Beth. To have her try and leapfrog this energy to her third chakra would have prevented her from finding her true power, the creative power that all women have. This power lays latent in a woman's uterus or second chakra. To have had her simply enjoy her awakened first chakra would have endangered her social standing and legal rights as a mother. Beth has since learned to handle her energy in a mature fashion, although she still struggles with it. She has begun to write a book, a task which appropriately directs and uses this awkward first chakra energy.

While the second chakra is obviously critical to men, it is the ultimate center for women. As explained to Carlos Castenada by la Gorda, a fellow student of sorcerer don Juan, a woman's method of power "Has to come from her womb, because that's her center." Don Juan, in Castenada's books, frequently makes reference to women as potentially more powerful than men because of the magnitude of the womb as a power center. Also, because the secret of warriorism is invisibility or selflessness, women have another advantage. As another of don Juan's students, Florinda, says, "I'm a woman, and that gives me a splendid advantage. I'm not accountable." Women's social invisibility liberates them to walk the path of power (Castaneda, Carlos. *The Eagle's Gift*. New York: Pocket Books/Washington Square Press, 1981, 136, 269).

A woman's kundalini must ultimately mold and meld more completely into her body than a man's. I believe this idea is supported by the fact that as a woman ages, her coccygeal vertebrae tend to merge with her sacrum. This fusion focuses her center of gravity and identity on her birthing center from which she must constantly draw the energy she needs for daily life. As the natural cycles of menstruation add to this need for constant energy renewal, the need for a strong energy source seems obvious. Red kundalini must feed this process; perhaps this is the purpose for which kundalini was even conceived. In *Uncoiling the Snake*, Janet Balaskas says kundalini energy belongs to women "through our biological processes of bleeding and birthing." Her statement that "kundalini is the foundation for our strength, courage, psychic power, and creativity" furthers the case that kundalini must stoke women's second chakra (Balaskas, Janet. "The Feminine Power of Birth." In *Uncoiling the Snake*, edited by Vicki Noble. New York: HarperCollins, 1993).

As the red kundalini or life energy passes through its four initial stages, symbolized by the four coccygeal vertebrae, we complete the initial entrance path of our own and the Divine Source's material energy.

The Sacral Vertebrae

We now move on to the next stage of growth, represented by the sacral spinal area. For women, this is the area of power. For men, this is the area of feelings.

The sacrum or hipbone is formed by the union of five vertebrae (figure 10b). In general, this vertebral area covers the second chakra area of the body. It forms the chalice that holds the *chi* or life energy that is poured in from the first chakra. This area is physically and metaphysically important to women and to men, but in different ways. For women, this spinal area regulates their life energy and serves as the pool from which they draw life energy for others, including babies, children, and life-purpose tasks. In men, this is the center for refining and maturing their physical energies. Here, feelings spill into passion, thus tempering drive, will, and action. In both sexes, this bone takes until age thirty to develop. At completion, it is shorter and wider in women than in men, underscoring that its function is different from gender to gender.

According to the Key Point System, the sacral vertebrae allow integration of Chakras Four through Eight into this, the creative center, of the body. I apply this information in many ways. First, it tells me that if a client is experiencing second chakra issues, such as low back pain, colitis, the flu, kidney or ovarian problems, he or she may also be reflecting issues related to one of the chakras integrating within that area. For instance, a client's colitis may relate to feelings being denied about a relationship (fourth-chakra vertebrae). Another client's ovarian cysts could pertain to repressed self-expression (fifth-chakra vertebrae). Low back pain might be a way for another client to keep himself from being physically active and looking fit, healthy, and attractive (a sixth-chakra vertebrae, self-image issue). Perhaps another client's kidney stones reflect childhood beliefs that it is not okay to do what she wants to do (seventh-chakra vertebrae), or the stones might relate to a past-life issue (eighth chakra).

Being able to differentiate issues to such a minute level is what makes this procedure helpful. If I am working on a client who seems to be experiencing second-chakra versus fourth-chakra difficulties, I can isolate the pertinent vertebrae. Yes, it can be difficult to actually pinpoint the correct vertebrae. (especially during Minnesota winters, when everyone wears thick sweaters). I may have the client picture these vertebrae in his or her own mind, either realistically or pictorially, or I may lay my hands over the entire chakra and energetically feel for the critical vertebrae. Typically, I like to have clients picture, touch, or diagnose their own issues. Healing, especially when conducted on the lower chakras, which often hold abuse or victimization issues, must be a self-empowering process.

I once worked with a female client, Marcy, who was suicidal. Yet another relationship had bit the dust, and she didn't want to go on. She experienced considerable low back pain and had been menstruating for a week longer than usual. In addition, she was unable to control her intense mood swings.

I asked Marcy to look within and find the root of her issues. She gasped, informing me that there was an incredible wound in her second chakra. She had been severely abused and rejected by her father at an early age. Without prompting she listed occurrences that correlated to each of the vertebrae within the sacral system. Her issues were relationship-based (fourth chakra), caused her to swallow her feelings and needs (fifth chakra), created an extremely low body image (sixth chakra), created confusion about whether she was spiritually supposed to have a relationship or not (seventh chakra), and had past life cords with at least the current flame (eighth chakra). To heal her wound, Marcy had to face each of these painful areas. Her body immediately responded by feeling better, and the back pain eventually disappeared.

The Lumbar Vertebrae

The vertebrae in the lumbar system are some of the largest in the spine. In general, they are also broader and have fewer features than other vertebrae (figure 10c). In relation to our chakric system, this means that they are good conductors and add stability to the overall energetic system. These vertebrae overlay part of our second chakra system and connect the second to the third. Because the individual vertebrae link our ninth chakra (at the lowest point) to the fourteenth energy point, Yang (at the highest point), they lock our purpose and male and female issues into our feeling state.

The attachment of these chakras to the second-chakra area links spiritual qualities to our feelings. With regard to the ninth-chakra connection, these vertebrae lock our purpose into our feelings. We can and should be able to "feel out situations" to distinguish if they are on purpose or not.

The tenth-chakra connection enables us to ground our spiritual and material self in our feelings. The eleventh chakra relationship allows us to draw elemental energies into our feeling body, and vice versa. The attachment between our twelfth chakra and the lumbar vertebrae bonds our feelings to each and every part of our physical body. As human beings, we may not actually be our feelings, but our feelings can tell us who we are.

The thirteenth and fourteenth energy point connections explain why many of our gender issues, especially those relating to our femininity or masculinity, affect our feeling state, and conversely, why our feelings can affect our views of our own femininity or masculinity. In general, the lumbar vertebrae connect our feelings to all aspects of our human condition, assisting

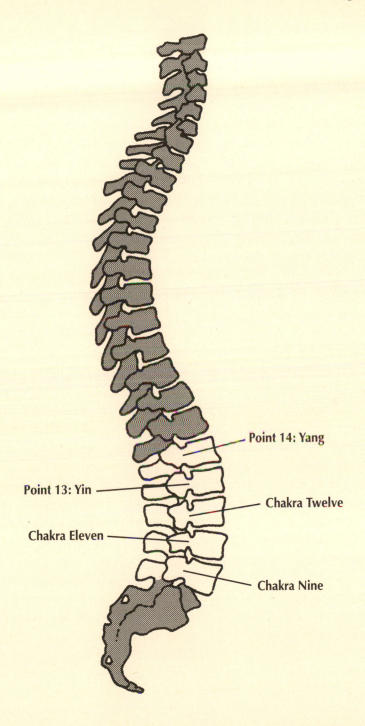

Point 14: Yang

Point 13: Yin

Chakra Twelve

Chakra Eleven

Chakra Nine

The lumbar vertebrae and their chakric connections.

us in healing through our feelings, and helping us heal our feelings through broader principles.

I believe that the principles associated with this vertebrae system are critical to healing our own unique masculine/feminine issues, and can provide assistance in helping men and women love and like each other. Though I cannot prove this assertion, a special case comes to mind.

I was asked to visit a friend's mother in the hospital. I went to support my friend, not to serve professionally. Her mother had broken her back in the lumbar area. Expecting to find her angry, despairing, or unhappy, I was surprised to find the mother smiling, with her husband by her side holding her hand. After a few minutes of small talk, her husband told me that in some ways, this accident was the best thing that could have happened. "It saved our marriage," he said. "I never knew how much I really cared—I had just been taking her for granted." In breaking open these vertebrae, this woman had broken herself open to the opportunity for true connection with her loved one.

The Thoracic (Dorsal) Vertebrae

The thoracic or dorsal vertebrae are intermediate in size, larger than the cervical vertebrate atop them, and smaller than the lumbar ones beneath them. They decrease in size as they progress up the spine. These vertebrae are located in the same region as the ribs, which place them in connection with the solar plexus and heart chakra, and in contact with the thymus (figure 10d). Their most distinguishing characteristic is their heart shape. Esoterically, this region's major function involves interlocking the higher energies related to heart's desires with our ability to manifest the success and relationships needed to breathe life into our dreams.

With regard to the particular energy connections, these vertebrae, from the bottom up, relate to the fifteenth through twenty-sixth energy centers. In general, those vertebrae that interface with the third chakra relate to balance, harmony, and free will; they interconnect with the heart itself via the Kundalini spiritual point (Point 19), and completely lock into the heart chakra through the energy of Mastery (Point 20). When men achieve focus in the third chakra section of this area, they are then automatically raised to compassion, the gift of the heart. Freed from the guilt and shame typically associated with the first chakra's basic drives, third-chakra-based men can actually be more, not less, successful than their counterparts.

As I've said, our third chakra is responsible for the input of ideas, intellectual knowledge, clairsentience (or clear knowing), and our relationship with worldly success. Because higher spiritual energies are attached to these concerns, through these vertebrae, we can all achieve the balance necessary to apply (free) will toward meeting our purpose.

When our ideas align with our purpose, we receive an additional zap of energy through the nineteenth energy center, Kundalini, located within this vertebral area. This Kundalini point is critical. It connects the red kundalini

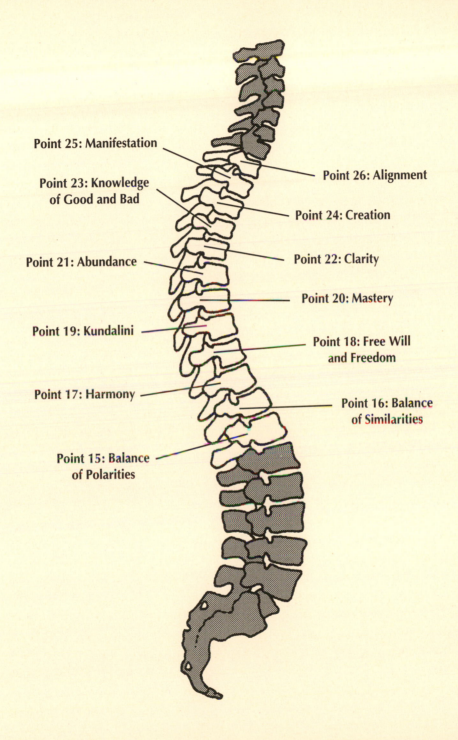

Point 25: Manifestation

Point 26: Alignment

Point 23: Knowledge
of Good and Bad

Point 24: Creation

Point 21: Abundance

Point 22: Clarity

Point 20: Mastery

Point 19: Kundalini

Point 18: Free Will
and Freedom

Point 17: Harmony

Point 16: Balance
of Similarities

Point 15: Balance
of Polarities

The thoracic (dorsal) vertebrae and their chakric connections.

coccygeal access point to the primary access point of golden kundalini, the crown. This entry point may also parallel the heart-based kundalini center referred to by several Indian yogic traditions. Leadbeater, in *The Chakras*, says this center is feminine, and called the "home of the world's mother" (Leadbeater, 33). Male or female, this center-point is both fertile and fueling. Thus, kundalini fuels our breath with life energy, imbuing us with the warm support of the Divine Source. We can now uplift our worldly goals to their highest level, through mastery of the task at hand.

Healing these vertebrae can be particularly helpful when we are experiencing doubt, confusion, or fears; when we seem stuck in regard to defining or achieving success; when we are experiencing low self-esteem, low energy, or metabolic problems. Often, the issue can relate to balance. We need to distinguish our ideas or our skills from those of others. This kind of self-appraisal, done through the eyes of our spiritual identity, brings us to a closer level of harmony with our true self. Once we grasp the idea that we really have free will and can choose what to believe or not, we can break the barrier of low self-esteem. Low self-esteem, more than any other issue, blocks our access to energy. When we energize ourselves with purpose and self-respect, we finally begin to master our own fates.

The lines of distinction between energy centers blur, of course, as one vertebra folds into another. Roughly, however, as we go from being energized through kundalini to realizing that we can master our own identities, we can recognize that we deserve abundance simply because we are who we are. The Abundance center vertebra is locked fully into the heart chakra. Just think of everything that relates to abundance. We want abundantly wonderful relationships. We desire abundance in regard to fun, fortune, and fame. We want abundant health. Believing in abundance is a heart's desire.

The thoracic vertebrae also assist the flow of abundance into our physical bodies. The trick is to realize that we desire and deserve abundance, and then receive clarity about how to achieve it. Clarity, in particular, relates to the lungs, one of the organs sharing the pericardium cavity with the heart. Clear thinking and clear breathing seem to go together, a truth understood by many yoga masters. Clarity as a reality braces us to make peace with our dual human nature—good and bad, light and dark, enlightened and unenlightened. Only by drawing fully on all the energies available to us—the dark as well as the light—can we go about creating and manifesting our heart and soul's desires—all under the protection of the top thoracic vertebra, Alignment (with Higher Purpose; Point 26).

Working with the thoracic vertebrae can be enlightening for anyone seeking relationship and manifesting assistance. Our heart is the meeting ground, a revolving door unto itself. It is the space in which our upper spiritual aspects meet our lower material aspects. Dhyani Ywahoo says that the energy of the earth and energy of heaven join in the heart, "expanding, radiating outward" (Ywahoo, 102). All of the heart-shaped thoracic verte-brae are concerned with helping us achieve what is truly best for us during this life.

The Cervical Vertebrae

The cervical vertebrae crown the spinal system. These individual vertebrae are generally smaller than those in other regions, yet each of them perform very important physical and metaphysical functions.

The cervical vertebrae compose the top upper back and the neck. These vertebrae cover the throat chakra and its connection to our heart chakra. They also attach the spine to the higher in-body centers or points; these points parallel the spine even though they are located outside the cranium. The seven vertebrae in the cervical system take us from the twenty-seventh energy point through the "Principle of the Thirty-third."

The twenty-seventh energy point is Peace. Serenity follows alignment with our purpose, which rounds out the heart's connection with the thy-mus. To achieve serenity, we must know that we are on track with our pur-pose. This vertebra, one of the odd-shaped cervical vertebrae, ties into our immune system. When experiencing immune deficiencies or disorders, we can use the spiritual energy of Peace to achieve the calm we need to regu-late our physical and chemical reactions. The connection between the Peace center and the lower neck area can help us achieve the balanced state we need to express ourselves appropriately and fairly.

The Wisdom center (Point 28) locks into the throat chakra. One of the higher goals of the throat chakra is to channel, know, and speak only wis-dom. Atop this, and still aligned with the throat, we link to Enjoyment and Forgiveness (Points 29 and 30). How many of our problems stem from hav-ing stifled our joy and life energy, or from not having spoken those difficult truths? The Forgiveness center is also well-placed. When we can say that we forgive ourselves and others, we break the cords or old tapes that enter all too often through the throat.

The cervical vertebrae complete at the **axis** or the second cervical verte-bra, which joins with the **atlas** or first cervical vertebra. These two vertebrae are extremely important, because they top off the spine, cradling our head. The axis forms a pivot upon which the atlas holds the head. This pivot allows the head to swivel. Along the back side of the body, the axis rises in a tooth-like form. The rest of the body looks almost like a bed that stretch-es out from a headboard. The axis and atlas also complete the spinal chakric system, and open us to life's higher principles.

The atlas links with our thirty-second energy point, the Grace and Divine Source-consciousness center. The Grace center is in direct opposition to the coccygeal bone connecting to the third coccygeal vertebrae, which contain our feelings and creativity. Channeling Divine Source-consciousness energy,

Figure 10e.

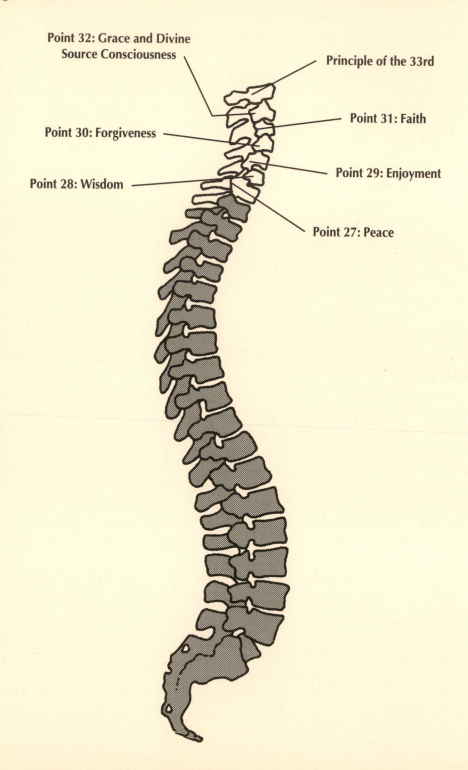

Point 32: Grace and Divine
Source Consciousness

Principle of the 33rd

Point 31: Faith

Point 30: Forgiveness

Point 29: Enjoyment

Point 28: Wisdom

Point 27: Peace

The cervical vertebrae and their chakric connections.

this connection with grace must align with our feelings and creativity, as well as the concerns addressed by our first chakric area. Shaped like a cradle, our atlas represents the cradle of our higher being, the cradle itself being made of grace.

The axis supports the globe of the head. It has neither a physical nor a spinal process. It is ring-like in shape with a front and back arch. Metaphysically, the axis pertains to the Principle of the Thirty-third, which is a protective energy that must be used to safely work with any of the higher energy points. This principle is that of Love. Not just love, the feeling we feel when infatuated, but the energy of Love, the feeling the Divine Source has for itself and for us.

Love depends upon grace to support the higher centers. It is also the doorway through which we journey to get to the higher planes of ourselves. It lies directly opposite the fourth coccygeal vertebrae, which relates to the first chakra, the force of primal life energy. When we draw our life energy up according to the principles of Love, our entire energy system automatically aligns.

The axis also serves as the spinal connection to golden kundalini, the spiritual energy feeding our purpose. This form of energy, referred to in works such as Ywahoo's *Voices of Our Ancestors*, based on Cherokee tradition, may be formed from energy like the *linga*, an Indian emblem of creative power that extends down from the heavens (as well as up through the earth). According to this tradition, the downward force ignites the top half of our body. I have experienced golden kundalini this same way. Entering through the crown chakra, it fuels the top half of our body, which houses our in- and out-of-the-body spiritual centers. Golden kundalini is so powerful and intense, metaphysical leaders such as Leadbeater have warned about kundalini that enters from above rather than below. He believes that one of the dangers of downward entering kundalini is that it can "excite the most undesirable passions," turning men into "monsters of depravity" (Leadbeater, 82).

I have found that the key to safely using golden kundalini is to bring it in with Grace, the energy point correlating with the atlas. We must also continue to pull red kundalini up until both mix with the spiritual kundalini in the heart. (See the "Coccygeal Vertebrae" section earlier in this chapter.) Thus, we blend our physical drive with the will of a higher power, the Divine Source.

I believe that several other cultures understand this concept. These cultures use the symbol of the shaman's portal to speak to this relationship between spiritual (kundalini) energy and the energy of the gods. This portal is shaped like a Celtic *dolman* or grave entrance, which is also comparable in form to the shape of a vertebra, and the shape of of the atlas and axis themselves. This portal is a logical door through which tribal healers venture to perform healings or gather knowledge. One shaman with whom I studied said that during trance he lifts his soul to the heavens through his neck. It is there, he said, that the bones "hollow into doors" so he can visit the "seven layers of reality." We can all reach these levels of higher consciousness, because these doorways are built into our own physical systems.

Working with the Key Point System

There are many ways to work with the Key Point System, several of which I have already mentioned. I will categorize these and others to better illustrate possible methods. There are three general approaches to working with this system:

Visual — Gathering pictures, images, or symbolic representations of an issue, belief, person, place, or thing.

Verbal — Hearing words or sounds from an aspect of ourselves, or from a source of visible or invisible guidance.

Kinesthetic — Feeling, sensing, or knowing information. Typically associated with one of the five senses.

The following Key Point System techniques may draw on any or all of the above approaches.

Isolating One Vertebra

If it is possible to pinpoint a particular issue, it can be beneficial to work with the vertebra relating to this issue.

Isolating a Chakric Area

When concentrating on the front-side, back-side, or combined energies of a particular chakra, it can be helpful to analyze the problem in connection with the vertebrae found in that chakric area.

Working with a Vertebrae Area

This technique is especially beneficial if someone is complaining about a pain or problem with his or her spine. For instance, if a client is experiencing low back pain, I would work with the centers located in the entire sacral vertebral area.

Working with Opposite Vertebrae, Chakras, or Spine Areas

Sometimes an issue associated with the physical dimension is mirrored in the spiritual dimension or vice versa. Also, an issue in one vertebra will be reflected in its direct spinal opposite. For instance, if a client is experiencing difficulties with his or her tailbone, it can be beneficial to also work on the cervical area. Our system is always attempting to achieve balance. Attacking the issue in a different way can help swing it back into equilibrium.

Applying the Child Development System

Our chakras awaken and open in stages. Our higher centers link into this process in stages via the vertebrae. Often, I will walk a client "up the spine," searching for repressed memories or issues at various ages. It can be helpful to have him or her open to the spiritual energies available through the vertebrae connections. For instance, when someone is dealing with an issue that has lingered since pre-teen years, tapping into the Peace center encourages a more expansive interpretation of that issue and its role. Clients healing traumatic issues can also benefit by opening to the higher spiritual energies available through the corresponding higher center.

Using the Rays

There are two major ways to work with the rays under the Key Point System. First, pinpoint the vertebrae that require healing, then select or intuit which rays will help heal the issue. Focus these rays on the injured vertebrae. Second, establish whether or not there is already a ray linked to the vertebrae in question, either as an in-point or an out-point. Use this ray energy to help fix the issue. (You can also use the ray energy nearest the vertebrae upon which you are working.)

Applying the Principles

Walking any issue through the Guardian Principles is an effective and meaningful way to heal ourselves or manifest our desires. As I suggested in Chapter Eight, the principles can be blended with the child development system. After using child development information to highlight the origin of an issue, we can walk ourselves through a healing process via the principles.

Working with the Kundalini

The spine functions best when red kundalini from the coccyx meets and works with the golden kundalini from the seventh chakra (and the nineteenth center thoracic vertebra) in the heart. This golden kundalini enters the spine through the axis. Any healing or manifesting process can benefit from making sure that the red and golden kundalini energy are mixing in the heart and/or in the thoracic vertebrae. This blended energy, which consists of spiritualized matter, can energize just about any process.

I would like to provide an example of how the Key Point System has helped someone heal. Bev, forty-five, was referred to me by a chiropractor. She had experienced intense back pain most of her life, ever since breaking her tailbone when she was seven years old. During the past decade, she had also suffered other chronic disorders, including headaches, fainting spells, digestive problems, and premenstrual syndrome. She complained about two other problems as well—she had never been able to get pregnant, and she often had sore feet due to having flat feet.

Bev and I worked together for about two months before the solution clicked. The core physical problem was her tailbone. Inherent in the tailbone are issues relating to the first, second, third, and tenth chakras, and Bev showed physical symptoms that could have stemmed from all of these chakras. Back problems, headaches, and fainting spells were symptoms of first chakra issues. Premenstrual and pregnancy difficulties stemmed from the second chakra. Digestive disorders were a product of a third chakra issue, and flat feet were a product of a tenth chakra concern.

The fact that all coccygeal vertebrae were affected gave me a clue. Bev's difficulties might have originated before birth, though they might have been aggravated at different points in this lifetime. I asked her if her physical symptoms were mirrored or affected by any one particular family member, or if they correlated with any problems experienced by family members as she was growing up. Bev shared story after story about her mother. Her mother had injured her own tailbone shortly before Bev had gotten hurt. Every time her mother became sick, so did she.

We followed these breadcrumbs to the core issue. Several lifetimes ago, Bev and her mother had created a soul contract. They had spiritually and physically tied themselves together by knotting their first chakras energetically. The result was that if one became sick, the other would provide her with life energy to help keep her alive.

To change this situation, Bev and I worked with the Divine Source. She established a different type of bond with her mother, one in which they shared love, but not life energy. Bev then connected her life energy with the Divine Source, and asked her mother's soul to do the same. Two weeks later, Bev came to see me. She had seen her chiropractor shortly after working with me. The chiropractor had spent one hour with her, amazed at how easily her spine, including her coccyx, adjusted. Three months later, Bev reported that her headaches, digestive problems, back pains, and other ailments had disappeared. Besides that, she said her relationship with her mother had never been better.

The moral of the story is not that working with the Key Point System can heal everything. Maybe it will; maybe it will not. If it is the right system for you or a client, if the timing is right, if you are open to change, it might help you heal yourself. There are many ways to feel good about yourself. If this system feels right, use it.

Chapter Eleven

Understanding Emotions

Many evolutionists assert that there are two traits distinguishing humans from the rest of the animal kingdom—our hands and our upper brain. Philosophers concur, but add that we are different because we can reason. Clergy insist that the difference is that humans have souls. I disagree with them all. If there is a determining factor (and one could argue this point), I think it would be that humans have emotions. Emotions provide us our greatest pleasure, but they also cause us most of our difficulties.

The Anatomy of Emotions

I believe that an emotion is a feeling plus a thought. I've also come to believe that feelings are the language of the body, while thoughts are the language of the mind. Emotions are produced when our body and mind communicate and reach agreement. When the body and mind link a feeling with a thought, we get an emotion—energy in motion. The result is expression.

Many scientific studies have underscored the idea that feelings truly are expressions of our body, and that they exist separate from our thoughts. Antonio R. Damasio, brain researcher and author of *Descartes' Error*, has found that feelings come from our sematic or body reactions to events. These reactions, based on past experiences and predictive responses "offer us a glimpse of what goes on in our flesh." Thus, feelings "let us mind the body" (Damasio, Antonio R. New York: G. P. Putnam & Sons, 1994, 159).

Examined more metaphorically, feelings could be likened to pure essence. In *Water Bears No Scars*, David Reynolds says that feelings are a "natural phenomenon" over which we have no more control than we have "control over earthquakes or summer breezes" (Reynolds, David K. *Water Bears No Scars: Japanese Lifeways for Personal Growth*. New York: William Morrow & Company, 1987). Not only do we have no control over these internal breezes, but we have a right to feel every feeling. We have a right to fully experience all of our feelings. Thoughts in and of themselves are also pure. We have a right to think every thought that forms. We have a right to fully explore each of our thoughts.

What exactly are thoughts? How do they in relate to feelings? Thoughts, like feelings, originate in the body. They differ from feelings, however, in that they are stored and built from "images in the mind," as Damasio explains. These images are originally laid down as "dispositional" representations of knowledge, innate and experiential. New knowledge is achieved by modification of these representations. Before these representations can be turned into words, they exist as "auditory or visual images in our consciousness" (Damasio, 104–106).

Mind equals consciousness. Thoughts express for this mind just as feelings express for the body. Damasio describes their relationship this way: as body changes happen, you can monitor these changes. "That process of continuous monitoring, that experience of what your body is doing while thoughts about specific contents roll by, is the essence of what I call feeling," he says. Therefore, an emotion is "a collection of changes in body state connected to particular mental images" (Damasio, 145).

Seen this way, emotions are natural and important vehicles for self-awareness. Feelings tied to thoughts provide us a glimpse into our inner and outer realities and needs. Together, they form the basis for our ability to reason, according to Damasio. Obviously, it is therefore in our best interest to allow both our feelings and thoughts to be freely felt.

Stuck Emotions

What? Express all of our feelings? All of our thoughts? Does this mean that if we are angry, it is okay to kill someone? Does this mean that if we think Polish or Afro-American or Caucasian people are stupid, we can be mean to them? No and no. Negative, self-destructive, or violent actions stem from stuck emotions, not free-flowing feelings or thoughts. We may feel angry, but we only get into trouble when we pair the feeling of anger with a destructive thought, such as "Being angry is bad, so I must stuff my anger," or "Being angry is macho. I better show how strong I am," and keep these feelings or thoughts paired or stuck together.

Stuck emotions are so tightly glued, they prevent us from rearranging either our feeling or thoughts to fit the circumstances presented to us. The truth is, any feeling will naturally disperse if we express it in alignment with the situation at hand. Any thought, even a negative one, will mature upon reflection if we examine it in alignment with the situation at hand. When our energy system is operating in alignment, we will always express our feelings and thoughts in a constructive fashion. Each feeling and thought will receive the input, advice, and healing it needs to be expressed authentically, because all our energy centers, not just certain ones, will be in on the act.

We are not fully open or aligned if we have cemented and failed to disengage critical feelings and thoughts. We become rigid, and lose our ability to adapt and be flexible. We easily allow ourselves to be triggered by external stimuli. New situations will often feel like recreations of prior events, events that probably caused the emotion to form in the first place. Our emotional responses have become habits or patterned reaction/responses. Our feeling and thought have become an enmeshed couple; they have grown too scared to operate independently. Because they are so ensconced, they are unavailable to pair up with other feelings and thoughts, the very feelings and thoughts that may be needed to address a current concern.

Healers train long and hard to deal with this problem. In *Kahuna Healing*, Serge King says, "Part of kahuna healing is concerned with helping the conscious mind learn how to perceive emotions without allowing the subconscious to engage in habitual action" (King, 94–95).

Feelings and thoughts usually marry for a good reason. Perhaps we felt threatened by someone during childhood. Certain feelings and thoughts bonded to best handle the situation. We created emotions that we perceived would help us through a dark experience. For example, say you were threatened by a drunk father when you were five. You felt scared. Who wouldn't? Your thinking self also reminded you that you were little and weak. The emotion that took care of you could be something like, "I am scared. I am not strong, so when I'm scared, I'd better be quiet."

This emotional response may have been appropriate for the original frightening situation. As an adult, however, you might be running into trouble if this response or emotion has become the only one triggered whenever you're scared. You're really not little anymore, but may believe you are whenever you're scared. Maybe you stay quiet when you're offered a promotion, threatened by a barking dog, or asked out on a date. Your quietness may cost you a raise, get you bit by a dog, or keep you sitting home on Friday night.

Given the obvious disadvantage to cementing emotions, we must wonder why we would ever let them stay stuck together. Well, perhaps we don't know any better. Maybe our mother did it this way. Maybe we were punished when we did it differently. Maybe the original situation remained constant for so long that we believed it could never be different. Remember, when it was formed, our emotion helped us, but if it has become a patterned response, a habit, we must change it. Holding onto an emotion that seemed to help us when in trauma will not prohibit additional trauma. In fact, evidence suggests that the opposite is true.

Yes, emotional patterns usually produce the opposite of what we desire. The feelings and thoughts composing the stuck emotions are unavailable for bonding with other thoughts and feelings. Our reactions are thereby inhibited and habitual. Because our situational responses have narrowed, we lose sight of additional choices. We make the same choice, therefore reinforcing our old habits.

Here are two examples of this emotional patterning. The first concerns Ryan, an energetic and highly successful video producer, who unfortunately hated his work. He found himself sabotaging his career by arriving late for shoots, talking back to clients, and displaying other self-defeating behaviors. Yet he wouldn't take steps to solidify his dream, which was to be a writer.

Upon probing, he discovered the heart of this situation was a stuck emotion. When Ryan was young, his dad would yell at him for writing poetry. He would shame his son at the supper table, insisting that "everything in the family would be better if Ryan would just stop wasting time and do what was important." Ryan's feeling response was anger, but his father was so rageful, Ryan decided that there must be something truly wrong with his desire to write. Anger became linked with the belief, "What I want to do causes trouble." As a adult, he found himself experiencing the turmoil of trying to reassert this soul-filled self, the writer self. He could give birth to the anger, but not get past it, until he detached it from being bad or wrong. He was living out the belief by causing trouble in his current profession.

Another example concerns my own life. Through the years, I'd become aware of an inability to stand up for myself. If, when trying to mediate for my own rights, my opponent pointed out something I'd done wrong, even things that happened as a child or teenager, I'd fall apart.

Through therapy, I came to understand that I was recreating a pattern begun between me and my mother. When young, I would attempt to argue against what was obviously an injustice. In response, my mother would tell me I was making her sick by arguing with her. She would go on to shame me for disagreeing with her and would eventually punish me. Therefore, my feeling of righteous anger became paired with three beliefs: "My anger hurts people," "Standing up for myself will result in punishment," and "I don't deserve to be heard." Unlocking these emotions has been a slow and arduous process, one that requires me to act out the new behavior and do some intense energy work. However, this work has resulted in the ability to run my own business, buy a home, and raise a son—activities which all require fighting against the odds.

Emotionalism Versus Emotional Sensitivity

I want to address another important issue regarding emotions. For years, women have gotten the rap for being emotional. We need to distinguish **emotionalism** from **emotional sensitivity**. Emotionalism occurs when our feelings are trapped within our belief system. If each time we are threatened we react the same way, if we cry no matter what, if we get angry every time someone confronts us, we are probably undergoing emotionalism. When this happens, we need to unlock our feelings from our thoughts and free ourselves from these imprisoning emotions.

However, if we empathize with others feelings, cry when it feels right, hold back tears when it does not, or get angry when our rights are being violated, we are being emotionally sensitive. Being emotionally sensitive, in contrast to being emotional, means the following:

Emotionalism

1. Reactions are based on feelings and thoughts that are automatically linked or permanently bonded.

2. Results in entrenched patterns that can be difficult to break, control, or manage.

3. Other people often end up feeling misunderstood, misperceived, misjudged, and ignored.

4. Leaves us feeling tired, exhausted, frustrated, spent, disconnected from ourselves or others, and incomplete regarding the experience.

Emotional Sensitivity

1. Reactions are based on feelings and thoughts that are bonded in response to the situation at hand.

2. Results in a fluid and appropriate response; typical responses may be changed if necessary.

3. Other people usually end up feeling cared about, listened to, and invited to agree or disagree.

4. Leaves us feeling refreshed, open, more connected with ourselves or others, and fulfilled regarding the experience.

When defined this way, emotionalism is no longer a female problem, but a human foible. Anyone who has experienced childhood dysfunction, who feels locked into old ways of doing things, or who senses that they are living the same situations, cycles, or relationships over and over again, may be locked into the old patterns and negativity associated with emotionalism. (For a complete overview on how childhood experiences can make us stuck, I would recommend John Bradshaw's series on healing family dysfunctions, including *Bradshaw On: The Family.* Deerfield Beach, FL: Health Communications,

Inc., 1988, and *Healing the Shame that Binds You*. Deerfield Beach, FL: Health Communications, Inc., 1988.)

Some of the problems that arise from emotionalism are obvious. Being emotional makes us feel bad. We experience difficulties communicating or bonding with others. I find that most people, but women especially, see this as a problem within themselves. Unfortunately, the typical response is to try and be cured of feelings, which is exactly the wrong approach. Feelings help us to be more rational and reasonable (the theme of *Descartes' Error*). We need to be free to feel our feelings and to think our thoughts, if for no other reason than to keep ourselves physically healthy.

Beliefs that cause us to repress our feelings, deny our passions, only take care of other people, or ignore our own needs, result in a feelings backlog. Remember, feelings are real energies. They are composed of physical matter, says the quanta theory. Therefore, these feeling backlogs not only jam our responses and thinking processes, but can also create build-ups in our body.

This belief that emotionalism can damage our bodies—and conversely, that positive thoughts and free feelings can heal it—is not new. One of my acquaintances, a chiropractor, speaks to the reality of feelings causing physical damage. Carla sees thousands of clients a year who primarily come because of physical complaints or problems. Rather than concentrating on relieving their physical symptoms, she tests the emotional basis of their problem, dividing it into feeling and belief. The reason her client base is so high is because this approach works. People get well.

When I worked with her, I lost thirteen allergies, all of which I had experienced since childhood. One vivid memory concerns a wheat allergy. With Carla's help, I isolated the basis of the allergy. When I was a child, my mother would give me a cookie every time I felt sad. Because the feeling component of my allergy was sadness, every time I ate a cookie later in life, I would feel despondent and "stuffed up." As soon as I uncovered this knowledge, I cried for days—everywhere. I then changed some of my beliefs about myself, and the allergy disappeared.

Besides affecting our physical health, patterned emotional responses can also inhibit our spiritual development. Thoughts such as "Good children respect their parents," are not necessarily negative. However, let's say our parents abused us when we were young, and we felt angry about it. Anger is a healthy and appropriate response to being abused. If we were told, for example, that our God doesn't love us when we don't listen to our parents and especially when we're angry, we could grow to believe that because we get angry when we were mistreated, God doesn't love us. How then could we let our soul or God into our body? Without our soul, we experience extreme difficulties in uncovering our purpose, allowing in abundance, and achieving self-love.

We need to free ourselves from our warped, rigid, or wrapped-up emotions, and allow our feelings and thoughts to flow within us. We want to heal our emotions, and by doing so, open to healing other aspects of ourselves and to manifesting our true desires.

The Ideal Feeling/Thought Chain of Reaction

Unhooking our feelings and thoughts (the subject of the next chapter) begins with understanding how they became linked in the first place. Remember, it's not bad to have emotions. We need them. We simply want them to form, then unform when their work is complete. Let's look at this ideal passageway of feeling-and-thought energy through our body. This description is based upon my own internal and professional work, and I hope it will help you better understand your own patterned responses.

The physical energy for both feelings and thoughts originates in the lower energy centers. I'll describe these steps via a real-life situation.

During preconception, the tenth chakra programs the material body (with the assistance of the ninth chakra) with fundamental beliefs and feelings. Let's say that my soul wants to experience true love during this lifetime. Through my tenth chakra, I may select genetic and psychic capabilities that will enhance this goal. I might plant feelings such as excitement and passion within my first chakra. I might make sure that my second chakra feeling bodies are diverse and intense. I might imbue my third chakra with beliefs such as "I deserve love."

My tenth chakra might also select genes that will provide me the type of body I need to be with or to attract an ideal mate. Imagining that my eighth chakra has karmically programmed this mate, I may make sure I'm blonde (or russet or brunette or whatever) if that will appeal to my potential mate. Thus prepared, I am born, and I mature. The groundwork is laid. My life is in place. Then I meet someone.

My first chakra quickly assesses this situation. Is this situation or person safe or not? Does my body need to invoke any security feelings, such as grief, rage, terror, or joy? The conclusions are sent through my spine to my brain. My brain, in turn, gives orders to my first chakra regarding what energy to send to the second chakra, which holds the feeling bodies, and to the third chakra, which operates like the "brain of the body."

The following occur simultaneously. My first chakra, responding to orders, strikes the appropriate notes in my second chakra. Certain feeling bodies are awakened; certain ones are overridden. The back of the second chakra opens to balance these energies and create a unified feeling. Beliefs and attitudes are passed down from the third chakra to the second chakra. (I remember this part of the process by picturing the red from the first chakra and the yellow from the third chakra mixing to make orange in the second chakra.)

In the second chakra, thoughts and feelings are paired up. I now have an emotion. More than one feeling or thought may be joined together. Remember, in an ideal situation, these bondings occur with the input from the entire energy system, under the advice of the spiritual energy points, and with the direction of intuition (a force we will discuss in more detail). Recall that our original response was sent up the spinal column, which means it received input, healing, and assistance from every single in-body chakra and spiritual chakra or energy point connected to the various higher energy centers. Returning from the brain, the command re-registered with all energy centers. This two-way process assures that the entire system falls into alignment regarding a response.

The resulting emotions are fully incorporated into my power center. As a woman, this is my second chakra. If I were a man, it should be my third.

My power center disperses emotions upward and downward. The emotion acts like a message that, when interpreted by the other chakras, stimulates a response. Because men and women have different power centers, our first responses would differ from each other. In women, downward messages register in the first chakra, resulting in a physical response, such as an action or a primary feeling. In men, downward messages register in the second chakra before passing to the first, resulting in a feeling or creative initial response. In women, the upward messages trigger responses in the third chakra, initiating a thought, belief, or act of personal power. In men, upward messages stimulate a heart response, calling for a relationship-oriented or compassionate result.

My responses continue on their upward and downward paths, eventually registering in a verbal response (fifth chakra), strategic response (sixth chakra), and philosophical response (seventh chakra). Even though this cycle seems linear, it really isn't. Emotions radiate from the power center in spirals, rather than straight lines.

The process continues to spin through this cycle as long as necessary. Emotions are formed, then evaporate. They should rotate freely, at least as long as it takes to decide if Mr. Perfect is or isn't.

In an advanced energy system, the power center shifts from the second or third chakra to the heart. Coming from our heart speeds up this internal processing, for we will be clear whether a stimulus meets a child-like desire or not. Some people operate with two power centers, their gender-based center and their heart center. In these cases, a two-fold response may be felt.

I have just outlined an ideal stimulus-response process. As you can see, by the time we are finished processing or acting upon an issue, our formal emotions have been disbanded. They have been acted upon and do not need to exist any longer. Our system has returned to a balanced state in which feelings and thoughts co-exist separately, available at all times for us and for each other.

For many of us, this process doesn't always go this smoothly. Rather than responding to the situation at hand, we react out of long-held, stuck emotions. We hook onto old emotions and patterns. We perceive all situations involving anger as the same situation, or all situations involving confrontation as dangerous to us. The best way to break our knee-jerk response is to understand how emotions can become injurious and entrenched.

Childhood Development of Emotions

Emotions are formed when our feelings are judged and we accept these judgments as true, and when we are exposed to lies and believe the lies. While this process can occur at any time in our lives, we are most vulnerable when we are children. Typically, the emotions formed during our first swing through the chakra development cycle are the ones that replay the rest of our lives, until we short-circuit the process.

Let's walk through our development chart from start to finish again, this time checking for problem points.

Pre-Conception — Chakra Ten

Before conception, our soul selects a set of parents, and contract is developed. Drawing upon the elements and a swirling mass of visible and invisible energy, our tenth chakra constructs the template for our physical form. Overseen by our ninth chakra and our guides, it chooses our genes and psychic traits. The chakra composes this template from our parent's genetic pools and characteristics from our past lives.

Unfortunately, emotional blockages can be programmed in even at this point. (Yes, we can get into trouble even before we are born!) Let's say that, in a past life, we failed to work through our anger issues with authority. Our soul knows that if we don't heal this issue, we may not be able to fulfill our soul purpose. In its infinite wisdom, our soul lifts this issue, part and parcel, and programs it into our current-life energetic system, hoping to force us to deal with it. We are now programmed to have anger issues with authorities—authorities we haven't even met yet.

Other emotional programs can stem from our genetic lineage. Perhaps most of our forefathers decided that in order to survive, they had to repress their sadness. They believed that being sad would weaken them. Wanting to survive, our body may have decided to incorporate this belief into our embryonic energetic system. "If that's what kept our forebears alive, maybe it will help us," might have been our reasoning.

Sometimes emotional issues are scripted during the actual conception process. Even while our body gathered together the threads of life, our soul interacted with those of our parents. If either of our parents experienced strong reactions to having a child, such as fear or resistance to getting pregnant, we may have concluded that we are not wanted, that we are troublesome, or that we don't deserve to be alive. These emotional conclusions could have locked into our system.

One of my students, Jill, is a good example of this. Jill always felt her mother tried to punish her for being enthusiastic and passionate about life. Later, in response to some questions that came up in therapy, Jill asked her mother about what was going on at the time she was conceived. Her mother replied that Jill was conceived out of passion; her mother threw caution to the wind and had unprotected sex. She conceived, then later had many doubts about having the child. It's no wonder Jill felt she was being punished for being passionate. Each time she was enthusiastic, she re-experienced the idea that being passionate can cause life-long consequences.

Another example concerns work I once did with a man who had dyslexia. Though he had made peace with this problem, he came to me to find out why it had afflicted him his entire life. During a regression, he remembered swirling around while his parents were making love (right before he was conceived). In a trance, he relayed that a guide had been in attendance during this conception time. They had discussed whether he was willing to take this body. The guide informed him that he would probably be learning disabled due to a genetic trait and a soul pre-disposition to such a disability. Apparently, he had been a teacher in a past life and was unable to understand students not capable of scholastic achievement. My client had decided to enter this body. After emerging from the regression, he seemed relieved to understand the cause of the dyslexia.

Womb to Six Months — Chakra One

At this time, our body is busy developing. Our soul is overseeing and busy deciding when to enter (or pondering how long it can delay the process). Unfortunately, the less available our soul is to our body, the less space it occupies within our body. The resulting emptiness creates a vacuum waiting to be filled. The feelings, thoughts, emotions, and awarenesses floating around us, whether they are ours or not, may enter to fill this void. Because our mother is currently our primary caregiver, we typically absorb more of her issues than anyone else's.

If she or other caregivers are worried about money, are disappointed about our gender, or are blocked in regard to meeting our needs, we may swallow these emotional issues whole, or create emotional issues of our own in response. If our primary caregivers are denying certain feelings, memories, or problems, they may also become ours. As we know, it is impossible to work through an issue which is not ours.

Womb and infantile regression has become an important therapeutic methodology. I know two doctors (friends of mine) who frequently regress clients back to in-womb or infantile states. They have said that the deep dysfunctions exhibited by many of their clients, from addictions to depression, clear up when early issues are faced. I've often done regression with my clients.

I once experienced a spontaneous regression during a shamanic ceremony in South America. I was suddenly back in the womb, and I could "see" the sounds of my parents' arguments. I re-experienced the terror and the despair associated with having this couple as my parents. To this day, I believe that the hopelessness I've struggled to clear, and my disbelief in healthy relationships, partly stem from those in-womb experiences and reactions.

Six Months to Two and One-Half Years — Chakra Two

During this time, our feelings are awakening, as are our creative responses to the people and situations surrounding us. Already intact, our feeling bodies are coming alive. We want each to be stimulated, supported, and nourished by our external environment, which assures that, as adults, we will have a well-rounded emotional life. If we can pass through this time period being assured that all our feelings are okay, we will have achieved a lot. The trouble is, few of us experienced this ideal situation. It is doubtful that our parents grew up in atmospheres that nurtured feelings. How could they have provided one for us?

There are many scenarios that can damage these developing feeling bodies. Our parents may teach us, inadvertently or directly, that certain feelings are not okay. We might displace these dirty feelings somewhere inside or outside of our body. Now our remaining, acceptable feelings will have to do double duty.

In contrast, we may be exposed to extreme displays of emotion, which frequently happens in alcoholic or dysfunctional families. We may decide that certain feelings are bad, or we may decide that to survive, we will model our own behavior after our parents' behavior. As perceptive as we are when children, we might also become psychically or kinesthetically aware of free-floating, unclaimed feelings. Children will do anything to bring balance to our environment. Our survival depends on it. Therefore, we absorb these rejected feelings.

Whatever the case, the end result is the same. Wounded, incomplete, or over-stimulated feeling bodies warp our energetic system. Now out of balance, our system seeks to right itself. The only way it knows how to do this is to compensate. Usually, our first and third chakras volunteer.

If our first chakra fills the role, we will inevitably act out our feelings. Addictions, crazy behavior, willfulness—there are any number of ways our system will try and throw off these over-stimulated feelings, and stimulate the repressed or apathetic ones. Unfortunately, the cure hurts worse than the cause. Our feelings become further damaged and strained. Furthermore, our own actions make us feel worse. We heap self-induced guilt, shame, terror, and rage upon the backlog already existing. The emotional attachments formed between these types of feelings and thoughts tend to be highly self-critical, self-loathing, and painful.

If our third chakra tries to fill the gap, we will probably try to reason through our feelings. We may attempt to dissociate ourselves from our feelings. The beliefs that are available to bond with our feelings will probably discredit, control, or discount them and us. Character traits usually include living in our head, never losing our cool, or being rational at all costs. The irony is, while we may not appear emotional, we are. It is just that in this system, thoughts, rather than actions, rule our feelings.

Sometimes people ask me, "How could a child make these kind of decisions?" We must remember that we are much older than our age. Our Divine Source self is eternal. Our soul is ancient. Our mind is old. Even though our bodies look young, they are composed of cells that are as old as this planet, if not the stars. As Deepak Chopra says in *Creating Health*, "You are not absolute, static matter. The matter itself was once interstellar dust, and nature has future uses for it in the cosmos" (Chopra, 108). Though our physical cells and in-body energy centers are just developing, they are tapping into our higher spiritual energy points, the rays, and the invisible realms that hold more knowledge than we could possibly imagine. They are linked to purposes that reach far beyond our imagination.

Even so, when we are young, we are vulnerable. Our auras are incomplete. Our crown chakra is still open. We are sponges. We absorb everything—good and bad. It's a wonder, actually, that as children, we can look as young as we are.

Two and One-Half to Four and One-Half Years — Chakra Three

As we develop, we become more conscious of the world around us. Our perceptions first crystallize into awarenesses, then thoughts, and finally beliefs. Our third chakra is initially involved in this growth. During ages two and one-half to four and one-half we learn the power of saying no and yes. We have experienced our feeling bodies, and we now add the other ingredient we need to make emotional soup—thoughts. These thoughts come from other people, our own experiences, and from our own perceptions. As we test our own power against the power of others, we weigh the responses we get from the world. We draw conclusions if the people around us react with consistency. This consistency is the basis for beliefs.

This is a critical age for us, especially because so few caregivers realize the cognitive abilities present in a two- to four-year-old. They think we are just emotional or throwing tantrums. What most fail to realize is that we are creating thoughts left and right. From these thoughts, we are forming beliefs which are then packaged into emotional states. We are asking ourselves, "What happens if I put this feeling together with this thought?" or "How about this belief with this feeling?" If we are safely supported throughout this process, we will learn two important facts:

1. Emotions are fluid. We can change our emotions to fit the situation.

2. Emotions can be released. We can unhook feelings from thoughts and bring ourselves back into balance.

Of course, few parents know these truths, so most of us emerge from the terrible twos with a basketful of feelings that are solidly linked with thoughts. These emotions can greatly inhibit our further development in that they become the foundation for our relationships (Chakra Four), our communication style and ability to receive guidance (Chakra Five), our self-image (Chakra Six), and our sense of purpose (Chakra Seven). They affect our twenties because they will call forth certain karmic patterns over others (Chakra Eight), and they can force our soul to create discordance in our lives in order to turn us to our path (Chakra Nine).

There are millions of emotions that can be formed during this time period. Here are a few that I consistently see with my clients. The emotive responses include the conclusions most often drawn from this environmental response, and the typical ways these conclusions manifest.

Feeling (usually the child's true reaction)	Thought (often the message given to the child)	Emotive Response (conclusion drawn from reactions to feelings)
Sadness	Being sad makes other people uncomfortable.	I can never be loved for who I am. (Often triggered by sadness, accompanied by sadness, or results in repressing sadness.)
Anger	It is bad to have strong feelings.	I am bad when I feel angry. (Can cause repression of anger, frustration, inhibition of power, build-up and acting out of rage, powerlessness, victimization, or displays of violence.)
Neediness	You are in the way.	I cannot get my needs met. (Can increase ploys to use negative or needy behavior to meet needs, or cause a shut-down in relation to self-care.)

Joy	No one else is this happy. Why are you?	I don't deserve to feel happy. Being happy makes other people feel bad. (Can cause repression of happy feelings, depression, avoidance of happy events, or the need to become the family clown to try and cheer everyone up.)
Fear	There is nothing to be afraid of.	My fears are stupid. My fears are bigger than I am. (Can lead to repression of fear, increase in fears, attempts to avoid scary situations at all costs, low or crazy risk-taking.)
Desire	It is not okay to want/demand/ask for something.	I don't deserve to get what I want. (Can set us up for failure, repression of will and success, or the opposite, an "I will succeed no matter what" hero syndrome.)

The most common emotional issues I see require more explanation. These involve the feelings of guilt and shame, often induced by authority figures to create a desired behavior. These figures wield power by telling us there is something wrong with us if we don't do or see it the same way as they do.

Guilt and shame work this way. Let's say we are taught that boys are violent and must be controlled. If we are a boy, we are naturally energetic because we are first chakra based. We might then conclude that being energetic or physical means we are violent, and therefore, bad. We will also conclude that our physical behaviors are also naturally violent. These conclusions make us feel shameful, like there is something intrinsically wrong with us. We will feel guilty for being a boy, for being physically active, or wanting to assert our own will. We may try to appease this guilt by controlling ourselves or inhibiting our natural and free personality. We may also buck against the system by becoming uncontrollable. Either way, we are reacting out of an emotional state that hooks us with guilt and shame.

Here is another example. Let's say that we are exposed to the messages "Good girls don't get messy" or "Good girls take care of other people before thinking about themselves." As a girl, we will feel bad every time we are creative, active, assertive, or self-caring. We are being bad, which produces shame. Likewise, we will feel guilty for breaking the commandment to be good. "If we can just be a little better..." will be the litany in our head. These stuck emotions can affect just about anything that we do.

My clients are constantly working on emotional issues stemming from this formative age. One of the strongest examples was Claire, who described her true self as full of energy and power until age four. It all changed when her family's attempts to control her worked. Claire only worked through her guilt when, during a session, she could picture herself, at age four, stuck on the precipice of a cliff, her family making fun of her. As she imagined herself confronting them, her guilt disappeared. Her life comletely changed, and her challenge now, she says, is trying to figure out what really motivates her, now that guilt doesn't.

Four and One-Half to Six and One-Half — Chakra Four

As we move into our heart chakra, relationships become all-important. We extend further into the world and seek bonding. Our circle of influence expands beyond the family. We associate more and more frequently with peers, friends, teachers, television action figures, book characters, and more.

We bring into these relationships some already-formed emotions. While our third-chakra stage involved drawing conclusions related to our individuality, fourth-chakra development encourages responses about "we." Some of the emotions we drag up to this level may be invalidated. We think we should feel guilty every time we have a need—but our friend Bobby doesn't think so. Positive reflections such as these will break up stuck emotions. They can help us loosen limiting strictures, teach us that all relationships are not the same, and help us become more free-forming in regard to our feelings, thoughts, and expressions.

On the other hand, our relationship experiences may deepen our current emotional issues. "See, even my teacher gets mad when I want something!" we might conclude. "See, even my friends think I am stupid when I cry!" Remember, people live within environments that mirror their own beliefs. Our community will probably reflect many of the issues, perceptions, beliefs, and attitudes that we experience within our own family unit. The programming begun by our families will probably be continued by our external environments.

The emotions we accept as reality at this point will have an impact on our relationship life later. During this stage, we select, learn, and practice the emotions that regulate our behavior with other people. We will carry these conclusions forward, using them to make adult choices about friends, lovers, and life mate(s).

One of my clients informed me, without prompting, that the reason she married or dated the same type of man over and over was that her father had severely wounded her heart. As she explained, he had convinced her that she was only acceptable and lovable if she acted "nice," meaning she never screamed, cried, or talked back. When she did show feelings about something at age twelve, he told her he wouldn't talk with her again, and pulled completely back for six years. With an emotional belief and experience this strong, little wonder she met men who upheld the core emotional belief that she was only acceptable if silent.

Six and One-Half to Eight and One-Half — Chakra Five

We are communicating—talking, sharing, learning, stating the truth of ourselves. In many ways, we are sensing out others' reactions to the feelings, thoughts, and emotions that we are putting forth. How will others respond? Will they like us or not? Are these emotional jettisons effective or not? We are in another time of testing.

The unique aspect of this developmental stage, in regard to our emotions, is that we are now capable of receiving even more spiritual guidance than ever before. Through the back fifth chakra, we can hear this guidance. Ideally, we are now able to receive the higher help we need to break down our emotional blocks. I remember surviving as a child because at this age I could hear voices "on the wind." I tried to be alone outside as often as possible because of them. I needed their messages, which contrasted with the life-threatening ones provided by my parents.

Many of us, however, have a difficult time hearing our guidance, or even if we do, the negative brainwashing is too strong to be overwhelmed. Still seeking the validation and love we did not receive when younger, we might make a dangerous sort of pact. Rather than take in higher wisdom, we lock into our parent's old tapes. These tapes are laden with explosive emotional conclusions, most of which relate to the thematic beliefs underlying our family systems and our cultural milieu.

These tapes lock in through the back of our neck. As we mature, they link us to our family's way of working, learning, and thinking about the world. Our manifesting abilities and needs succumb to the dreams and desires our parents may have for us. If these emotionally charged contracts remain in place, our emotions become more and more locked in. Our free feelings and thoughts may be shamed into hiding, shamed by the inner critic now growing within us.

It can be helpful to work with the back of the neck when seeking to heal emotional patterns. When I say this in class, invariably one-third or more of the participants complain that their neck has just started hurting. I ask them to check if the pain locks in the left, right, or center: mom/female, dad/male, or systemic, respectively. Short reflection almost always clarifies the exact message causing the discomfort.

Eight-and-One-Half to Fourteen — Chakra Six

Visions. Dreams. Possibilities. Fantasies. What do we want? What do we want to be? How do we want to be? A rainbow of delights entices us to try new things, act new ways, dress in wild clothes, experiment with who we are. "Potential" is our operating word.

"Potential" should be our operating word. Stuck emotions not only prevent us from reaching toward stars, but they also block our view of the skies. Cultural beliefs carry considerable impact during this stage. Our internal vision is so open, so fresh, it often lacks the protection necessary to properly screen beneficial from destructive programs.

These societal messages, garnered from the school system, religious institutions, television, magazines, peer groups, and more, can be extremely narrowing. For girls, these messages encapsulate beliefs that females must be sexy, demure, contrite, and petite. For boys, these messages engineer them toward becoming macho, strong, smart, and monetarily successful. When these beliefs square off against our innate feelings and desires, we usually lack the support and knowledge necessary to reject or alter them. Rather, we swallow them whole. Inside us, they tangle with our natural feelings and dreams. It is not feminine to have anger or rage or want to build a business. It is not masculine to feel sad or scared or want to become a daddy. The remaining emotional mess anchors our loyalty to societal standards, but drowns us in the process.

In many ways, feminism or any other kind of social movement "ism" are attempts to uncover and dispel the programs instilled by society, the programs affecting self-image, and therefore, achievement of potential. However, these movements tend to turn into emotional tragedies. When you take a stand, you immediately draw a battle line. Perhaps it would be helpful to examine the emotional (feeling plus thought) components of image issues—then, if necessary, join a movement, not the other way around.

I think a lot of adults suffer from emotions surviving from this developmental stage. I often have clients look inside their third eye to see who they really are inside. I then have them imagine their current self-concept. The difference is typically drastic. When I had one client perceive such a difference, she didn't recognize the self in the real picture. With time, she began to address the feelings she had been stifling by living down to her mentally low standards. When last I heard from her, she called to tell me I wouldn't recognize her. She had cut her hair, changed its color, lost thirty pounds, and started wearing bright colors instead of pastels.

Fourteen Through Twenty-One — Chakra Seven

As we pass into adolescence, we enter the world of purpose. During this time period, we are invited into the realm of our own spirit. Our soul and Divine Source self will be encouraging us to individuate ourselves, even while we learn how to bond with the visible and invisible supports around us.

Any conflict between our soul purpose and our already-established emotions will arise or increase during this period. One reason is that as we progress through the seven years in this stage, we recycle through each of our chakras. At age fourteen, the feelings generated from pre-conception through six months will resurface. At age fifteen, we will re-experience our second chakra feeling life, and so on.

The downside of this recycling is that our formed emotions are extremely strong. They can feel and appear out-of-control; they can seem more powerful than our inner wise self. This is because we are re-testing our emotionally-based judgments about ourselves and the world by acting them out. Strong emotions tend to scare other people. If we experience these emotions as true or if others try to shut them down, we will probably swallow them once and for all, resigning ourselves to our fate.

The upside of this recycling is that we can change. Our emotions are resurfacing to be healed, to be cleaved. At some level, we want our emotional conclusions to be challenged by our loved ones. We want different training. We want our beliefs to be transformed. We want our feelings to be acknowledged. We want freedom—a cry often heard from teenagers. We do not really want freedom from responsibility. We want freedom from our imprisoning belief systems, from our imprisoning emotions.

I have often noticed that my clients' emotion-based issues, even in adulthood, fulfill this child development process. I once worked with a twenty-year-old woman experiencing severe emotional pain and fear of abandonment. She said they came from an experience with a boy she had known at age fifteen. Interestingly enough, she had developed uterine polyps at this age, which represented the second chakra in play (in the seventh chakra) at age fifteen. Using psychic techniques, she determined that her feelings of fear originated at age three, the beliefs at age fifteen. She had put these together in such a way that they still affected her.

EXERCISES
Sketching Your Past

We all have emotional patterns that interfere with our success and happiness. Let's take a walk through memory lane and uncover some of them.

I. You are going to make a time line. Create or buy a sheet of paper about two feet long. Draw a line horizontally across the middle, then make eight marks on the line. Each mark will represent one of the chakras. (Number ten will be on the far left, and you will conclude with number seven.) Label each of these with the age associated with the chakra. Gather writing and drawing instruments.

   A. Settle into a meditative state. Taking each age group one at a time, begin with the latest age (Chakra Seven) and finish with the earliest (Chakra Ten), you are going to pinpoint the emotion originating during the stage that affects you the most.

   To do this, write or sketch the feeling associated with the emotion above the line; the belief associated with this emotion under the line; and write the emotive response on the line.

   B. When you are done, take another sheet of paper. Analyzing each emotion, write down how it is currently affecting you and what you must do to heal it.

II. Select an emotional issue you are facing. Decide:
   - The primary feeling.
   - The primary thought or belief.

Use this checklist to see if you can decide at which chakra, and, therefore, at which age this emotion may have originated, and heal from this point.

Feelings	Thoughts
Rage, terror, joy, shame, desire, guilt, etc. —*Primal Feelings*	About existence, right to be, life and death, abundance, our needs, etc.
Fears, anger, creativity or blocks of such, sensuality or lack of contentment. — *Softer Feelings*	About body, creativity, children, birth (of self, ideas, projects).

Fear, anxiety, phobia, low
self-confidence or esteem,
caution, prudence, courage.
   —*Action Feelings*

Regarding place in world,
success and abilities, power.

Love, bonding, distance,
hurt and pain.
   —*Relationship Feelings*

About relationship with self
and others, childish and innate
dreams and desires.

Feelings regarding abilities
or drive to share feelings,
communicate, listen, or
understand.
   — *Expression Feelings*

Regarding expression,
communication, manifesting,
responsibility, saying yes or no.

Self-acceptance or self-loathing,
excitement, or despair.
   — *Self-Image Feelings*

Concern about self-image, body
image, desires for future.

Spiritual or religious awareness,
sense of self in relation to higher
good, fitting in, acceptance,
rejection (by the Divine Source).
   —*Self-Fulfillment Feelings*

About the Divine Source,
religious or spiritual figures
or directions, purpose, meaning,
values, or principles.

Chapter Twelve

Freeing Your Emotions

Being emotionally stuck is no fun. It hurts. It keeps us trapped in obsolete, self-destructive patterns. An imprisoning emotion prevents us from achieving our heart's and soul's desires.

Remember, though, we want feelings. We want thoughts. Feelings spice up life. They keep it fluid. They are the stream upon which we flow. Thoughts mark our life events. We think them, and know where we are and who we are being. We remember them to know who we were and who we can become. When feelings fuel us, we feel alive. When thoughts guide us, we are wise.

Inevitably, the question arises. Once our emotions become stuck, once we become emotional, once the patterns become imprinted and impressed, can we heal ourselves? How can we ever return to being and feeling free? How can our feelings and thoughts ever become free if they never have been?

The answer is simple. We must spring our feelings loose from our thoughts and allow them to act again as free agents. That sounds simple, but only if we understand the basic concept introduced in the last chapter. An emotion is created from a feeling and a thought, but it is not a feeling and a thought. When we feel, we are experiencing a feeling; we are not being the feeling itself. When we think, we are the thinker of the thought, not the thought itself; a thought is not the same as the thinker. Emotions are a projection of a feeling and a thought. The glue that keeps them together is the energy we breathe into this projection.

I believe that emotions, feelings, and thoughts work the same way that a movie does. The image we see on the screen is a created by projections from two film reels. Each of these reels rolls film, upon which are inscribed images, past a light. The interaction of these images with the light creates the picture that we see on the screen. Alone, the unfolding images have no life. They don't capture feelings or thoughts; they show pictures resulting from feelings and thoughts. The reality of these images comes from us. We lend our energy to the script, the play, the pictures of light. The images only have life because we send our own life energy into them.

Now let's back up even more. Let's pretend that we are working with two types of projectors. One contains imprints of feelings, the other is a sound-track upon which thoughts are recorded. Let's call the first one our second chakra, and the second one our third chakra. The photographic material in the second chakra reel are really only snapshots taken of our feeling bodies. The stream of thoughts on the third chakra reel are only images solidifying our mind's musings. Our body has mailed us the second chakra reel, as if to tell us, "Here. This is what is going on with me." Our mind has shipped us the third chakra reel, saying, "This is the information I've been compiling." The feelings we experience feel real because we give them that power. Thoughts seem right because we decide we want to believe them.

Once in a while, problems arise in either the recording, observation, or interpretation process. Maybe someone messes with our reels. They stick feelings onto our second chakra reel that are not ours. They splice beliefs onto our third chakra reel that don't come from our own mind. Sometimes the two projections, those of our feeling and those of our thoughts, conflict with each other. We can't separate the feelings from the thoughts, what our body needs from what our mind needs. Perhaps our hardware is damaged, and the light doesn't work. What we see on the screen is confusing. The screen can even look blank. Physical impediments, energy-system imbalances, and traumatic emotions can all result from damaged hardware. Whatever the case, there are many potential hazards to our feeling, thinking, and emotional processes.

Healing our emotions is now starting to look like a complicated process, isn't it? Do we have hardware damage? An ailment in our liver can impair third chakra processing. Feelings convoluted from childhood dysfunction can injure second chakra feeling bodies. Are the original feelings and thoughts recorded clearly? Beliefs drawn from an unhealthy system will be unhealthy in and of themselves. Feelings twisted by our parent's reactions will mar the final picture. Are we interpreting the final picture correctly? Our other energy centers may see the scene differently than our body and mind intended it to be seen. Our desires can alter our perceptions, causing us to blur the meaning of the emotion.

Face it. Most of us are past twenty-one and by now, we have experienced a great many hardware, software, and programming disasters. Most of us have probably already made inroads to healing these problems. Perhaps we have seen a therapist, counselor, pastor, alternative healer, holistic-care provider, or a psychic. Perhaps we have gone on vision quests, read self-help books, or visited sacred sites. Maybe we have looked for assistance through meditation, guided imagery, business seminars, Outward Bound courses, self-reflection, or support groups. The list of healing avenues goes on and on. You, here we are—still stuck. What are we supposed to do about it?

All possibilities boil down to one primary healing strategy. The only way through an emotional mess is to go through it. It will not work to jump over it, to try and rationalize it, or to just feel our way through it. Sooner or later, like a good technician, we must start checking each point for error and make corrections as we go. The Guardian Principles may work in and of themselves. We can also walk ourselves through our energetic system, building off the emotional development process we described in the previous chapter.

Sometimes, however, we need a more psychological approach—a more emotive approach, if you will. We need to peel away the layers of a problematic emotion or emotional pattern, and follow the lights and lines back to the participatory feeling and thought. It does help, of course, to conduct these steps in a safe manner. I think the conditions covered by Carl Rogers in *On Becoming A Person* most succinctly express the internal and external standards necessary to do true healing work (Rogers, Carl D. Boston: Houghton Mifflin Company, 1961). Although he relates them as conditions for constructive creativity, I think they apply to healing endeavors as well. His three "inner conditions" are:

1. Openness to experience.
2. An internal locus of evaluation.
3. The ability to toy with elements and concepts.

His external conditions are:

1. Psychological safety.
2. Psychological freedom.

My read on these conditions is that as we press forward, we must stay open to allowing our self-respect and imagination to teach us what we need to know. To alleviate the fear of change, we must constantly reassure ourselves, internally and externally. With this is mind, I suggest the following four steps for freeing emotions.

Step One: Put Your Emotion at Center Stage

All emotional healing begins with recognizing where we are. Are we stuck in an emotion, being emotionally sensitive, or just having a bad day?

We have explored the different indicators for being emotional versus being emotionally sensitive. We know that we are probably emotional instead of sensitive when our way of being is interfering with our good, when we can't seem to cope, get what we want, feel understood, or understand others. We are probably dealing with an emotional pattern when these or other conditions are chronic, when we can't seem to get rid of them or out of them, no matter what we do.

Emotionalism, in a rather ridiculous sort of way, is an attempt to bring balance to our system. Here is a plain and simple example. If no one in our childhood family expressed anger, we might become belligerent in an attempt to fill the gap. In this situation, our emotion, which might combine the feeling of anger with the belief that "I must take care of my family's anger," is trying to pull us one way over another to achieve balance. The trouble is, our family system is out of whack, not us. Trying to right a wrong in a system will leave us out of balance, even as it smoothes out the family.

All emotionalism pulls us off-center. It takes us away from our center-point—our sense of self—in one of two directions. When working with a stuck emotion or an emotional pattern, it is beneficial to get a sense of which direction we are being pulled. This can help us decide what we need to let go of or add to achieve equilibrium. The two directions of emotionalism are:

- **Over-Drive**: the state of over-exertion.
- **Under-Drive**: the state of being pulled-in and shut-down.

Over-Drive

When we are in over-drive, we feel like we are working all the time. Even in our sleep, we seem to be constantly processing, thinking, feeling, moving, or sensing. Over-drive is a state of over-exertion. The overriding belief is that it is our job to compensate for other people or for those parts of ourselves that are not fulfilling their functions. The feelings associated with over-drive tend to be overwhelming. When in over-drive, we will experience intense, passionate, or painful feelings.

When we are in an over-drive emotional pattern, we may:

- Feel crazy or confused.
- Feel out of control.
- Often feel irrational or stuck in a patterned response.
- Have a hard time differentiating our reality or boundaries from someone else's.
- Have difficulty separating our issues, feelings, or desires from someone else's.
- Experience all our feelings intensely, which can confuse us when the situation does not seem to merit this strong response.
- Feel compelled to take care of someone else; make them feel a certain feeling or have them see things our way.
- Experience problems with physical or psychic boundaries.

- Have a hard time staying in the present situation; our mind or feelings stray to the past or to the future.
- Feel stuck in a reactive mode and seem unable to get out.
- Experience flashbacks.
- Experience mood swings, sometimes for no apparent reason.
- Often feel over-stimulated or hyper.
- Experience waves of exhaustion; feel tired underneath all our activity.

One of my most popular classes is called "Intuitive Development for Over-Intuitors." In it, I meet hundreds of people who say they have lived their lives feeling crazy, seemingly unable to differentiate themselves from other people. Almost all have benefited from learning about the intuitive dimensions of reality. By learning how to set psychic boundaries, they make significant inroads on their psychological and physical well-being. In general, these people have had to learn how to change their beliefs so as to better manage their feelings.

Under-Drive

When we are in under-drive, we operate robotically; our responses will seem automated to ourselves or to other people. We might be unable to react to a situation, respond emotionally, or come up with something to say.

Sometimes, under-drive may appear as over-intellectualism. Try as we might, we cannot get to the feeling at hand, only a thought process. This process will probably seem terribly familiar. Do we always play the same tapes over and over? When in under-drive, our feelings may be difficult to reach, feel, or sense. When we are in an under-drive emotional pattern, we might:

- Live in our head, responding out of rationality or logic.
- Feel disconnected from our feelings.
- Get stuck in one feeling or a set pattern of feelings over and over.
- Experience a sense of deadness, lethargy, or apathy.
- Have a hard time motivating ourselves to do something new or creative.
- Receive feedback that we are too cold or unfeeling.
- Experience bouts of self-doubt and waves of discontent.
- Notice that most of our beliefs about ourselves or others are negative or critical.
- Have difficulty connecting with our intuition, sense of awareness, vision, or empathy.
- Have pent-up energy and lack a motive for expressing it.
- Have a difficult time getting in touch with or believing in the psychic or the spiritual.

When working with under-drive people, I have usually had to help them uncover the situation(s) that originally caused them to shut down their feelings. Often, this requires therapeutic assistance. Upon increasing the flow of feeling energy, they can better regulate the power they give to their beliefs.

Those of us with extreme personalities may consistently operate in over-drive or under-drive. Others of us are mixed bags. During certain situations, such as parties, we may shut down or go into under-drive. During other times, such as visits to family members, we may become hyper-active or go into over-drive. It is easier to recognize over-drive tendencies as emotionalism because we appear more emotional, both to ourselves and to others. We are more active. Our feelings are on the surface. We are expressive. It might be difficult for ourselves or others to realize that under-drive is an emotional state, rather than just a personality trait. If our low state of energy interferes with our well-being, creates unhappiness within us, or impairs our mental or relationship life, it is a symptom of emotionalism. When we are in over-drive, we are emoting outwardly. When we are in under-drive, we are emoting inwardly. Our emotions are hiding within us rather than being displayed outside of us.

Once we have recognized that we are being emotional or are stuck in an emotional pattern, we must begin to separate the thought from the feeling. After sorting the emotion into its components, we will be much more ready to address and heal it. Step Two and Step Three are interchangeable, depending on whether we are working in over-drive or under-drive. When working with an over-drive emotion, I tend to first isolate the feelings, then the thoughts. When working with an under-drive emotion, I first work with the thoughts, then the feelings. I work these different ways because an over-drive emotional state is run on feelings; an under-drive emotional state is powered by thoughts. It is easier to pinpoint the top rather than bottom layer of an issue.

Step Two: Isolating the Feeling

Whenever we are in an emotional state, we are stuck in a certain feeling. When trying to decipher the feeling caught in an emotion, we must remember that the pertinent feeling comes from the past, not the present. Even if a current situation has hooked a feeling, the intensity, the flavor, the breadth and depth of the feeling lies in our past, not in our present. The rule of thumb for recognizing that a feeling is old or entrenched is one shared by my therapist. If a feeling seems too big for the situation, it probably is.

Sometimes, it is relatively easy to acknowledge the major feeling player. More often, however, the causal feeling is covered by a layer or layers of secondary feelings that blanket the primary feeling. We layer feelings to bandage the original wound, to protect the self that was injured in the past, so that it cannot be injured again.

In general, the more intense and difficult the emotion, the older and more damaged the feeling is, the younger we were when our feelings became hurt or misused. It is important to get to the age at which we were injured, the age at which we formed the emotion that causes us current harm. That self is crying for help, even though it might also be simultaneously pushing it away. We want to heal and prevent more pain. This tension can cause us to feel terrified about being healed, confused about the process, and eager to be helped. Sounds like an emotional state right there, doesn't it?

When working with clients who are sorting through their feelings, I often like to apply hands-on therapies, or have them work with a healer or massage therapist while working with me. Feelings are the language of the body. If we are willing to listen to it, the body can be of great help in the healing process. It can help us locate our feelings, uncover repressed feelings and memories, and repair damaged feelings.

My favorite method is to use non-intrusive therapeutic touch. Usually, I put a hand on each chakra, working from the top down. I ask the client to describe the feeling state this touch brings up in regard to the emotional state he or she has been experiencing. We go down the chakras, searching for the feeling that brings up the undesired emotional state, looking for the feeling that triggers the entire emotion.

I can often sense where this feeling is by the hot and cold spots in the person's body. A hot spot means that a feeling is brewing within this area. A cold spot frequently indicates that a feeling is absent or hiding. When I or the client feel a hot spot, I have him or her go into this feeling to see if it connects to the emotional state. If it does, we begin our work here. When I or the client sense a cold spot, I lightly stimulate this area. I shoot energy into it, and I ask the client to bring his or her consciousness into it. I might flip the person and work on the back-side chakra until the person gets some feelings. Once we have arrived at the feeling, I bring the client further into it, encouraging him or her to feel, be, and act the age associated with that feeling. Often, my intent is to enable the person to remember the experience, state, person, or situation linked to that feeling.

There are many other ways to pinpoint a feeling. I may ask a client to simply point to the area that holds the feeling locked within the emotion. I may use my knowledge of the child development/chakra system to guide the person into a childhood state. If the client seems truly blocked, I may work mainly with the back-side system, encouraging help from the person's unconscious and guides. I may have the person sit in a chair and begin talking to another chair. I support him or her by directing whatever feeling comes into the body to the "person" sitting in the other chair. Whatever the case, our objective is two-fold.

1. We want to help isolate the major feeling wrapped up in the undesirable emotional state or pattern.

2. We want to get a fix on the age and situation at which this feeling became stuck.

Sometimes, a client will take weeks getting to the formative feeling, and that is okay. I will support the person no matter what, or encourage him or her to work with another professional. The person might get stuck in fear for a while. If that is the case, I tell the client to feel as scared as he or she can. The person might become unbelievably sad; I tell them to go to sad movies. The person might sense the need to be angry, but doesn't feel he or she can let the anger out. I have the person beat pillows until the feeling comes up on its own. We want to peel away the layers of feelings until we get to the one that seems right, until the client can say, "Yes! This is the feeling I feel when I'm emotional about XYZ."

Step Three: Isolating the Thought Form

The thought connected into the troublesome emotion may or may not have originated with us. It may well represent our personal reaction to a certain situation. If this is the case, it will probably be phrased like an observation. "I see that everyone is unhappy." "I just caused pain to my mother." "I didn't have an answer when the teacher called on me." Thoughts such as these don't cause an emotional reaction in and of themselves; they must be teamed with a feeling to create difficulties.

Take our first example: "I see that everyone is unhappy." Imagine that this thought originated in a family event at which we expressed some anger. If we then perceived that everyone is unhappy that we are angry, we might have formed the core belief and emotion "Everyone becomes unhappy when I am angry." This emotion may clear if we can discuss it with someone, raise it to our heart chakra for a second opinion, or experience a family event at which we saw a very different reaction when we became angry. Unfortunately, especially with family matters, we tend to receive the same reactions and judgments over and over. At some point, our perception of others' unhappiness links with our anger, and they become permanently cemented together. Our energy system can become muddled every time we see someone angry and rekindle the thought that someone outside of us is unhappy.

Thoughts may also come from the people around us. Some thoughts we swallow whole; others we digest over time. For instance, if we were raised in a family that decried a certain ethnic group, believed that everyone with money was bad, or proposed that artists must be poor, we could understandably take on these points of view wholeheartedly. We might also select pieces of the belief system swirling around us. Our father, for instance, might insist that women are stupid. Our mother, who seems intelligent enough to us, may have trouble balancing the checkbook. We might put two and two together, then subtract one of each to create the hybrid belief "Women are stupid about money." Often, these types of beliefs are more difficult to isolate than wholly owned ones. Because they are composites, they can be quite complicated.

Distinguishing the most important thought or belief form can be a troublesome process. We might have thousands of thoughts swimming in our head at any given time, hundreds of which might be subsidiary conclusions forming the emotion at hand. The belief that women (or men) are stupid about money may the key ingredient in our own struggles to make a decent living. With time, we may have added a number of tributaries to this belief. "Women should be kept away from money." "Women shouldn't have any money of their own." "Women should feel stupid if they make money." What we want to do is to get to the core belief, not get lost in the myriad of secondary beliefs threading themselves throughout our energy system.

The best way to do this is to isolate the belief in tangent with one of the other emotional indicators. While feeling the feeling associated with our problematic emotion, or feeling/being/acting the age at which we incorporated the emotion, we can simply ask our younger self to tell us what conclusion we drew from the circumstances around us. Then we must listen. We must hear ourselves talk to ourselves.

I will often have clients dealing with confusion conduct a belief exercise. Using pen and paper, I have them write their understanding of the emotion affecting them. I then have them make a statement of thought or belief about this emotion. For instance, a female client might write:

> Statement regarding the emotion: "I often feel bad when I am spending money. I tell myself I shouldn't be doing it, but the worse I feel, the more I spend."
>
> Corollary belief: "I am bad with money."

To make sure we have really gotten to the bottom, I have the client continue. After writing "I am bad with money," I have her rewrite this statement, add a "because," and fill in an answer. I have her continue on this path until she hits pay dirt, until she feels an "Ah-hah!" and knows that we have hit bottom. For example:

> Corollary belief: "I am bad with money because *I can never hang onto it*."
>
> Corollary belief: "I can never hang on to money *because I am a girl*."
>
> Corollary belief: "As a girl, I can never hang on to money *because girls are bad with money*."
>
> Corollary belief: "Girls are bad with money *because my father says so*."

Corollary belief: "My father says so *because he believes it*."

Corollary belief: "My father believes girls are bad with money *because he's scared of letting them have it*."

Corollary belief: "He's scared of letting girls have money *because then they wouldn't need men*."

Corollary belief: "If they didn't need men, *he could be left*."

Ah-hah! See how this brings the issue to its core?

If I want to go one step further, I can use this place as a springboard for regression work. I may now be able to dive into the situation that locked up the emotions. Regarding the above example, this might involve remembering what age the client was when she perceived that females were bad with money. She will want to recall who demonstrated this behavior, taught her this, or forced her to believe it.

Step Four: Uncovering the Pay-Off

Once we have our emotion pared down into its raw components, we want to free our body and mind from the clutches in which they have been confined. The only way to do this is to love the emotion—to death. That's right. We must assume that the problematic, troublesome, and hated emotion we have been experiencing was meeting a need, and so has the feeling and thought battling within it. If we are to truly become free from the emotion, we must do more than destroy the emotion. Hammering it into oblivion will only leave us empty. This emptiness, this void, will seek to be filled. The original need will call out. Even if we succeeded in unsticking our stuck emotion, but fail to find a new way to meet the old need, we will just design a new emotion to fill the vacuum. This new emotional state will create just as much havoc as the original did.

When we understand the need our troublesome emotion is filling and create a new, more self-loving way to fill it, we become more willing to allow our feelings and beliefs to detach. We open to the energies and help that we need to allow damaged feelings and beliefs to heal. We allow the stuck parts of ourselves to grow up. At first glance, most of us can't believe that we are receiving benefit for being unhappy, hating ourselves, or picking only alcoholics as mates, but we are. We may not be proud of our reasons, but they are there. The types of needs or pay-offs I run across vary widely, but there are two basic types: fear-based pay-offs and love-based pay-offs.

Fear-based pay-offs are based on fears of consequence. They stem from an internal drive to avoid responsibility, self- or other-care, or truthfulness. We all have fears. That doesn't mean we are bad people. It probably means that, when we were growing up, our energy systems didn't fully develop because something or someone in our environment didn't support the maturing process. Fear-based pay-offs keep us frozen in time. The two-year-old girl or boy that was hurt will remain within us, locked within our second chakra. This two-year-old will run the show, scared to let go of control until we meet its needs and let it be a child again.

Love-based pay-offs are sacrificial in nature. They involve making choices to hurt ourselves so that someone else may feel better or avoid being hurt. A case in point is one of my clients who decided to take on her mother's physical issues. She truly loved her mother and thought that was the best way that she could help. Even though this client manifested this choice through physical illness, the disease itself was emotional because it was motivated by a belief ("My mother will die without my help") and a feeling (love for her mother).

Overall, I see fewer love-based problems than I do fear-based. It does happen, however. I remember several times deciding to not "speak my truth" because it would hurt my father. I recall a client who mirrored her mother's back pain so her mother would have it easier. I had another client decide she was bad because if she wasn't, her mother, who had ritually abused her, would be the bad one; she was willing to "go to hell" so her mother wouldn't. I more commonly find clients absorbing a parent's pain, because doing so assures their own survival. I think this absorption happens because we exist in a fear-based society. Love is not mirrored or reflected back to most of us on a daily basis. Unconditional love may be heard of, but seldom experienced. It is difficult to build a foundation without blueprints.

The most common pay-offs of both types I see in my work include the following:

Fear-Based Pay-Offs

- Don't have to grow up.
- Don't have to take risks.
- Avoid getting hurt.
- Won't have to feel (certain) feelings.
- Get to avoid responsibility.
- Won't have to remember a painful experience.
- Won't have to repeat a painful experience.
- Don't have to confront an issue.
- Can get taken care of by other people.
- Get to feel sorry for self.
- Avoid success.
- Avoid failure.
- Get attention.
- Don't have to admit being wrong.

Love-Based Pay-Offs

• Save someone's life.

• Ease someone's pain.

• Put another person first.

• Atone for guilt.

• Fulfill karmic debt.

• Be of service.

• Learn a lesson.

• Learn how to be compassionate.

• Experience the positive use of power.

• Practice a healing art.

• Make the world a better place.

Determining the pay-off involved in an emotional issue requires complete honesty with oneself or another human being. The Twelve-Step Programs are designed to help people achieve this level of honesty. One of the steps these programs direct people to undertake is a thorough overview of themselves and their actions. They are asked to make a list of all the people they have wronged, and to make amends if appropriate. These steps invite seekers of truth to bare their own souls, to peer within, and to admit failures of spirit. Forgiveness is inevitable, because we are children of the Divine Source. Children make mistakes. Children display false pride. Children need guidance. It is prideful and grandiose to think that we would be the only human being alive to escape making mistakes, now wouldn't it? Personally, I find great relief in admitting when I'm being dishonest or manipulative in an emotional way. Even experiencing others' feelings is manipulative, because it controls the situation.

Typically, once a client accepts the fact that he or she is a student of the Universe, a child of the Divine Source, and a self in development (not just a completed self), the pay-off simply pops into his or her mind. Of course, there are other techniques for unearthing it. I might regress clients to the point of injury; use applied kinesiology, a system for testing the body's response to questions; have clients ask for an informative dream; or have the client write a fable or fairy tale. When using the story-writing technique, I have them center the storyline on the emotional issue in question and freely write whatever comes into their heads. The pay-off usually leaps off the page.

Once the pay-off is clear, we know what we need to know. We have assembled our character cast. We know the emotion, the feeling, the thought (or belief), and the pay-off. I would like to be able give a quick and easy method for healing from this point on, but I can't. This is because the first and most important part of healing the apparent emotion is to become willing to part with it.

Here, we must return to our Guardian Principles. I will frequently walk clients through a few of these principles in question form when healing the emotion-based problem. I will ask them if they are willing to be healed and to manifest their desires. I will ask them if they are willing to change or accept a new way to meet their needs. I will ask if they are willing to let go of the old patterns and pay-offs. I will ask them if they are willing to feel the feelings they need to feel, to create a new thought for themselves, and to be free rather than imprisoned. I will ask them if they are willing to allow the Divine Source or their Divine Source self to serve as a guide throughout the process. Sometimes, I even ask if they are willing to allow miracles to happen, to let people become magical, and to do the work they must do to become the people they want to become. At this point, I go with the flow. I must trust my own sense of process and encourage the client to do the same, to actually allow the energy system to change and to shift.

Support is an important part of an emotional change process. Long-held feelings may rise to the surface, causing bouts of grief, anger, rage, or terror. Crusty, debilitating thoughts may storm up, reciting litanies of criticism about themselves or others. My experience is that if these old energies are provided a space or place for safe expression, they soon evaporate, mature, or transform. Left in their wake is usually a somewhat tired, but ecstatic, new person who, male or female, looks much like a mother who has just gone through labor and given birth to an incredibly beautiful baby—the self.

EXERCISE
Writing the Story of Your Life

A. Take out a pad of paper and a pen. Now, think of an issue that is causing you frustration or dissatisfaction. You are going to take a journey of words on the land of paper before you.

You will be writing your own journey as you go. You will be writing the story of your life in relation to this issue. To do this, you might want to follow the path of the "Hero's Journey." A hero is someone who learns something (the hard way) and becomes a better, stronger person for it, a person able to share his or her learnings with others.

You are the hero in this story. You are the major character. You are the person affected by the emotional problem; you are the hero who rides straight into it. You are the hero who struggles and overcomes the problem. You are the hero who lives to tell about it and returns home. You are the hero who creates good out of the difficulty.

B. The points of your journey will be these:

1. Begin "at home," describing your background and the situations that set you up for your difficulties.

2. Leave home. What happens to you, the hero, as you journey forth into the world?

3. Fight the dragon. The emotional issue is your dragon. Describe it. Know it. How must you approach it? Deal with it? Combat it?

4. Defeat the dragon. How will you overcome the obstacle this emotion/dragon represents? What powers must you draw forth from yourself to defeat it? What help must you ask for or accept to master the dragon? What wisdom must you have to transform the emotion/dragon?

5. Cut off the dragon's head. What have you learned from struggling with this dragon?

6. Accept your reward. What does your struggle mean for you within the greater context of your life? What new energies, knowledge, or riches must you accept to change your life?

7. Return home. All heroes return to their points of origin. What does this beginning point look like to you now? Can you see it with compassion?

8. Teach others. All heroes bring their learnings, their riches, their wisdom back to the community. What must you do, know, or understand to do this?

C. After writing your story, reflect upon its meaning for you today.

Alternate Exercise

A. Select a problem that you can't seem to shake. Ask yourself these questions:

   1. What feeling(s) do I feel when I think about this problem? Write these down in list format.

   2. What belief relates to each feeling? These beliefs should be written in statement form, such as:

Problem Feelings	Problem Beliefs
Sadness	I hurt others when I say my truth.
Fear	I can be hurt by others if I ask for something.
Panic	Nothing can stop this pattern.

B. Take each belief and pare it back to a thought, such as:

Problem Beliefs	Thoughts
I hurt others when I say my truth.	I can hurt others. I can say my truth.
I can be hurt by others when I ask for something.	I can be hurt. I can ask for something.
Nothing can stop this pattern.	I have patterns. Patterns can't be stopped by anything I know.

C. Take the thoughts and put them together with the feelings as perceptions, such as:

   • I feel sad when I say my truth and others hurt me, and so, I can decide when to share something or not.

   • I feel scared when I ask for something, and I get hurt. So I can ask someone else, until I find someone willing to help me.

   • I feel panicked that I have patterns, and I don't know how to stop them. So I will ask people without these patterns to help me.

Chapter Thirteen

Being Your Divine Source Self: Living as an Everyday Shaman

When seeking to heal or to manifest, we must often unravel years upon years of emotional, physical, and spiritual issues or blocks. These blocks (points of resistance) are aptly named, because they block the natural flow of energy revolving between our spiritual and physical selves. Because we come from the Divine Source, are the Divine Source, and seek the Divine Source within ourselves, the best way to clear out our resistance is to work with this knowledge.

Unfortunately, there is something in the way. It is the something that underlies most of our emotional issues, physical disorders, and spiritual misperceptions. That something is denial. Denial exists whenever we ignore our true nature, our Divine Source self. When we accept anything less than that which the Divine Source desires for us or that which our Divine Source self deserves, we are buying into a pay-off. By thinking or hoping that a pay-off will fill our needs, we deny ourselves the power, energy, and love that will really meet our needs—our essential needs.

How did or does denial enter our existence, and what are we supposed to do about it? This grandiose question begs both esoteric and practical responses.

The Role of Denial

To deny something is to turn our back on it. In relation to our feelings, we are in denial when we refuse to recognize, affirm, or feel our feelings. In relation to our thoughts, we are in denial when we refuse to think, attend, or review our thoughts. In relation to our emotions, we are in denial if our emotions remain unexpressed or continue to recycle. There is a state of denial behind all of these circumstances, however: we are in denial when we refuse to affirm our Divine Source self.

Getting to the Divine Source self underneath the layers of denial, emotion, misperceptions, diseases, and bad relationships can be a painful process. It is painful not because being our Divine Source self is painful, but because it comes from combating the years of programming that convince us that the best way to heal or manifest is the hard way. We cure cancer by ingesting drugs. We make money by working at jobs that we hate. We learn about love by being in relationships that make us feel bad. We have fun by doing what other people tell us is fun. We struggle with life so that we can deny death. In other words, we work very, very hard to do it right—only to end up miserable.

There are layers to our denial. When working with clients, I often find that many of them uncover one level only to plunge to the next. These layers appear with clients sorting through health, relationship, career, psychological, religious, and all other concerns. I believe that all these levels relate to our spiritual and child development.

In my world, it works like this. At some point, our soul was damaged by an original wound. That wound caused us to turn our backs on the reality of the Divine Source, at least in part. Feeling guilty about turning our backs, we went forth in denial of our true Divine Source and our true self, true purpose, and true will. Denying these, we heaped one feeling upon another, one emotion upon another, one physical ailment upon another—each layer blanketing the layer beneath. Healing involves uncovering these layers of denial so that we can touch back into our original wound or misperception. Manifesting is the process whereby we receive or gain that which we need to reach this centerpoint.

The following are the layers of denied emotion that I most typically see. I have listed them from top to bottom, and described each layer according to its three major components. The denied feeling indicates the feeling state that covers up the layer beneath. The predominate thought indicates the primary belief associated with this layer. The cause relates to the wound that occurred at this layer.

The Basic Layers of Denial

Denied Feeling	Predominant Thought	Cause
1. Fear	I am not strong enough to see what lies beneath my fear.	Fear serving as a protection mechanism.
2. Sadness	I have lost something important or valuable.	Loss of self, others, or dreams due to hardships.

3. Anger	I have been wronged.	The cause of our pain, usually a person who doesn't seem to care.
4. Hurt	Something has happened to me that cannot be repaired.	Our spirit is injured; part of our true self is disregarded.
5. Rage	I am impotent; I am unable to keep myself safe.	Rage, a combination of hurt and anger, will exist underneath or over the layers of sadness and anger, if these unexpressed feelings become bonded with powerlessness.
6. Shame	I am bad.	We have been treated badly; we own the blame for this treatment. Shame fills the gap caused by abandoning ourselves.
7. Guilt	I caused myself to be hurt.	We abandon ourselves; we repress, renege, splinter, or deny a part of ourselves to better cope with that which is causing us pain.
8. Terror	I am powerless to stop that which is outside of me from hurting me.	We perceive that something or someone is going to damage us, and believe we are unable to stop it or call for help.
9. Judgment/ Guilt	There is something wrong with me; I do not deserve to be part of the Divine Source.	We hold this belief because we perceive that we are separate from the Divine Source. It leads us to believe that we cannot call on the Divine Source for help.
10. Denial	I am not the Divine Source.	Believing we separated ourselves from the Divine Source, we deny our true power and potential.

I help clients process these layers and rewrite the original scripts in a number of different ways. In my opinion, the clients who experience the most growth are those able to get to the basic root of guilt. The clients who become their true selves, however, are those who allow themselves to fall all the way into their denial of the Divine Source—and come up again.

A case in point concerns Fred. A medical doctor, Fred was an alcoholic. During the past few years, his successful practice had fallen in half. His marriage was barely limping along. His children were displaying the typical characteristics of adult children of alcoholics—their lives were messy and out-of-control. For his part, Fred swam in a continual bath of self-pity. Anytime he was confronted, he would slump into his chair and begin to mutter. "I know, I know. I'm a failure. I can't do anything right."

Fred came to me out of desperation. During our first session, I asked him to throw himself into his feelings of self-pity and uselessness. At first, he was scared. After a while, he became sad and began to cry, calling himself a failure over and over. Assuming that we had unearthed at least part of his emotional issue, I asked him if he really thought of himself as a failure. "Yes," he said. "I am. That is all I ever have been."

Even though we had rested on an emotionally laden belief, I didn't feel like we had gotten to the core emotion. After all, he had been in this state before, and it had not stopped his drinking. During the next session, I asked him to pretend that he was drunk. I then spoke with his drunk self, asking it why it needed to drink. Fred immediately moved from sadness to anger. He began ranting and raving. Life was unfair, his wife didn't understand him, everyone expected something from him, but no one cared about him.

I decided we needed to go for the core. Guiding Fred into his lowest chakra, I asked him to be the age at which this issue had originated. To my surprise, he immediately, curled up in a ball. He was a small child. The feeling connected to feeling like a failure? Guilt. He hadn't been able to make his parents get along with each other and felt bad about it. After processing his guilt and forgiving himself, Fred's progress leaped ahead. He voluntarily began attending Alcoholics Anonymous. He checked himself into a treatment program and asked his wife to get help for herself, too.

Despite these heroic moves, a year later, Fred was still experiencing waves of self-pity. His business was still slow. He was still confused about whether or not he deserved money, a good relationship, and, most of all, his own existence. Then I saw a miracle occur. At some level, I believe that Fred continuing to process guilt and shame. One day, he came into my office, aglow. He had been sitting at a stop sign, impatiently waiting for an older woman to cross the street. For "no reason," he said, she stopped and turning toward him, she smiled. All of a sudden, he "got it!"

"For some reason, that smile did it. I realized that she was a part of the human race, not just somebody out to slow me down. She was, well, a part of God!" He looked down, as if still somewhat embarrassed by this revelation and then, his eyes shining, added, "I thought, well, if she is a part of God, then I must be, too. No matter what I have done." Fred had taken the leap—he had jumped from denial to truth. Needless to say, his life was never the same after that.

Integrating Our Selves

While it can be effective to journey our energy systems chakra by chakra, ray by ray, age by age, and emotional layer by emotional layer, I often draw on a concept that is much simpler for my clients (and me) to grasp. I encourage clients to think of themselves as having three aspects. To keep it easier, I don't label them body, mind, and soul, although these three aspects of self are obviously still involved. Instead, I have clients decide which of the following describes their current self:

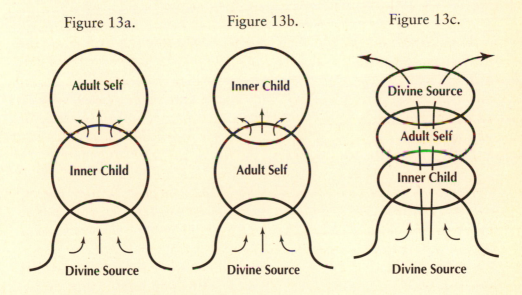

Figure 13a.   Figure 13b.   Figure 13c.

Everyone can relate to the idea of having an inner child or many inner children. These are the selves who have become lost within our energy system. These are the child parts of ourselves who have remained imprisoned within our developing chakras. These are the selves that, gifted as they are, must be rescued. Our inner children are the children that we have been and who have not grown up. Usually, we experience these children selves as very intense. They are so loud! Their feelings are so intense! They are so needy! Because they seem so demanding, we often put these children selves in the driver's seat, giving them responsibility for our lives (figure 13b).

The trouble is, having too much responsibility only scares these children selves all the more. They need guidance, which requires that we assume an adult self. This adult part of us must make sure that we don't make crazy decisions. If our children selves are to feel safe, this adult self must keep our car in running order, pay the bills, say hello to the boss, and drive us to our therapist's office. As long as we keep the adult part of us in working order, the children parts of us can calm down and do what children need to do—play, heal, laugh, and make magic (figure 13a). However, most of our adult parts feel as lost as do our children parts. We have limited vision. We feel like we are faking it. We don't understand the world any better than the next person. We screw up.

This is where our Divine Source self comes in. If our adult self can establish a bond with our Divine Source or essential self, it will be able to act responsibly, for it will receive the mentorship and guidance it needs. After all, our Divine Source self has a much higher perspective. It knows all there is to know. It knows what we need to know right now and what can wait. Our Divine Source self also has the ability to see our final destination and chart the course to it. All aspects of ourselves—the children parts that need healing, the adult part that learns how to manifest, and the Divine Source self that seeks integration—can fall into alignment when they work together (figure 13c).

By working as a trilogy, the following occurs:

1. Our Divine Source self can heal our soul. Our soul draws miracles into our lives.

2. Our adult self can heal our mind. It can manifest through work.

3. Our children selves can heal our body. They can manifest through magic.

The key to all of the above is to allow our Divine Source self into us (figure 13d). Left alone, our adult/mind self and children/body self run rampant, cause chaos, become emotional. How do we do this? How do we know whether or not our Divine Source self is linked in? How do we hear what this Divine Source self has to say? It's simple. We open to our intuition.

The Voice of Our Spirit Self

Thoughts communicate for our adult/mind self, and feelings speak for our childlike/body selves. Intuition, however, is the voice of our soul. Actually, intuition is the voice of the Divine Source self, the essential spirit self, that speaks through our soul. Intuition tells our soul what to do. In turn, our soul directs us toward our purpose.

Despite the recent interest in the mind/body connection, there are still few professionals willing to assert that there is a mind/body/soul connection. If our soul isn't represented, we are cut off from the infinite sources of invisible

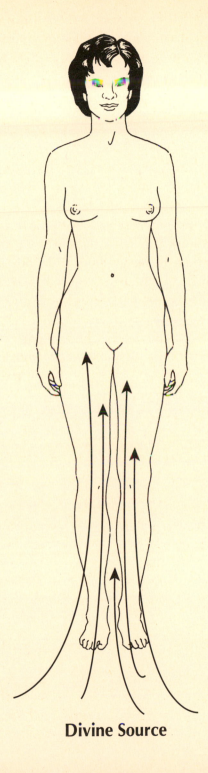

Divine Source

**Allowing the Divine Source into us
is the key to integrating our selves.**

and powerful assistance that we need to survive and thrive. Intuition is the one medium that can free us from everything and anything. Neither our body nor mind can do it, because they were unable to keep us from getting emotionally trapped in the first place.

How do you recognize your intuition? You could read books and books on the subject, take class after class, but inevitably, you must still answer your own question. Because each of our Divine Source selves is unique, our intuitive style is unique. In a positive vein, I have never met anyone who was not acquainted with his or her intuition. At first, many people have insisted that they haven't the slightest idea what their intuitive voice sounds like. These same people, after understanding a bit about intuition, have all provided me examples of how intuition has affected their lives.

It is helpful to understand a few facts about intuition. First, it comes in many forms. Most people experience intuition in one of three ways. They visually see pictures, they verbally hear voices, or they kinesthetically sense, feel, or know answers. However, if you look back on our pages describing the major human chakras, you will notice that each chakra functions as an intuitive center. Each chakra has a link with our soul and our Divine Source self, and is capable of channeling information, healing energy, and messages from our highest forms of guidance. The first chakra, for instance, will understand intuition through physical sensations. The second will pick up on feelings. The fifth can travel to the astral plane for assistance. The sixth will provide us with pictures.

Traveling from center to center for guidance could drive us crazy. When we move our power center from a lower chakra to the heart, we realign our energy system. We allow our intuitive messages to converge in the heart. We can therefore access any guidance that we need from one place—our heart, the meeting ground of our spiritual and physical selves.

Following our senses of knowing, feeling, hearing, and seeing, we can gain the insight necessary to separate the beliefs and feelings that cause us trouble. We can gain the guidance our adult self needs to monitor our daily lives. We can obtain the reassurance our children selves desire to feel safe and secure. Sometimes our intuition will tell us that we need to cry, to hold our inner child, to regress to another time and place, to read a certain book, or to go out dancing. Intuition not only tells us how to heal damage, it can help us prevent further damage.

The other important reason for incorporating intuition into our emotional life is that it represents our soul. Our essential self has certain needs and drives. Our intuition's job is to help us fulfill these dreams by keeping us on track with our soul purpose. If we live in purposeful process, we will automatically be involved in healing situations. When we are following our purpose, following our meaning, expressing our essential self, we will also be able to manifest anything we need to heal. When we do this, we are living as our own shamans. We are being our own creators and healers.

Living as a Shaman

A shaman's purpose is to walk in both the spiritual and physical worlds. Since ancient times, communities all over the world selected representatives to link the spiritual and physical planes for the benefit of all. In *The Celtic Shaman*, John Matthews describes a shaman as "one whose work is so integrated into everyday life that the 'join' does not show" (Matthews, John. Rockport, MA: Element, Inc., 1992, 92) The shaman's job was to help individuals heal physical and spiritual issues, and assist the community in doing the same. To do this, the shaman had to negotiate the revolving doors between the two dimensions.

Our energy systems are designed to enable each of us to be our own shamans. Our in-body chakras have front sides and back sides. The centerpoints in the spine act like portals connecting our conscious and unconscious, our spiritual and tangible selves. We really are wheels of light, spinning in the stillness of our own being. As shamans for ourselves, it is our responsibility to keep the doorways between both worlds open at all times. By doing this, we can receive the "other-world" messages we need to heal and to manifest, and we can project the reality-based energies necessary to move through the world.

Our shaman self is the one capable of stretching to the stars, often via our uppermost energy points. This capability would be worthless to our here-and-now self if we could not ground these energies into practical reality. How can our kundalini help us pay the bills? How can the feeling of peace soothe a difficult relationship? Conversely, how can having a disease teach us about faith or grace? Whether we work these questions through our spine, our feelings, our thoughts, or anything else, work them through we must.

We have auras that exist on both the material and immaterial planes. These energy layers seam together our insides and outsides. Our physical energies ride these waves to the spiritual dimensions. In turn, spiritual energies can convert into physical matter. Our aura protects, defines, heals, and holds. In relation to our aura, we must walk the line between being inside and outside of our own body, and it is our shaman self who must do this for us. Our mind, connected as it is to the brain, unfurls into limitless realities, and it is our shaman self who must negotiate these boundaries. Our soul is planted both inside and outside this plane, and it is our shaman self who must combine the two.

There are many tools a shaman may draw upon. Traditionally, these props included the drum, dance, animals, and plants. The form used was often called "journeying," and consisted of ritually visiting the under- or overworld. Our personal shamanic tools must be gleaned from our own lives. We all have props that are meaningful to us. Reggae or classical music may invite our own soul into a healing state. Housekeeping or carpentry can lull our body into serenity, encouraging inspiration. A book, a child's smile, a snappy outfit, a well-done work proposal may be the triggers for our own reverie. Whatever and however we do it, we are all on a journey of our own making. We are all seeking not just to understand our purpose, but to fulfill it. To do this, we must tap both worlds. We must become both worlds.

As we journey forth, let us remember that we journey together, hand-in-hand. As we allow the magic, mystery, and work of the path to unfold, let us remember we can call for help from our neighbors, our families, our spiritual guides, the rays, and, of course, the Divine Source itself. As we evolve, let us remember that we are not so much changing as we are revolving from one aspect of ourselves to another. Ultimately, the purpose is one of enjoyment.

Appendix

The aura of a person with chronic fatigue syndrome, described in Chapter Six, is one example of how an existing or potential medical condition in the physical body can also be perceived in the energetic and spiritual bodies.

I and other intuitive people have hundreds of stories of perceiving potential illnesses this way, which all beg the question: is there really potential illness present? I reply, maybe. Through the seventh auric layer scan (described in Chapter Six), I have seen enough cancerous conditions that later proved to be really there to ascribe it validity. The seventh layer scan and other intuitive views of the energy/spiritual bodies are helpful as long as I (or other intuitive people) don't pretend to have the "right" answer. I use my gifts to direct individuals to help, rather than playing doctor.

The following are examples of physical and mental conditions I have intuitively perceived in the energetic and spiritual bodies.

Breast and Prostate Cancer

There are many types of cancer—enough for an entire book. In general, the development of breast cancer can be seen in the auric layers as one or more dark shapes pointed at the breast and moving through the aura. The darkness almost always points to or parallels the exact area a cyst or tumor might grow or is growing (figure 14a).

Tumors usually have three colors associated with them: black, white, and red. Black indicates absent or unexpressed emotions. It may signify the root of the problem or a secondary symptom of the causal issue. If a person is healthy, white indicates the presence of the soul; if a person is unhealthy, white indicates a spiritual misperception—often the case when a there is a tumor. Red indicates pain or source of the trauma.

With cancer, there is often another color present, depending on the type of cancer and the reason it exists. For instance, blue is often present if the malignancy is caused by holding onto another's issues. Sometimes it can be difficult to psychically distinguish these secondary colors because cancer itself is an elusive, out-of-control force. (In fact, it is undifferentiated tissue or cells, like fetal tissue.)

There may be energy lines linking the breast tumor(s) to various organs or glands. These lines often descend to the second chakra (to the ovaries, for instance), reflecting my awareness that breast cancer is often associated with misperceptions or repressions of feminine power. Lines may also ascend to the sixth chakra (the pituitary gland), reflecting that a woman's self-image affects her well-being. If both areas are linked to the diseased breast, I would say this woman is affected by identity issues involving sexuality and feminine power. These issues were probably caused by a relationship to another person, which leads me to search for cords.

Sickly yellow, slightly white energy in the prostate area, and white, yellow, and grey splotches between the second and third auric layers are indications of prostate cancer (figure 14b). Psychologically, this yellow color reflects inappropriate perceptions about power and a lack of clarity regarding the best use of male energy. Was this man raised to be a "good guy?" Was he made to feel shame about his first chakra energy? Did he misuse his sexuality at some time, or was he victimized for it (through sexual abuse, for example)? Issues such as these might also be reflected by a dark spot in the third eye (the sixth chakra).

It is possible to see splotchy orange and greyish or dark hues in the second chakra, which indicates that feelings were not integrated or were shamed. These discolorations night exist in or between the second and third auric layers around the first chakra. Also, red spots might be detected in the third chakra, indicating displaced passions.

Heart Disease

Heart illnesses often reflect issues about love, because the heart is located in the relationship (fourth) chakra. Before it strikes, heart disease can sometimes be seen in the etheric auric layer or in the tenth chakra, where the inherited diseases are found and where disease patterns might be held until they become too intense. The issues are then dumped into the body. In general, the key to heart issues is to locate the fear-based responses to relationships. Fear is the motivator for a person's inability to give or receive love.

There are several indicators of heart disease. One is a grey color and black spots in the fourth auric layer (figure 14c). Another is the appearance of dark energy in one or more of the heart chambers, right outside the heart itself (somewhere in the pericardium). This darkness becomes more defined

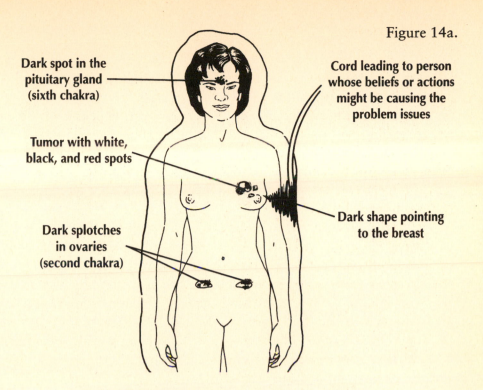

Figure 14a.

Dark spot in the
pituitary gland
(sixth chakra)

Cord leading to person
whose beliefs or actions
might be causing the
problem issues

Tumor with white,
black, and red spots

Dark shape pointing
to the breast

Dark splotches
in ovaries
(second chakra)

Energetic indications of breast cancer.

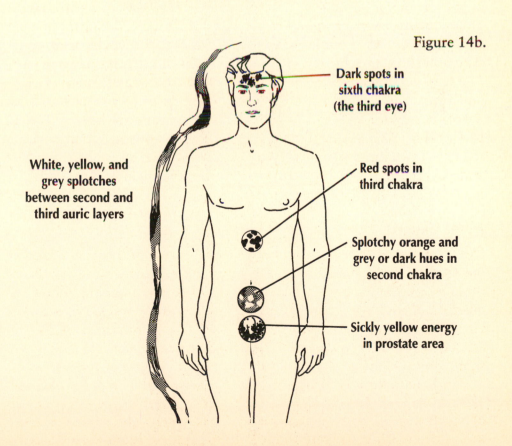

Figure 14b.

Dark spots in
sixth chakra
(the third eye)

White, yellow, and
grey splotches
between second and
third auric layers

Red spots in
third chakra

Splotchy orange and
grey or dark hues in
second chakra

Sickly yellow energy
in prostate area

Energetic indications of prostate cancer.

Figure 14c.

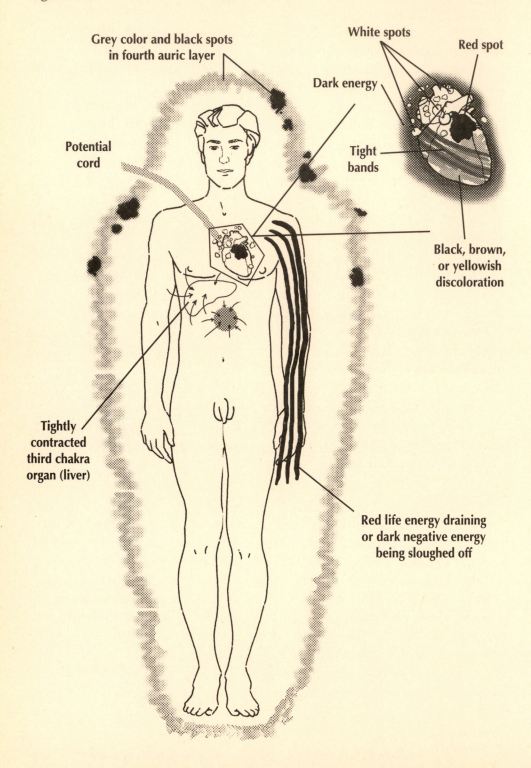

Grey color and black spots in fourth auric layer

White spots

Red spot

Dark energy

Potential cord

Tight bands

Black, brown, or yellowish discoloration

Tightly contracted third chakra organ (liver)

Red life energy draining or dark negative energy being sloughed off

Energetic indications of heart disease.

and pronounced as the disease progresses, finally turning into a series of tight bands that squeeze the heart during or right before a heart attack.

I might see one or more intense red spots in the heart area. Because these red spots indicate where the heart is concentrating or trying to contain energy, they become deeper-colored as the series of bands grow tighter. In this case, the heart is trying to preserve its life energy.

Often, there are also spots of white in the heart area. These white spots, if healthy and bright, indicate the presence of the soul. Either the soul is trying to work on the heart and its issues, or it is preparing to dissociate (just before death). If the white is unhealthy looking, I have the client examine what spiritual misperceptions they hold. These could be the very issues causing the problem.

With chronic heart issues, the green color of a healthy heart chakra tends to discolor, becoming sort of black, brown, or yellow.

Dark or light red energy often emerges out of the left hand. This is an energy leak, signifying that the heart is not circulating energy as it should. The red is life energy draining from the body; the dark is negative energy that the body is trying to slough off.

As a person gets closer to a heart attack, the other organs contract tightly within the body. For instance, the liver may become rigid and collapse inward. Before my father had a heart attack, I warned him: every organ in his body was contracted so tight, it could have sprung.

When dealing with heart disease, one should also look for cords in the heart area. These cords may also connect to a lower part of the body and a prior experience causing difficulties, or to a person (alive or not) who, in a relationship, created these fear-based responses to love.

Depression

There are probably hundreds of types of and reasons for depression, at least from an energetic perspective. In general, depression signifies a repression of feeling responses or a hidden aspect of the self whose feelings were/are perceived to be unacceptable or dangerous (to the self or others).

Depression in its generic form is one of the easiest problems to spot energetically. It always appears to me as a dark spot or chamber in the head, usually deep within the brain itself. Some important part of that person is locked away in a corner of his or her mind.

The key to working with depression is to view the inside of this box. Usually, I lead a client inside. Sometimes, I may look inside myself, and find the following:

- Feelings, represented by their associated colors.
- Pictures of the client at the age associated with a trauma or fear-related experience. (I want to see the primary wound, not just those which hook onto the initial reaction.)

Figure 14d.

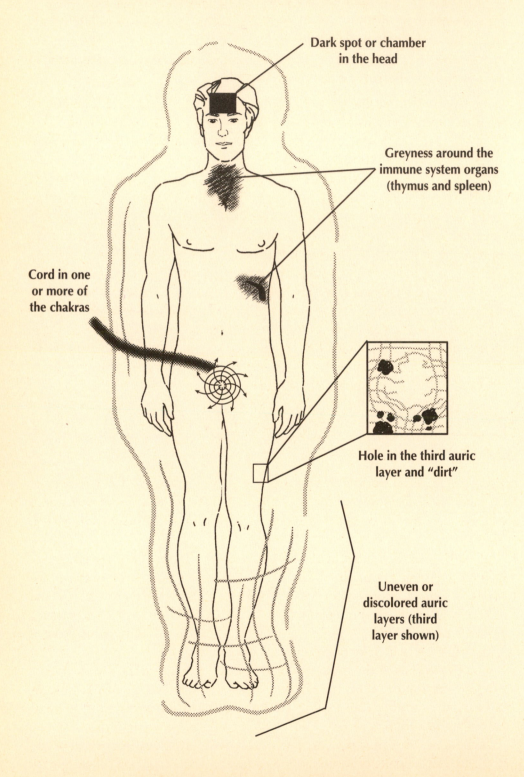

Dark spot or chamber
in the head

Greyness around the
immune system organs
(thymus and spleen)

Cord in one
or more of
the chakras

Hole in the third auric
layer and "dirt"

Uneven or
discolored auric
layers (third
layer shown)

Energetic indications of depression.

- Symbols or representation of gifts which have been locked away. (This is more common than you might believe; gifts such as compassion or intuition are often too dangerous or unacceptable to be acknowledged or used.)
- A soul fragment, an aspect of the soul that has not been integrated or was never truly born during this life.

I also might trace energy lines linking the box to other sites. Sometimes the lines extend from this box to another part of the body and provide a clue as to the date, location, or cause of a trauma, and show me what organ might be chemically affecting this person. Depression, remember, becomes a chemical condition over time. If feelings from age four have been hidden, organs in the third chakra may be affected, thus chemically altering the body. The energy lines may also connect to a part of the brain which has been altered because of the depressed state. In some cases, depression may actually be the result of a chemical imbalance. In these cases, it is even more critical to trace these energy lines to body organs and glands.

Aurically, the feelings repressed by the depressed person are often picked up from other people. This results in discolorations and heaviness in the emotional auric layer (the second layer). It can also result in holes in the mental auric layer (the third layer) which can attract the "dirt" or negative feelings from others. Sometimes these feelings are picked up through cords attached to one or more of the chakras.

A greyness around the immune system and its organs, such as the thymus and the spleen, signifies a depleted immune system.

AIDS

Acquired Immune Deficiency Syndrome (AIDS) displays itself in a variety of energetic symptoms. Depending on how advanced the disease has become, I can see some or all of the following indicators in an HIV-positive person (figure 14e).

A white box-like form in the head indicates a "spiritual depression"— a misconception about the spirit and the body (a mirror of first chakra issues). I usually see a constriction in the heart. A constriction on the left side indicates relationship judgments from a man/male authority or self issues regarding masculinity. A right side constriction shows judgments from a woman/female authority or self issues about femininity.

Dark splotches in the immune centers indicate deficiencies in these areas. A concentration of red in the abdominal area (second chakra) is an indication of pain, usually from an in-utero trauma regarding issues such as sexuality or gender choice.

The genital area (first chakra) also has a pool of blackish, pulsating energy, which equals judgments about the self regarding sexuality, spirituality, or gen-

Figure 14e.

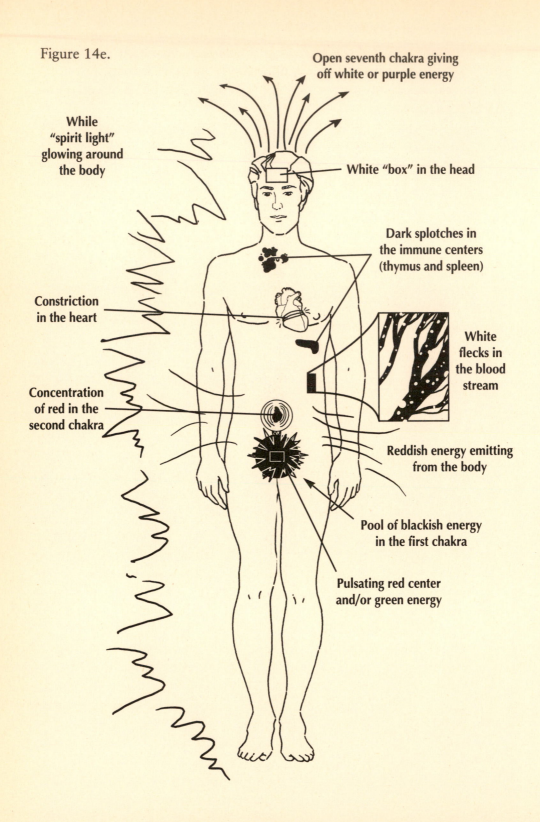

Open seventh chakra giving off white or purple energy

While "spirit light" glowing around the body

White "box" in the head

Dark splotches in the immune centers (thymus and spleen)

Constriction in the heart

White flecks in the blood stream

Concentration of red in the second chakra

Reddish energy emitting from the body

Pool of blackish energy in the first chakra

Pulsating red center and/or green energy

Energetic indications of AIDS.

der. If this pool has a red center, there is a "survival depression"—a misperception about the spirit's right to live and express through the body. Any green color around this energy pool represents AIDS as a force that is trying to heal a first chakra issue.

White flecks in the blood stream and a reddish energy emanating from the body indicate the spirit's presence in the body. The life blood dissipates as the spirit takes over the body. In some cases, the seventh chakra opens to give off white or purple energy.

As the AIDS reaches its more advanced stages and the person draws closer to death, the entire energy body glows with white spirit energy, which means that the spirit is slipping from the body into another world.

Bibliography

Andrews, Ted. *Imagick: The Magick of Images, Paths & Dance*. St. Paul, MN: Llewellyn Publications, 1989.

Bach, Richard. *Illusions: The Adventures of a Reluctant Messiah*. New York: Dell Publishing Company, 1977.

Balaskas, Janet. "The Feminine Power of Birth." In *Uncoiling the Snake*, ed. Vicki Noble. New York: HarperCollins, 1993.

Bradshaw, John. *Bradshaw On: The Family*. Deerfield Beach, FL: Health Communications, Inc., 1988.

Bradshaw, John. *Healing the Shame That Binds You*. Deerfield Beach, FL: Health Communications, Inc., 1988.

Brennan, Barbara Ann. *Hands of Light: A Guide to Healing Through the Human Energy Field*. New York: Bantam Books, 1987.

Bruyere, Rosalyn L. *Wheels of Light: A Study of the Chakras*, ed. Jeanne Farrens. Arcadia, CA: Bon Productions, 1989.

Castaneda, Carlos. *The Eagle's Gift*. New York: Washington Square Press, 1981.

Chopra, Deepak. *Creating Health*. Boston: Houghton Mifflin Company, 1987.

Damasio, Antonio R. *Descartes' Error*. New York: G. P. Putnam & Sons, 1994.

Gerber, Richard. *Vibrational Medicine*. Santa Fe, NM: Bear & Company, 1988.

Gray, Henry. *Gray's Anatomy*. Philadelphia: Running Press, 1974.

Kalweit, Holger. *Dreamtime & Inner Space: The World of the Shaman*. Boston: Shambhala Publications, Inc., 1984.

Katz, Richard. *Boiling Energy: Community Healing Among the Kalahari Kung*. Boston: Harvard College, 1982.

King, Serge. *Kahuna Healing*. Wheaton, IL: The Theosophical Publishing House, 1983.

Lansdowne, Zachary F. *The Rays and Esoteric Psychology*. York Beach, ME: Samuel Weiser, Inc., 1989.

Leadbeater, C. W. *The Chakras*. Wheaton, IL: The Theosophical Publishing House, 1927.

Matthews, John. *The Celtic Shaman*. Rockport, MA: Element, Inc., 1992.

Men, Hunbatz. *Secrets of Mayan Science/Religion*, trans. Diane Gubiseh Ayala and James Jennings Dunlapp II. Santa Fe, NM: Bear & Company, 1990.

Morgan, Marlo. *Mutant Message Down Under*. Lees Summit, MO: MM Co., 1991.

Reynolds, David K. *Water Bears No Scars: Japanese Lifeways for Personal Growth*. New York: William Morrow & Company, 1987.

Rogers, Carl D. *On Becoming A Person*. Boston: Houghton Mifflin Company, 1961.

Stein, Diane. *Women's Psychic Lives* (formerly *Stroking the Python*). St. Paul, MN: Llewellyn Publications, 1988.

Stetler, Alfred. *PSI-Healing*. New York: Bantam Books, 1976.

Talbot, Michael. *The Holographic Universe*. New York: HarperCollins, 1991.

Whistler, W. Arthur. *Polynesian Herbal Medicine*. Kauai, HI: National Tropical Botanical Garden, 1992.

Wiedermann, Frederic. *Between Two Worlds: The Riddle of Wholeness*. Wheaton, IL: The Theosophical Publishing House, 1986.

Ywahoo, Dhyani. *Voices of Our Ancestors*. Boston: Shambhala Publications, Inc., 1987.

☾ REACH FOR THE MOON

Llewellyn publishes hundreds of books on your favorite subjects! To get these exciting books, including the ones on the following pages, check your local bookstore or order them directly from Llewellyn.

Order by Phone

- Call toll-free within the U.S. and Canada, 1-800-THE MOON
- In Minnesota, call (651) 291-1970
- We accept VISA, MasterCard, and American Express

Order by Mail

- Send the full price of your order (MN residents add 7% sales tax) in U.S. funds, plus postage & handling to:

  Llewellyn Worldwide
  P.O. Box 64383, Dept. 1–56718–200–3
  St. Paul, MN 55164–0383, U.S.A.

Postage & Handling

- **Standard** (U.S., Mexico, & Canada)

If your order is:
  $20.00 or under, add $5.00
  $20.01–$100.00, add $6.00
  Over $100, shipping is free
(Continental U.S. orders ship UPS. AK, HI, PR, & P.O. Boxes ship USPS 1st class. Mex. & Can. ship PMB.)

- **Second Day Air** (Continental U.S. only): $10.00 for one book + $1.00 per each additional book
- **Express** (AK, HI, & PR only) [Not available for P.O. Box delivery. For street address delivery only.]: $15.00 for one book + $1.00 per each additional book
- **International Surface Mail:** Add $1.00 per item
- **International Airmail:** Books—Add the retail price of each item; Non-book items—Add $5.00 per item

Please allow 4–6 weeks for delivery on all orders.
Postage and handling rates subject to change.

Discounts

We offer a 20% discount to group leaders or agents. You must order a minimum of 5 copies of the same book to get our special quantity price.

Free Catalog

Get a free copy of our color catalog, *New Worlds of Mind and Spirit.* Subscribe for just $10.00 in the United States and Canada ($30.00 overseas, airmail). Many bookstores carry *New Worlds*—ask for it!

Visit our website at www.llewellyn.com for more information.

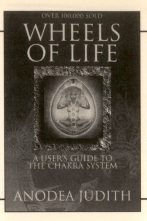